The Clinical

DOCUMENTATION
SOURCEBOOK

The Clinical
DOCUMENTATION
SOURCEBOOK

The Complete Paperwork Resource for
Your Mental Health Practice

THIRD EDITION

Donald E. Wiger

WILEY

John Wiley & Sons, Inc.

Note about Photocopy Rights
The publisher grants purchasers permission to reproduce handouts from this book for professional use with their clients.

ISBN: 0-471-68931-9

Printed in the United States of America.

10 9 8 7 6 5 4 3 2

This third edition is dedicated to the late Drs. K.T. Puramore and Cassie Fraffer,
who have been an inspiration to both my professional and personal life.
No words could adequately describe their level of encouragement
and example to me and many others.
The world needs role models like you.
Thank you.

Contents

Contents

Chapter 3   Assessment Forms 3.1

Chapter 4   Psychological Evaluations 4.1

Chapter 5   Treatment Planning Forms and Procedures 5.1

Contents

CD Contents

CD Contents

Acknowledgments

Special thanks are given to Argosy/Twin Cities—Minnesota School of Professional Psychology graduate student Katie Kohlman for helping with the research for this edition.

Preface to the Third Edition

Each edition of the *Clinical Documentation Sourcebook* has improved in providing concise and well-integrated mental health forms designed to meet the most stringent criteria. The positive response to the initial text led to publication of the *Psychotherapy Documentation Primer,* which provided thorough documentation training in psychological assessment, treatment planning, and progress notes. The first edition focused on providing a set of forms that were interrelated and thorough, thus reducing redundancies in clinical documentation. The second edition added 30% more forms and increased its focus to the documentation requirements of third-party payers and accreditation agencies. With the onset of HIPAA requirements many therapists have expressed concern as to what additional documentation and confidentiality procedural changes might be necessary. This edition contains 52 mental health forms. It has expanded in three major ways: (1) several new forms have been added or revised; (2) the focus has expanded to include not only adults but also children, families, and relationships; (3) it includes an emphasis on HIPAA compliance; and (4) increased outcomes and chart review forms.

Introduction

Few mental health professionals have received graduate training in documentation procedures. Learning to write case notes, treatment plans, and other documentation is usually a trial-and-error process, often resulting in vague treatment plans, case notes, and therapy. Historically, case notes and treatment plans have been required in most mental health care settings, but few standardized procedures have been acknowledged. In many cases, the mere existence of various forms and documents in clients' files was sufficient.

Historically, documentation procedures in medical fields other than mental health have been quite stringent, requiring that specific interventions be accurately charted. Without such documentation, physicians and nurses are understandably vulnerable to litigation. But prior to the emergence of managed care, most mental health professionals received little scrutiny by third-party payers in areas of accountability. Managed care changed the rules by raising the standards of documentation procedures in the mental health field.

For managed care companies to obtain contracts and stay in business, they must attempt to provide the best services for the least money. Often, a few managed care companies cover a significant number of people in a given geographic area. To receive a sufficient number of referrals, mental health providers contract with these companies, but may become dissatisfied with demanding documentation rules and regulations.

Graduate training programs have concentrated on traditional therapeutic methods, teaching therapists to attend to clients, conceptualize cases, listen empathically, render interpretations, ease clients' emotional pain, provide direction, and slowly taper off the sessions to prevent relapse. Although such procedures and interventions are therapeutically necessary, third-party requirements rarely mention them because in themselves they do not necessarily document the efficacy and course of therapy. Instead, terms often not learned in graduate school such as "medical necessity," "functional impairment," and "discharge criteria" have become the criteria for continued services.

Procedural requirements and changes catalyzed by managed care for documentation of therapy have increased cognitive dissonance in mental health professionals. Dissonance has developed because therapists are being challenged by discrepancies between their established mental health procedures and seemingly conflicting new requirements that are often viewed as limiting the clinician's therapeutic freedom. The resulting cognitive dissonance leads to stress, discomfort, worry, and complaints. To say that managed care regulations and procedures have caused cognitive dissonance is an understatement like the observations that "Sigmund Freud had some sort of effect on psychology" or "Albert Einstein was smart."

It is possible to reduce cognitive dissonance by focusing on the benefits of documentation procedures. Effective documentation holds mental health professionals accountable for accurate diagnosis, concise treatment planning, case notes that follow the treatment plan, treatment reflecting the diagnosis, and documentation of the course of therapy.

Introduction

Effective case notes can be written in a manner that would enable a new therapist to review a file and clearly determine specific impairments, the effectiveness of previous treatment strategies, client compliance, progress and setbacks.

Treatment does not necessarily have to change, but documentation procedures validating the effectiveness of treatment must be learned in order for mental health services to survive in the world of managed care. The ethical implications of being accountable (or not being accountable) for work deserves attention.

Managed care has brought the mental health profession up to par with other health care professionals in accountability procedures. In other areas of health care, the "black box" treatment approach—in which specific interventions are not documented—would be considered unethical, not reimbursable, and open to litigation. Without clear documentation procedures there is little or no accountability, leaving professionals open to allegations of fraud due to lack of specific evidence that necessary services are being provided.

For example, one major insurance provider (Blue Cross/Blue Shield) has established the following (selected) requirements and criteria for mental health services to be eligible for benefits:

1. "Services must be medically and/or therapeutically necessary." Medical necessity is determined by "the presence of significant impairment or dysfunction in the performance of activities and/or responsibilities of daily living as a result of a mental disorder." Note that the emphasis is on the impairment, not simply the diagnosis. Although most third-party payers require an Axis I diagnosis, it is the resulting impairment that is the focus of interventions.

2. "Therapeutic necessity is defined as services consistent with the diagnosis and impairment which are non-experimental in nature and can be reliably predicted to positively affect the patient's condition." Therapeutic interventions must have a positive track record for the particular diagnosis and impairments. Charting procedures that do not clearly and consistently reflect such interventions do not document therapeutic necessity.

3. "The intensity of treatment must be consistent with the acuity and severity of the patient's current level of impairment and/or dysfunction." Without regular documentation of current functioning (session by session) and a rationale for the intensity of treatment, no evidence exists.

4. "There must be documentation of reasonable progress consistent with the intensity of treatment and the severity of the disorder." Case notes must validate the effectiveness of the current therapeutic interventions and justify the frequency of sessions.

5. ". . . documented, specific evidence of a diagnosable mental disorder (based on current *DSM*). The diagnosis must be validated by *Diagnostic and Statistical Manual of Mental Disorders (DSM)* criteria. A diagnosis is more than an opinion: Specific symptoms must be documented according to current *DSM-IV* criteria.

6. "The treatment plan includes specific, objective, behavioral goals for discharge." Both the client and the therapist have agreed on discharge criteria, stated in behavioral measures.

7. Justification to continue treatment includes "persistence of significant symptoms and impairment or dysfunction resultant from mental illness which required continued treatment including impaired social, familial or occupational functioning or evidence of symptoms which reflects potential dangers to self, others and/or property." Case notes must regularly document the persistence of impairment. Without this documentation, there is no evidence and therefore the impairment and diagnosis no longer exist (as far as documentation is concerned). It is possible that a significant impairment may exist, but if it is not appropriately documented, payment for services could be discontinued.

8. "Insufficient behavioral and/or dysfunctional evidence is present to support the current diagnosis." Not only must impairments be documented, but the *DSM-IV-TR* Axis I diagnosis must be documented with evidence throughout the course of therapy. If the diagnosis is not supported throughout the case notes, there is no evidence, and therefore third-party payment may be halted.

9. "Lack of therapeutic appropriateness and/or lack of therapeutic progress." Evidence of therapeutic gains and setbacks are required documentation procedures.

10. Noncovered services include services without a "definite treatment plan," services without corresponding documentation, medically unnecessary services, services without a diagnosable mental disorder, and several other uncovered services.

This summary of third-party documentation procedures indicates specific requirements that are designed to document the efficacy of therapy in such areas as validation of diagnosis, functional impairments, symptoms, treatment, client cooperation, and providing behavioral evidence of gains and setbacks in treatment. Benefits of learning these procedures range from increased prior authorization approval for additional sessions, to clearer focus in therapy, to audit survival.

Sample forms and related examples of several documentation procedures from the initial client contact to the discharge summary are included. Blank forms are provided along with several of the forms filled out. Unless a form is self-explanatory, explanations are provided on its use. Special emphasis is placed on treatment plans and case notes.

Mental health forms are much more than simply extra work for therapists. A well-designed form allows the clinician to save time by organizing information in a standardized format. Without efficiently written forms, one can easily forget to inquire about important clinical information or focus too much on other areas. They provide an organized flow of information to monitor treatment, aid in communication with other professionals, help determine outcomes of treatment, and can aid in complying with state and federal requirements.

Historically, mental health professionals have made concerted efforts to protect client information. That is, the need for protecting client information both understood and agreed upon. However, knowledge of how to implement specific HIPAA procedures to safeguard client information is unfamiliar to many therapists. The forms presented in this text are specifically designed to comply with HIPAA requirements.

Organization

This text is divided into nine chapters, including forms in areas of administrative, HIPAA compliance, assessment, psychological evaluations, treatment planning, progress notes, the course of treatment, chart review, outcomes documentation, termination, chart review, and aftercare. The table of contents notes where the forms are intended for adults, children/adolescents, and/or relationships.

Brief explanations are provided for each form. Forms which are more complex include a filled-out example. Blank forms are provided on the CD at the end of the book. An ongoing case example of Judy Doe is used in many of the documentation procedures and forms.

The Clinical
DOCUMENTATION
SOURCEBOOK

Chapter 1

Administrative and Intake Forms

The mental health clinic's intake information forms elicit demographic and payment information about the client. They also communicate business, legal, and ethical issues and responsibilities. Although initial intake forms do not provide specific clinical information, they do provide an understanding of the responsibilities of both the client and the clinic. In each case, these forms are taken care of prior to the first counseling session. All insurance and financial agreements are contracted with the client before services begin. The clinic's financial policies must be clearly spelled out. In addition, the client should be made aware of, and agree to, the limits of confidentiality in a counseling session.

Common client questions are: "What if my insurance company does not pay?," "How confidential is the session?," "Do parents have the right to their children's records?," "What happens if payment is not received?," "What happens if suicide is mentioned?," and "What is the price of therapy?" These and other questions are not only answered, but also documented and signed. Any of these issues, if not covered, could lead to misunderstanding, subsequent premature termination of treatment, ethics changes, or a lawsuit. Intake forms provide clear communication between the client and clinic, with the aim of eliminating misunderstandings detrimental to the therapeutic process and clinic survival.

FORM 1
Screening Information

The screening information contains demographic information which is generally held by office personnel for administrative reasons. It is kept separately from the client's confidential medical records. The information contained is used for ongoing office and billing procedures in which a quick reference is needed without having to access the client's medical records. It excludes private clinical information and is typically readily accessible to administrative/office/billing personnel. The form also provides emergency contact information as required by accrediting agencies. For example, if a client has a medical problem or becomes suicidal, information such as emergency contacts, the primary physician, and other background information must be readily available. Referral source information may be used for tracking purposes.

FORM 2
Notice of Appointment

This form serves to remind the client of an upcoming initial appointment and instructs the client on what information to bring to the session.

FORM 3
Consent to Treatment and
Recipient's Rights

A statement of consent for treatment and the client's rights are common requirements of accreditation agencies. The client further acknowledges reading and understanding their rights as a patient. The form further explains various situations in which the client could be discharged from treatment non-voluntarily and the limits of confidentiality.

FORM 4
Recipient's Rights Notification

The information contained in this client handout includes disclosures often required by accreditation agencies that inform clients of their rights as consumers of mental health services.

FORM 5
Initial Client Information

The initial client information form (Form 5) is filled out at the time of the referral or initial client contact with the mental health care provider. Information solicited from the client includes basic demographic, plus insurance identification information. For insurance reasons, information requested from the client should minimally include:

- Policyholder information: name, date of birth, social security number, policy number.
- Similar information from family members receiving services.
- Name of employer.
- Name and telephone number of each third-party payer.

If the mental health care provider processes insurance information, it is crucial to verify benefits from the insurance company. Specific questions should be asked of the third party, minimally including the following:

- Persons covered by the policy.
- Deductible amount and amount currently satisfied.
- Co-payment amounts.
- Limits of policy.
- Covered/noncovered services (e.g., individual, family, relationship).
- Prior authorizations needed.
- Coverage and policies for testing.
- Supervision required for various providers.
- Type(s) of provider(s) covered for services (e.g., psychologist, social worker, counselor).
- Policy anniversary date.

When this information is unclear or unknown, there is room for misunderstanding between the mental health care provider and the client. Clients usually believe that all services performed in therapy are covered by their insurance. But mental health benefits from several sources are decreasing, and only specific, limited services are now covered. For example, just a few years ago several third-party payers paid for testing; today testing is seldom considered a standard procedure and often needs prior approval. Another trend is that most managed-care companies approve only a few sessions at a time, while in the past few restrictions were made.

Initial insurance information provided by third-party payers is not a guarantee of benefits. Each mental health care provider should have a clear financial policy and payment contract (possibly on the same form) to explain conditions of payment in the event that the third-party payer denies payment.

FORM 6
Financial Policy

Clinical skills are necessary, but not the sole component in the overall scope of mental health services. A concise, written financial policy is crucial to the successful operation of any practice. Clear financial policies and procedures eliminate much potential discord (and premature termination of services) between the client and the therapist and clinic. Clinics that thrive financially and are self-sufficient have few accounts receivable at any time. An adequate financial policy statement addresses the following:

- The client is ultimately responsible for payment to the clinic. The clinic cannot guarantee insurance benefits. (*Note:* Some managed-care contracts forbid client payment to the clinic for noncovered services without permission.)

- Clinics that bill insurance companies should convey to clients the fact that billing third-party payers is simply a service—not a responsibility—of the clinic.

- There are time limits in waiting for insurance payments, after which the client must pay the clinic. Some clinics collect the entire amount initially from the client and reimburse the client when insurance money is received.

- The clinic's policy regarding payment for treatment of minors should be noted.

- The policy regarding payment for charges not covered by third-party payers should be addressed.

- The financial policy form should be signed by the person(s) responsible for payment.

- Assignment of benefit policies should be addressed.

- The financial policy statement should specify when payments are due and policies for nonpayment.

- Methods of payment should be listed.

Request clients to read and sign the financial policy statement (Form 6) prior to the first session. Some mental health providers ask clients to come to the first session 15 to 20 minutes early to review the initial policies and procedures. Take care of all financial understandings with the client before the first session begins; otherwise, valuable session time might be taken up reviewing financial issues.

FORM 7
Payment Contract for Services

Along with the financial policy statement, the payment contract is vital for the clinic's financial survival. Without a payment contract, clients are not clearly obligated to pay for mental health services. The following payment contract meets federal criteria for a truth in lending disclosure statement for professional services and provides a release of information to bill third parties (Form 7).

The contract lists professional fees that will be charged. (A clinical hour should be defined by the number of minutes it covers rather than stating "per hour.") Interest rates on late payments must be disclosed. Other services provided by the mental health care provider must also be listed, and costs should be disclosed. Fees for services such as testing should be listed, either by the test or at an hourly rate for testing and interpretation time. The contract should cover specific clinic policies regarding missed appointments, outside consultations, and other potential fees related to the mental health care provider.

The mental health care provider may choose to include or omit estimated insurance benefits in the payment contract. Since the mental health clinic is not directly affiliated with the third-party payer and their changing policies, it is important to clearly state that payment is due regardless of decisions made by the third-party payer and that the client is financially responsible to the clinic for any amounts not paid by the third-party payer within a certain time frame.

FORM 8
Code of Ethics and
Mission Statement

Accreditation agencies require that clinics post a mission statement. This form contains a sample mission statement and the ethical stance of a clinic. Typically this is posted in a conspicuous place in the waiting room.

FORM 9
Therapist's Ethics Statement

This form is signed by each therapist in the clinic as a means to document their compliance with the ethical stances of the clinic and their professional association.

FORM 10
Agreement Regarding Minors

This form provides an agreement that parents will respect certain rules of privacy regarding what their children disclose in therapy.

FORM 11
Preauthorization for
Health Care

Charge cards are an effective means of collecting fees for professional services. The following form provides several benefits. It allows the clinic to automatically bill the charge-card company for third-party payments not received after a set number of (often 60) days. It eliminates expensive—and often ineffective—billing to the client and successive billing to the insurance company. It further allows the clinic to bill the charge-card company for recurring amounts such as co-payments. This policy is often welcomed by clients because it eliminates the need to write a check each time services are received.

Most banks offer both VISA and MasterCard dealer status, but established credit is needed. Some therapists have become vendors for credit-card companies by offering to back the funds with a secured interest-bearing account (e.g., $500) for a set period while their credit becomes established with the bank.

Fees for being a charge-card dealer vary and may be negotiated, so competitive shopping for a bank is suggested. Some banks charge a set percentage of each transaction, while others include several hidden fees. The process is simpler though when the same bank is used in which the mental health professional has a checking account, because charge account receipts are generally deposited into a checking account.

Form 1   Screening Information

SCREENING INFORMATION

Please Print Clearly   **THIS SHEET MUST BE FILLED IN COMPLETELY**   Readmit: __Yes   __No

Date_____   Client's Social Security #_____   Case #_____

Client's First Name_____   Last Name_____   MI_____

Address_____   City_____   State_____   Zip_____

Telephone (Home)_____   (Work)_____

Birthdate____/____/____   Age_____   Gender __F __M   Race_____

Name of Spouse/Guardian_____   Phone_____

Address_____   City_____   State_____   Zip_____

Person Responsible for Payment_____   Soc. Sec. #_____

Signature of Person Responsible for Payment **X**_____ (Must be signed for services to begin)

Emergency Information

In case of emergency, contact:

Name (1) _____   Relationship_____   Phone_____Work_____

Address_____   City_____   State_____   Zip_____

Name (2) _____   Relationship_____   Phone_____Work_____

Address_____   City_____   State_____   Zip_____

Physician_____   Phone_____

Address_____   City_____   State_____   Zip_____

Psychiatrist_____   Phone_____

Address_____   City_____   State_____   Zip_____

Other Physicians_____   Phone_____

Current Medications_____

Allergies_____

Employment Information (If client is a child, use parent's employment)

Client/Guardian: Place_____   Phone_____   Hrs_____

Spouse: Place_____   Phone_____   Hrs_____

Insurance Information

Primary Insurance_____   Secondary Insurance_____

Phone_____   Phone_____

Contract/ID#_____   Contract/ID#_____

Group/Acct#_____   Group/Acct#_____

Subscriber_____   Subscriber_____

Subscriber Date of Birth _____   Subscriber Date of Birth_____

Client's relationship to Subscriber   Client's relationship to Subscriber

__Self __Spouse __Child __Other_____   __Self __Spouse __Child __Other_____

Referral Source

How did you hear of our clinic (or from whom)?_____

Address_____   City_____   State_____   Zip_____

Phone_____   Relationship to referral source_____

Form 2   Notice of Appointment

Date: _____

Dear _____

This is to confirm your appointment with _____(therapist's name)_____ at our clinic.

on _____(date)_____ .

Your appointment time is at _____, however, please arrive _____ minutes early to fill out insurance

and clinical forms. The appointment will last approximately _____ minutes.

Address of clinic   _____

                             _____

                             _____

Please bring the following information to the clinic.

_____   _____

_____   _____

_____   _____

If you have any questions or must cancel your appointment please phone the clinic at

_____(phone number)_____ at least _____ hours in advance.

Sincerely,

_____

Form 3   Consent to Treatment and Recipient's Rights

Client_____   Chart #_____

I, _____, the undersigned, hereby attest that I have voluntarily entered into treatment, or give my consent for the minor or person under my legal guardianship mentioned above, at _____(name of clinic)_____, hereby referred as the Center. Further, I consent to have treatment provided by a psychiatrist, psychologist, social worker, counselor, or intern in collaboration with his/her supervisor. The rights, risks and benefits associated with the treatment have been explained to me. I understand that the therapy may be discontinued at any time by either party. The clinic encourages that this decision be discussed with the treating psychotherapist. This will help facilitate a more appropriate plan for discharge.

Recipient's Rights: I certify that I have received the Recipient's Rights pamphlet and certify that I have read and understand its content. I understand that as a recipient of services, I may get more information from the Recipient's Rights Advisor.

Non-Voluntary Discharge from Treatment: A client may be terminated from the Center non-voluntarily, if: A) the client exhibits physical violence, verbal abuse, carries weapons, or engages in illegal acts at the clinic, and/or B) the client refuses to comply with stipulated program rules, refuses to comply with treatment recommendations, or does not make payment or payment arrangements in a timely manner. The client will be notified of the non-voluntary discharge by letter. The client may appeal this decision with the Clinic Director or request to re-apply for services at a later date.

Client Notice of Confidentiality: The confidentiality of patient records maintained by the Center is protected by Federal and/or State law and regulations. Generally, the Center may not say to a person outside the Center that a patient attends the program or disclose any information identifying a patient as an alcohol or drug abuser unless: 1) the patient consents in writing, 2) the disclosure is allowed by a court order, or 3) the disclosure is made to medical personnel in a medical emergency, or to qualified personnel for research, audit, or program evaluation.

Violation of Federal and/or State law and regulations by a treatment facility or provider is a crime. Suspected violations may be reported to appropriate authorities. Federal and/or State law and regulations do not protect any information about a crime committed by a patient either at the Center, against any person who works for the program, or about any threat to commit such a crime. Federal law and regulations do not protect any information about suspected child (or vulnerable adult) abuse or neglect, or adult abuse from being reported under Federal and/or State law to appropriate State or Local authorities. Health care professionals are required to report admitted prenatal exposure to controlled substances that are potentially harmful. It is the Center's duty to warn any potential victim, when a significant threat of harm has been made. In the event of a client's death, the spouse or parents of a deceased client have a right to access their child's or spouse's records. Professional misconduct by a health care professional must be reported by other health care professionals, in which related client records may be released to substantiate disciplinary concerns. Parents or legal guardians of non-emancipated minor clients have the right to access the client's records. When fees are not paid in a timely manner, a collection agency will be given appropriate billing and financial information about client, not clinical information. My signature below indicates that I have been given a copy of my rights regarding confidentiality. I permit a copy of this authorization to be used in place of the original. Client data of clinical outcomes may be used for program evaluation purposes, but individual results will not be disclosed to outside sources.

I consent to treatment and agree to abide by the above stated policies and agreements with _____(name of clinic)_____.

_____   _____
Signature of Client/Legal Guardian   Date
(In a case where a client is under 18 years of age, a legally responsible adult acting on his/her behalf)

_____   _____
Witness   Date

Form 4   Recipient's Rights Notification

As a recipient of services at our facility, we would like to inform you of your rights as a patient. The information contained in this brochure explains your rights and the process of complaining if you believe your rights have been violated.

Your rights as a patient
1. Complaints. We will investigate your complaints.
2. Suggestions. You are invited to suggest changes in any aspect of the services we provide.
3. Civil Rights. Your civil rights are protected by federal and state laws.
4. Cultural/spiritual/gender Issues. You may request services from someone with training or experiences from a specific cultural, spiritual, or gender orientation. If these services are not available, we will help you in the referral process.
5. Treatment. You have the right to take part in formulating your treatment plan.
6. Denial of services. You may refuse services offered to you and be informed of any potential consequences.
7. Record restrictions. You may request restrictions on the use of your protected health information; however, we are not required to agree with the request.
8. Availability of records. You have the right to obtain a copy and/or inspect your protected health information; however we may deny access to certain records in which we will discuss this decision with you.
9. Amendment of records. You have the right to request an amendment in your records; however, this request could be denied. If denied, your request will be kept in the records.
10. Medical/Legal Advice. You may discuss your treatment with your doctor or attorney.
11. Disclosures. You have the right to receive an accounting of disclosures of your protected health information that you have not authorized.

Your rights to receive information
1. Medications used in your treatment. We will provide you with information describing any potential risks of medications prescribed at our facility.
2. Costs of services. We will inform you of how much you will pay.
3. Termination of services. You will be informed as to what behaviors or violations could lead to termination of services at our clinic.
4. Confidentiality. You will be informed of the limits of confidentiality and how your protected health information will be used.
5. Policy changes.

Our ethical obligations
1. We dedicate ourselves to serving the best interest of each client.
2. We will not discriminate between clients or professionals based on age, race, creed, disabilities, handicaps, preferences, or other personal concerns.
3. We maintain an objective and professional relationship with each client.
4. We respect the rights and views of other mental health professionals.
5. We will appropriately end services or refer clients to other programs when appropriate.
6. We will evaluate our personal limitations, strengths, biases, and effectiveness on an ongoing basis for the purpose of self-improvement. We will continually attain further education and training.
7. We hold respect for various institutional and managerial policies, but will help improve such policies if the best interest of the client is served.

Patient's responsibilities
1. You are responsible for your financial obligations to the clinic as outlined in the Payment Contract for Services.
2. You are responsible for following the policies of the clinic.
3. You are responsible to treat staff and fellow patients in a respectful, cordial manner in which their rights are not violated.
4. Your are responsible to provide accurate information about yourself.

What to do if you believe your rights have been violated
If you believe that your patient rights have been violated contact our Recipient's Rights Advisor or Clinic Director.

Form 5   Initial Client Information

Name: _____   Intake date: _____   Time: _____

Address: _____   Therapist requested: ___ Y ___ N

_____   Therapist: _____   Office: _____

Source of referral: _____   Type(s) of service: _____

Phone number: _____   Work phone: _____   Date of birth: ___ / ___ / _____

(___)   Primary insurance company: _____

      Address: _____   City: _____   State: _____   Zip: _____

Phone number: _____   Persons covered: _____

Contact person: _____   M&F covered: _____

Policy holder: _____   Policy number: _____

Employer/Group: _____   SS number: _____

PROVISIONS: Client pays $ _____ Deductible amount   Amount satisfied: $ _____

      Insurance pays _____ % for visits ___ - ___ and _____ % for visits ___ - ___

Type(s) of providers covered: _____   Supervision: _____

Prior authorization needed: _____

Effective date: _____   Policy anniversary: _____

Coverage for testing: _____   Annual limit: _____

Other third-party coverage: _____

Address: _____   City: _____   State: _____   Zip: _____

Phone number: _____   Persons covered: _____

Contact person: _____   M&F covered: _____

Policy holder: _____   Policy number: _____

Other provisions: _____

_____

(___)   Personal payment amount: $ _____   Terms: _____

Payment method (Insurance and cash clients; deductibles, co-payments, etc.)

___ Check   ___ Cash   ___ Charge card (type) _____   Number: _____

Cardholder's name: _____   Expires: _____

Completed procedures: ___ Entered system   Date: _____

                        ___ Confirmed insurance   Date: _____

                        ___ Confirmed with client   Date: _____

Name: _Judy Doe_   Intake date: _3/8/2005_   Time: _9:00 A.M._

Address: _123 Main St._   Therapist requested: ___ Y _X_ N

Pleasantville, NJ 99999   Therapist: _DLB_   Office: _SP_

Source of referral: _YP_   Type(s) of service: _Individual_

Phone number: _555-5555_   Work phone: _555-5544_   Date of birth: _7_ / _6_ / _1954_

(_X_) Primary insurance company: _United Cross Healthcare_

      Address: _5678 9th St._   City: _Pleasantville_   State: _NJ_   Zip: _99998_

Phone number: _555-5555_   Persons covered: _All family members_

Contact person: _Sheryl Sperry_   M&F covered: _No_

Policy holder: _Judy Doe_   Policy number: _1234567_

Employer/Group: _Pleasantville School Dis. 22_   SS number: _999-99-9999_

PROVISIONS: Client pays $ _100_ Deductible amount   Amount satisfied: $ _50_

      Insurance pays _80_ % for visits _1_ - _10_ and _75_ % for visits _11_ - _30_

Type(s) of providers covered: _Indiv, Family, Group, Assessment_   Supervision: _None if licensed_

Prior authorization needed: _After session 5 need PA. All testing_

Effective date: _Jan. 1, 2005_   Policy anniversary: _Dec. 31, 2005_

Coverage for testing: _Annual limit: $400_   Annual limit: _(total) $2,000.00_

Other third-party coverage: _None_

Address: _____   City: _____   State: _____   Zip: _____

Phone number: _____   Persons covered: _____

Contact person: _____   M&F covered: _____

Policy holder: _____   Policy number: _____

Other provisions: _____

(_X_) Personal payment amount: $ _____   Terms: _as incurred_

Payment method (Insurance and cash clients; deductibles, co-payments, etc.)

___ Check   ___ Cash   _X_ Charge card (type) _Discover_   Number: _1234-5678-9012-3456_

Cardholder's name: _Judy Doe_   Expires: _8/02/2006_

Completed procedures: _X_ Entered system   Date: _3/5/2005_

                     _X_ Confirmed insurance   Date: _3/5/2005_

                     _X_ Confirmed with client   Date: _3/5/2005_

Form 6   Financial Policy

The staff at (_____) (hereafter referred to as the clinic) are committed to providing caring and professional mental health care to all of our clients. As part of the delivery of mental health services we have established a financial policy which provides payment policies and options to all consumers. The financial policy of the clinic is designed to clarify the payment policies as determined by the management of the clinic.

The Person Responsible for Payment of Account is required to sign the form, *Payment Contract for Services,* which explains the fees and collection policies of the clinic. Your insurance policy, if any, is a contract between you and the insurance company; we are not part of the contract with you and your insurance company.

As a service to you, the clinic will bill insurance companies and other third-party payers, but cannot guarantee such benefits or the amounts covered, and is not responsible for the collection of such payments. In some cases insurance companies or other third-party payers may consider certain services as not reasonable or necessary or may determine that services are not covered. In such cases the Person Responsible for Payment of Account is responsible for payment of these services. We charge our clients the usual and customary rates for the area. Clients are responsible for payments regardless of any insurance company's arbitrary determination of usual and customary rates.

The Person Responsible for Payment (as noted in the Payment Contract for Services) will be financially responsible for payment of such services. The Person Responsible for Payment of Account is financially responsible for paying funds not paid by insurance companies or third-party payers after 60 days. Payments not received after 120 days are subject to collections. A 1% per month interest rate is charged for accounts over 60 days.

Insurance deductibles and co-payments are due at the time of service. Although it is possible that mental health coverage deductible amounts may have been met elsewhere (e.g., if there were previous visits to another mental health provider since January of the current year that were prior to the first session at the clinic), this amount will be collected by the clinic until the deductible payment is verified to the clinic by the insurance company or third-party provider.

All insurance benefits will be assigned to this clinic (by insurance company or third-party provider) unless the Person Responsible for Payment of Account pays the entire balance each session.

Clients are responsible for payments at the time of services. The adult accompanying a minor (or guardian of the minor) is responsible for payments for the child at the time of service. Unaccompanied minors will be denied nonemergency service unless charges have been preauthorized to an approved credit plan, charge card, or payment at the time of service.

Missed appointments or cancellations less than 24 hours prior to the appointment are charged at a rate noted in the Payment Contract for Services.

Payment methods include check, cash, or the following charge cards: _____ .
Clients using charge cards may either use their card at each session or sign a document allowing the clinic to automatically submit charges to the charge card after each session.

Questions regarding the financial policies can be answered by the Office Manager.

I (we) have read, understand, and agree with the provisions of the Financial Policy.

Person responsible for account: _____ Date: ____/____/____

Co-responsible party: _____ Date: ____/____/____

Form 7   Payment Contract for Services

Name(s): _____

Address: _____ City: _____ State: _____ Zip: _____

Bill to: Person responsible for payment of account: _____

Address: _____ City: _____ State: _____ Zip: _____

Federal Truth in Lending Disclosure Statement for Professional Services

Part One   Fees for Professional Services

I (we) agree to pay _____ , hereafter referred to as the clinic, a rate of $ _____ per clinical unit (defined as 45–50 minutes for assessment, testing, and individual, family and relationship counseling).

A fee of $ _____ is charged for group counseling. The fee for testing includes scoring and report-writing time.

A fee of $ _____ is charged for missed appointments or cancellations with less that 24 hours' notice.

Part Two   Clients with Insurance (Deductible and Co-payment Agreement)

This clinic has been informed by either you or your insurance company that your policy contains (but is not limited to) the following provisions for mental health services:

Estimated Insurance Benefits

1) $ _____ Deductible amount (paid by insured party)
2) Co-payment _____ %   ($ _____ /clinical unit) for first _____ visits.
3) Co-payment _____ %   ($ _____ /clinical unit) up to ___ visits.
4) The policy limit is _____ per year: ___ annual ___ calendar

We suggest you confirm these provisions with the insurance company. The Person Responsible for Payment of Account shall make payment for services which are not paid by your insurance policy, all co-payments, and deductibles. We will also attempt to verify these amounts with the insurance company.

Your insurance company may not pay for services that they consider to be nonefficacious, not medically or therapeutically necessary, or ineligible (not covered by your policy, or the policy has expired or is not in effect for you or other people receiving services). If the insurance company does not pay the estimated amount, you are responsible for the balance. The amounts charged for professional services are explained in Part One above.

Part Three   All Clients

Payments, co-payments, and deductible amounts are due at the time of service. There is a 1% per month (12% Annual Percentage Rate) interest charge on all accounts that are not paid within 60 days of the billing date.

I HEREBY CERTIFY that I have read and agree to the conditions and have received a copy of the Federal Truth in Lending Disclosure Statement for Professional Services.

Person responsible for account: _____   Date: _____/_____/_____

Release of Information Authorization to Third Party

I (we) authorize _____ to disclose case records (diagnosis, case notes, psychological reports, testing results, or other requested material) to the above listed third-party payer or insurance company for the purpose of receiving payment directly to _____ .

I (we) understand that access to this information will be limited to determining insurance benefits, and will be accessible only to persons whose employment is to determine payments and/or insurance benefits. I (we) understand that I (we) may revoke this consent at any time by providing written notice, and after one year this consent expires. I (we) have been informed what information will be given, its purpose, and who will receive it. I (we) certify that I (we) have read and agree to the conditions and have received a copy of this form.

Person(s) responsible for account: _____   Date: _____/_____/_____

Person(s) receiving services: _____   Date: _____/_____/_____

Person(s) or guardian(s): _____   Date: _____/_____/_____

Form 8   Code of Ethics and Mission Statement

Mission Statement

We, at _____(name of clinic)_____ are dedicated professionals committed to providing quality mental health and substance abuse services. It is our overall goal to enhance the quality of life for individuals and families. Our belief is that all people are valuable and unique and should be treated with dignity and respect. While recognizing the potential for change, an assessment of the client's emotional, physical, spiritual, and life experience is provided in a caring environment. The growth of the individual is promoted through a course of treatment developed and executed in a timely and cost effective manner.

Ethical Stance

We, at _____(name of clinic)_____ dedicate ourselves to serving the best interest of each client.

We, at _____(name of clinic)_____ will not discriminate between clients or professionals based on age, race, creed, disabilities, handicaps, preferences, or other personal concerns.

We, at _____(name of clinic)_____ maintain an objective and professional relationship with each client.

We, at _____(name of clinic)_____ respect the rights and views of other mental health professionals.

We, at _____(name of clinic)_____ will appropriately end services or refer clients to other programs when appropriate.

We, at _____(name of clinic)_____ will evaluate our personal limitations, strengths, biases, and effectiveness on an ongoing basis for the purpose of self-improvement. We will continually attain further education and training.

We, at _____(name of clinic)_____ hold respect for various institutional and managerial policies, but will help improve such policies if the best interest of the client is served.

If you believe any of your rights have been violated, please ask to speak to our Recipient Rights Advisor or Clinic Director.

Form 9   Therapist's Ethics Statement

I fully understand and agree that any information I provide to _____(name of clinic)_____ concerning my background and work history shall be accurate. Client information shall not be discussed with or revealed to any non-clinic individuals. I will only discuss client information with the clinic staff, on a need to know basis. When I am responsible for professional service provision, I shall provide these services with dignity and respect. I understand and agree to be bound by applicable state laws and relevant accreditation standards, and to avoid any conflict of ethics or beliefs, which conflict with those of a client, to the extent that it influences my ability to provide appropriate treatment. I understand that I have the right and ethical obligation to request case transfer in such situations. Further, I agree to familiarize myself with the Recipient Rights law and policies, to be accountable for conducting myself in accordance with said laws and polices, and to report any client care concerns to my supervisor or the Recipient Rights Officer.

I agree with and support the following statements from the Mission Statement and Ethical Stance.

We, at _____(name of clinic)_____ dedicate ourselves to serving the best interest of each client.

We, at _____(name of clinic)_____ will not discriminate between clients or professionals based on age, race, creed, disabilities, handicaps, preferences, or other personal concerns.

We, at _____(name of clinic)_____ maintain an objective and professional relationship with each client.

We, at _____(name of clinic)_____ respect the rights and views of other mental health professionals.

We, at _____(name of clinic)_____ will appropriately end services or refer clients to other programs when appropriate.

We, at _____(name of clinic)_____ will evaluate our personal limitations, strengths, biases, and effectiveness on an ongoing basis for the purpose of self-improvement. We will continually attain further education and training.

We, at _____(name of clinic)_____ hold respect for various institutional and managerial policies, but will help improve such policies if the best interest of the client is served.

I pledge to uphold the ethical standards of the following:

_____ American Psychiatric Association
_____ American Psychological Association
_____ American Counselors Association
_____ National Association of Social Workers
_____ Other(s) _____

Furthermore, all business activities conducted at _____(name of clinic)_____ will be conducted in a professional, ethical manner. Therefore, _____(name of clinic)_____ specifically prohibits the following: 1) falsification of documents (time cards, charting, reports, etc.), 2) billing for services not rendered, 3) providing or receiving bribes, and 4) soliciting.

Name of Therapist (print) _____

Signature of Therapist _____ Date_____

Name of Administrator (print)_____

Signature of Administrator_____ Date_____

Form 10   Agreement Regarding Minors

The involvement of children and adolescents in therapy can be highly beneficial to their overall development. Very often, it is best to see them with parents and other family members; sometimes, they are best seen alone. I will assess which might be best for your child and make recommendations to you. Obviously, the support of all the child's caregivers is essential, as well as their understanding of the basic procedures involved in counseling children.

The general goal of involving children in therapy is to foster their development at all levels. At times, it may seem that a specific behavior is needed, such as to get the child to obey or reveal certain information. Although those objectives may be part of overall development, they may not be the best goals for therapy. Again, I will evaluate and discuss these goals with you.

Because my role is that of the child's helper, I will not become involved in legal disputes or other official proceedings unless compelled to do so by a court of law. Matters involving custody and mediation are best handled by another professional who is specially trained in those areas rather than by the child's therapist.

The issue of confidentiality is critical in treating children. When children are seen with adults, what is discussed is known to those present and should be kept confidential except by mutual agreement. Children seen in individual sessions (except under certain conditions) are not legally entitled to confidentiality (also called privilege); their parents have this right. However, unless children feel they have some privacy in speaking with a therapist, the benefits of therapy may be lost. Therefore, it is necessary to work out an arrangement in which children feel that their privacy is generally being respected, at the same time that parents have access to critical information. This agreement must have the understanding and approval of the parents or other responsible adults and of the child in therapy.

This agreement regarding treatment of minors has provisions for inserting individual details, which can be supplied by both the child and the adults involved. However, it is first important to point out the exceptions to this general agreement. The following circumstances override the general policy that children are entitled to privacy while parents or guardians have a legal right to information.

- Confidentiality and privilege are limited in cases involving child abuse, neglect, molestation, or danger to self or others. In these cases, the therapist is required to make an official report to the appropriate agency and will attempt to involve parents as much as possible.

- Minors may independently enter into therapy and claim the privilege of confidentiality in cases involving abuse or severe neglect, molestation, pregnancy, or communicable diseases, and when they are on active military duty, married, or officially emancipated. They may seek therapy independently for substance abuse, danger to self or others, or a mental disorder, but parents must be involved unless doing so would harm the child. *(These circumstances may vary from state to state, and the specific laws of each state must be followed.)*

- Any evaluation, treatment, or reports ordered by, or done for submission to a third party such as a court or a school is not entirely confidential and will be shared with that agency with your specific written permission. Please also note that I do not have control over information once it is released to a third party.

Now that the various aspects surrounding confidentiality have been stated, the specific agreement between you and your child/children follows:

I, (name) _____ (relationship to child) _____

I, (name) _____ (relationship to child) _____

agree that my/our child/children

(name) _____

(name) _____

(name) _____

should have privacy in his/her/their therapy sessions, and I agree to allow this privacy except in extreme situations, which I will discuss with the therapist. At the same time, except under unusual circumstances, I understand that I have a legal right to obtain this information. To increase the effectiveness of the therapy, I agree to the following:

The goals of the therapy are as follows:

(by parent) _____

_____

(by child) _____

_____

_____

I will do my best to ensure that therapy sessions are attended and will not inquire about the content of sessions. If my child prefers/children prefer not to volunteer information about the sessions, I will respect his/her/their right not to disclose details. Basically, unless my child has/children have been abused or is/are a clear danger to self or others, the therapist will normally tell me only the following:

• whether sessions are attended
• whether or not my child is/children are generally participating
• whether or not progress is generally being made

The normal procedure for discussing issues that are in my child's/children's therapy will be joint sessions including my child/children, the therapist, and me and perhaps other appropriate adults. If I believe there are significant health or safety issues that I need to know about, I will contact the therapist and attempt to arrange a session with my child/children present. Similarly, when the therapist determines that there are significant issues that should be discussed with parents, every effort will be made to schedule a session involving the parents and the child/children. I understand that if information becomes known to the therapist and has a significant bearing on the child's/children's well-being, the therapist will work with the person providing the information to ensure that both parents are aware of it. In other words, the therapist will not divulge secrets except as mandated by law, but may encourage the individual who has the information to disclose it for therapy to continue effectively.

Parent(s): Please make any additions or modifications as desired: _____

_____

Signature: _____ Date: _____/_____/_____

Signature: _____ Date: _____/_____/_____

Minor(s): Please make any additions or modifications as desired: _____

_____

Signature: _____ Date: _____/_____/_____

Signature: _____ Date: _____/_____/_____

Signature: _____ Date: _____/_____/_____

Therapist Signature: _____ Date: _____/_____/_____

Form 11   Preauthorization for Health Care

I authorize (_____) to keep my signature on file and to charge my
_____(type of charge card)_____ account for:

___ All balances not paid by insurance or other third-party payers after 60 days. This total amount cannot
exceed $ _____ .

___ Recurring charges (ongoing treatment) as per amounts stated in the signed Payment Contract for
Services with this clinic.

I assign my insurance benefits to the provider listed above. I understand that this form is valid for one
year unless I cancel the authorization through written notice to this clinic.

Client's name: _____

Cardholder's name: _____

Cardholder's billing address: _____

          City: _____   State: _____   Zip: _____

Charge card number: _____   Expiration date: _____

Cardholder's signature: _____   Date: ____/____/_____

Chapter 2

Forms Designed for HIPAA Compliance

The following information is not intended to constitute comprehensive HIPAA training, but rather, it briefly summarizes the rationale for the guidelines. HIPAA guidelines specifically state that there are no approved training courses, and consumers are cautioned to be aware of programs that present themselves as such. The material presented in this text is the author's best effort to present forms designed to follow HIPAA regulations, but ultimately, the service providers are responsible for compliance. The U.S. Department of Health and Human Services (HHS) implemented the Health Insurance Portability and Accountability Act (HIPAA) in 1996. HIPAA is designed to both protect people's health information and provide standards to regulate the flow of information. Complete rules may be found on the Office of Civil Rights (OCR) website at http://www.hhs.gov/ocr/hipaa.

A number of terms used in the HIPAA material will be incorporated into the forms designed for compliance with specific HIPAA regulations. The bulk of the additional forms since the second edition are designed to this criteria.

HIPAA's "Privacy Rule" refers to the standards of disclosure of "protected health information" by "covered entities" (those subject to the regulations). The covered entities include health care clearinghouses, health plans, and health care providers who transmit health information electronically or use billing services that transmit electronically.

The covered entity must have a written contract with each business associate to safeguard the protected health information. All individually identifiable health information held or transmitted by a covered entity or its business associate (non-member of covered entity's workforce who has access to protected health information; e.g., billing service, utilization review) requires this contract. The OCR website provides a sample at http://www.hhs.gov/ocr/hipaa/contractprov.html.

Health care providers who are covered entities must disclose protected health information in two broad situations. These include providing the information to 1) the individual (or personal representative) who requests his or her records, and 2) to HHS in a compliance action. The covered entity may disclose protected health information without the individuals consent in the following situations.

1. The individual who is the subject of the protected health information (i.e., client, patient) is not required to authorize information sent to self.

2. Treatment, payment, and health care operations. Protected health care information that is used in the normal operation of providing services, consultation, and referral does not need a specific authorization.

3. Payment operations, such as premiums, determination of benefits, and billing services are not subject to an authorization.

4. Health care operations such as quality improvement, case management, competency assurance activities (e.g., credentialing, accreditation), audits, reviews, insurance functions, business development, and administrative activities may use a "limited data set" in which records are "de-identified" (patient information does not include identifying information, such as name, social security number, or other specific identifiers).

5. The public interest can override confidentiality in situations such as when the health, welfare, or safety of others may be in jeopardy. Certain civil operations such as court orders, crimes, essential government services necessary for the public's best interest do not require an individual's authorization for disclosing protected health information.

The covered entity is required to treat the individual's "personal representative" with the same rights as the individual in matters of disclosure. The personal representative is legally allowed to make health care decisions for the individual, except in cases of suspected abuse. In general, parents are the personal representatives of their minor children, and have access to protected health information, except in cases where the law would allow discretion on behalf of the licensed health care professional.

Disclosure of Information

A written authorization from the individual (or authorized representative) to the covered entity must precede a release of protected health care information. The content of the authorization must be in specific terms, written in plain language. The authorization must designate what information is being requested (rather than asking for an entire file), include an expiration date, and describe the individual's right to revoke the authorization.

In most cases an individual must consent to disclose psychotherapy progress notes. Exceptions include ongoing psychotherapy with the originator of the progress notes, training, legal matters brought on by the individual, legal reasons, and the public interest.

The practice of routinely requesting an individual's entire record is discouraged. The Privacy Rule requires limiting the amount of information disclosed to the "minimum necessary." The covered entity is required to develop and implement policies to set guidelines for determining what is the minimum amount of information necessary for the intended purpose of the disclosure. It's also essential to have policies and procedures that spell out which employees of the covered entity will have access to which level of protected health information in order to adequately perform their duties. When covered entities receive requests for specific information, it can be assumed that the level of information requested is reasonable.

Covered entities are required to provide a notice of privacy practices that describes people's rights to privacy, the duties of the covered entity, and the complaint process. This notice must be distributed to the individual at their first encounter (e.g., office, electronic, mailing). It must be posted in a prominent space where the individual can read it. The covered entity must make reasonable efforts to obtain the individual's signature that the notice was received.

The covered entity has the right to review their medical records (designated health set). However, the covered entity may choose not to disclose 1) psychotherapy progress notes, 2) information from legal proceedings, and 3) laboratory results, when it is deemed as not being in the individual's best interest.

Individuals have a right to amend information in their protected health information when they consider the information to be inaccurate or incomplete. If the information is amended, a reasonable effort must be made to provide the revised information to those who rely on this information for treatment and to any others identified by the individual as needing the information. When the request for an amendment is denied, the individual has the right to include a statement of the disagreement in the record.

FORM 12
Privacy of Information Policies

The Privacy Rule describes various covered entities that are required to comply with confidentiality requirements. Information may be disclosed to the individual, and for treatment, payment, and health care operations, for the public interest and safety, public health activities, health oversight activities, judicial and administrative proceedings, law enforcement purposes, serious threats to public safety, essential government functions, and when complying with worker's compensation laws. In addition, a number of practical areas are included specifically in this form.

1. *Duty to warn and protect.* When a client discloses intentions or a plan to harm another person, health care professionals are required to warn the intended victim and report this information to legal authorities. In cases in which the client discloses or implies a plan for suicide, health care professionals are required to notify legal authorities and make reasonable attempts to warn the family of the client.

2. *Public Safety.* Health records may be released for the public interest and safety, public health activities, judicial and administrative proceedings, law enforcement purposes, serious threats to

public safety, essential government functions, and when complying with worker's compensation laws.

3. *Abuse of children and vulnerable adults.* If a client states or suggests that he or she is abusing or has recently abused a child or vulnerable adult, or a child or vulnerable adult is in danger of abuse, health care professionals are required to report this information to the appropriate social service and/or legal authorities.

4. *Prenatal exposure to controlled substances.* Health care professionals are required to report admitted prenatal exposure to controlled substances that are potentially harmful. State laws may vary.

5. *In the event of a client's death.* In the event of a client's death, the spouse or parents of a deceased client have a right to gain access to their child's or spouse's records.

6. *Professional misconduct.* Professional misconduct by a health care professional must be reported by other health care professionals. If a professional or legal disciplinary meeting is held regarding the health care professional's actions, related records may be released in order to substantiate disciplinary concerns.

7. *Court orders.* Health care professionals are required to release records of clients when a court order has been issued.

8. *Minors/guardianship.* Parents or legal guardians of nonemancipated minor clients have the right to gain access to the client's records.

9. *Collection agencies.* Although the use of collection agencies is not considered unethical, there may be ethical concerns if a client is not informed that the clinic uses collection agencies when fees are not paid in a timely manner. If use of a collection agency causes a client's credit report to list the name of the counseling agency, it is not uncommon for the client to threaten a lawsuit against a therapist claiming that confidentiality has been violated.

   A clear financial policy signed by the client prior to receiving services is crucial in the operation of a clinic. Clear financial policies and procedures eliminate much potential discord (and premature termination of services) between the client and the therapist and clinic. Clinics which thrive financially and are self-sufficient have few accounts receivable.

10. *Third-party payers.* Many clients using insurance to pay for services are not aware of potential drawbacks. They may not realize which of their mental health records may be available to third-party payers. Insurance companies may require and be entitled to information such as dates of service, diagnosis, treatment plans, descriptions of impairment, progress of therapy, case notes and summaries. The documented existence of an Axis I diagnosis could have adverse future effects on such areas as insurance benefits.

11. *Professional consultations.* Clients should be informed if their cases are discussed in staff meetings or professional consultations. Assure them that no identifying information will be disclosed.

12. *Typing/dictation services.* Confidentiality might be violated when anyone other than the therapist types psychological reports. In many cases office staff have access to records. There have been several cases in which office personnel have reviewed files of relatives, neighbors, and other acquaintances. This is difficult to prevent, so inform clients that clerical personnel might have access to records and are held accountable for confidentiality. Records should be available within a clinic only on a "need to know" basis.

13. *Couples, family, and relationship counseling.* Separate files should be kept for each person involved in any conjoint or family counseling. If more than one person's records are kept in one file, it is possible that a serious breach of confidentiality could take place. For example, when couples enter counseling for marital issues, there is a potential for divorce and a child custody battle. If one of the partners requests "their file" and receives confidential material about the spouse, confidentiality has been violated. A clear policy indicating the agency's procedures in such situations is needed.

14. *Telephone calls, answering machines, and voice mail.* In the event that the agency or mental health professional must telephone the client for purposes such as appointment cancellations, reminders, or to give/receive information, efforts must be made to preserve confidentiality. The therapist should ask the client to list where the agency may phone the client and what identifying information can be used.

FORM 13
Request to Amend Health Records

Clients (or representatives) have the right to request an amendment to information in their medical records. The provider of services reviews the request, leading to a decision whether to make the amendment. The client is then notified of the decision. If it is decided that the amendment will not be made, the client has a right to have their request included into the medical records. The request or amended material is then sent to those whom the client (or representative) lists.

FORM 14
Request for Restricted Use/ Disclosure of Records

Clients (or representatives) have the right to request a restricted use or disclosure of their medical records. The provider of services reviews the request, leading to a decision whether to honor the request. The client is then notified of the decision.

FORM 15
Request for Alternative Means of Confidential Information

Under HIPAA regulations, clients (or representatives) have the right to have alternative means of communication from the provider. This request generally stems from confidentiality reasons in which the client requests a different address and/or telephone number be used to contact the client.

FORM 16
Release of Information Consent

This form incorporates both legal and ethical obligations. No protected client health information should be discussed with anyone without the written permission of the client or their personal representative except in areas defined in HIPAA regulations. A violation of confidentiality could lead to ethical, professional, and legal problems.

Clients have the right to know how the information will be used and which files will be released. A release of information is typically valid for one year (check state requirements), and may be cancelled at any time.

A significant change from HIPAA notes that progress notes are kept separately from other protected information. A request for a client's entire file, in itself, is not sufficient to obtain progress notes. A separate request for the progress notes must be included.

The legal guardian of a child must sign the release unless the child is an emancipated minor. It is necessary to determine whether a client has a personal representative. Evidence should be presented in written form prior to releasing protected health information.

FORM 17
Record of Requests for
Client Information

The purpose of this form is to comply with the HIPAA requirement of keeping a record of each request for the client's medical records from within and outside the agency.

FORM 18
Request for Listing of Disclosures
of Client Records

Under HIPAA regulations, clients (or representatives) have the right to request a listing of who has requested their medical records.

Form 12   Privacy of Information Policies

This form describes the confidentiality of your medical records, how the information is used, your rights, and how you may obtain this information.   Effective 4-14-03

Our Legal Duties
State and Federal laws require that we keep your medical records private. Such laws require that we provide you with this notice informing you of our privacy of information policies, your rights, and our duties. We are required to abide these policies until replaced or revised. We have the right to revise our privacy policies for all medical records, including records kept before policy changes were made. Any changes in this notice will be made available upon request before changes take place.

The contents of material disclosed to us in an evaluation, intake, or counseling session are covered by the law as private information. We respect the privacy of the information you provide us and we abide by ethical and legal requirements of confidentiality and privacy of records.

Use of Information
Information about you may be used by the personnel associated with this clinic for diagnosis, treatment planning, treatment, and continuity of care. We may disclose it to health care providers who provide you with treatment, such as doctors, nurses, mental health professionals, and mental health students and mental health professionals or business associates affiliated with this clinic such as billing, quality enhancement, training, audits, and accreditation.

Both verbal information and written records about a client cannot be shared with another party without the written consent of the client or the client's legal guardian or personal representative. It is the policy of this clinic not to release any information about a client without a signed release of information except in certain emergency situations or exceptions in which client information can be disclosed to others without written consent. Some of these situations are noted below, and there may be other provisions provided by legal requirements.

Duty to Warn and Protect
When a client discloses intentions or a plan to harm another person or persons, the health care professional is required to warn the intended victim and report this information to legal authorities. In cases in which the client discloses or implies a plan for suicide, the health care professional is required to notify legal authorities and make reasonable attempts to notify the family of the client.

Public Safety
Health records may be released for the public interest and safety for public health activities, judicial and administrative proceedings, law enforcement purposes, serious threats to public safety, essential government functions, military, and when complying with worker's compensation laws.

Abuse
If a client states or suggests that he or she is abusing a child or vulnerable adult, or has recently abused a child or vulnerable adult, or a child (or vulnerable adult) is in danger of abuse, the health care professional is required to report this information to the appropriate social service and/or legal authorities. If a client is the victim of abuse, neglect, violence, or a crime victim, and their safety appears to be at risk, we may share this information with law enforcement officials to help prevent future occurrences and capture the perpetrator.

Prenatal Exposure to Controlled Substances
Health care professionals are required to report admitted prenatal exposure to controlled substances that are potentially harmful.

In the Event of a Client's Death
In the event of a client's death, the spouse or parents of a deceased client have a right to access their child's or spouse's records.

Professional Misconduct
Professional misconduct by a health care professional must be reported by other health care professionals. In cases in which a professional or legal disciplinary meeting is being held regarding the health care professional's actions, related records may be released in order to substantiate disciplinary concerns.

Judicial or Administrative Proceedings
Health care professionals are required to release records of clients when a court order has been placed.

Minors/Guardianship
Parents or legal guardians of non-emancipated minor clients have the right to access the client's records.

Other Provisions
When payment for services are the responsibility of the client, or a person who has agreed to providing payment, and payment has not been made in a timely manner, collection agencies may be utilized in collecting unpaid debts. The specific content of the services (e.g., diagnosis, treatment plan, progress notes, testing) is not disclosed. If a debt remains unpaid it may be reported to credit agencies, and the client's credit report may state the amount owed, the time-frame, and the name of the clinic or collection source.

Insurance companies, managed care, and other third-party payers are given information that they request regarding services to the client. Information which may be requested includes type of services, dates/times of services, diagnosis, treatment plan, description of impairment, progress of therapy, and summaries.

Information about clients may be disclosed in consultations with other professionals in order to provide the best possible treatment. In such cases the name of the client, or any identifying information, is not disclosed. Clinical information about the client is discussed. Some progress notes and reports are dictated/typed within the clinic or by outside sources specializing in (and held accountable for) such procedures.

In the event in which the clinic or mental health professional must telephone the client for purposes such as appointment cancellations or reminders, or to give/receive other information, efforts are made to preserve confidentiality. Please notify us in writing where we may reach you by phone and how you would like us to identify ourselves. For example, you might request that when we phone you at home or work, we do not say the name of the clinic or the nature of the call, but rather the mental health professional's first name only. If this information is not provided to us (below), we will adhere to the following procedure when making phone calls: First we will ask to speak to the client (or guardian) without identifying the name of the clinic. If the person answering the phone asks for more identifying information we will say that it is a personal call. We will not identify the clinic (to protect confidentiality). If we reach an answering machine or voice mail we will follow the same guidelines.

Your Rights
You have the right to request to review or receive your medical files. The procedures for obtaining a copy of your medical information is as follows. You may request a copy of your records in writing with an original (not photocopied) signature. If your request is denied, you will receive a written explanation of the denial. Records for non-emancipated minors must be requested by their custodial parents or legal guardians. The charge for this service is $_____ per page, plus postage.

You have the right to cancel a release of information by providing us a written notice. If you desire to have your information sent to a location different than our address on file, you must provide this information in writing.

You have the right to restrict which information might be disclosed to others. However, if we do not agree with these restrictions, we are not bound to abide by them.

You have the right to request that information about you be communicated by other means or to another location. This request must be made to us in writing.

Your have the right to disagree with the medical records in our files. You may request that this information be changed. Although we might deny changing the record, you have the right to make a statement of disagreement, which will be placed in your file.

You have the right to know what information in your record has been provided to whom. Request this in writing.

If you desire a written copy of this notice you may obtain it by requesting it from the Clinic Director at this location.

Complaints
If you have any complaints or questions regarding these procedures, please contact the clinic. We will get back to you in a timely manner. You may also submit a complaint to the U.S. Dept. of Health and Human Services and/or the _____ (therapists state licensing agency) _____. If you file a complaint we will not retaliate in any way.

Direct all correspondence to: _____

I understand the limits of confidentiality, privacy policies, my rights, and their meanings and ramifications.

Client's name (please print): _____

Signature: _____   Date: ____/____/____

Signed by: __client __guardian __personal representative

Form 13   Request to Amend Health Records

The purpose of this form is to request an amendment in medical records maintained at _____ (name of clinic)_____. Upon receiving your request, the information will be reviewed and a decision letter will be sent to you or the person designated.

Request to amend information for

Name: _____

Address: _____ City: _____ State: _____ Zip: _____

Phone: _____ DOB: _____

Your relationship to client: __Self   __Parent/legal guardian   __Legal representative
                            __Other (describe)_____

Please list which information you desire to be amended in the following format.

1. Identify the information (preferably a copy of the information or document)
If no copy is available describe the information in detail (e.g., date of service, type of document)

2. Indicate what is inaccurate or incomplete

3. Describe what amendment(s) should be made

Please list who should receive copies of the amended information

Mail to: _____ Relationship: _____
Address: _____ City: _____ State: _____ Zip: _____

Mail to: _____ Relationship: _____
Address: _____ City: _____ State: _____ Zip: _____

Mail to: _____ Relationship: _____
Address: _____ City: _____ State: _____ Zip: _____

If you are the legal guardian or representative appointed by the court for the client, please attach a copy of this authorization to receive this protected health information.

I authorized the above-listed amendments to be sent to me and others listed

Client's Signature: _____ Date: _____/_____/_____

Parent/guardian/legal representative (if applicable)

   Signature: _____ Date: _____/_____/_____

Witness (if client is unable to sign):

   Signature _____ Date: _____/_____/_____

Form 14   Request for Restricted Use/Disclosure of Records

The purpose of this form is to request that a restriction be placed on how the client's medical records maintained at _____(name of clinic)_____ are used or disclosed. Upon receiving your request, the information will be reviewed and a decision letter will be sent to you or the person designated.

Request restrictions for the records of

Name: _____ _____

Address: _____ City: _____ State: _____ Zip: _____

Phone: _____ DOB: _____

Your relationship to client: __Self   __Parent/legal guardian   __Legal representative
                              __Other (describe)_____

Please describe the restrictions you desire for the use/disclosure of these records. Include the reasons for the restrictions.

_____
_____
_____
_____
_____
_____
_____

I authorize the above-listed restrictions.

If you are the legal guardian or representative appointed by the court for the client, please attach a copy of this authorization to receive this protected health information.

Client's Signature: _____ Date: _____/_____/_____

Parent/guardian/legal representative (if applicable)

    Signature: _____ Date: _____/_____/_____

Witness (if client is unable to sign):

    Signature _____ Date: _____/_____/_____

Form 15   Request for Alternative Means of Confidential Information

The purpose of this form is to request alternative means of _____ (name of clinic) _____
providing confidential communication to the client,

Client

Name: _____

Address: _____   City: _____   State: _____   Zip: _____

Phone: _____   DOB: _____

Your relationship to client: __Self   __Parent/legal guardian   __Legal representative

__Other (describe)_____

Check those which apply:

__Alternative address. Send client communication material to

Name: _____

Address: _____   City: _____   State: _____   Zip: _____

__Alternative phone. Make phone calls to

Phone: _____

I authorize the above request.

If you are the legal guardian or representative appointed by the court for the client, please attach a copy of this authorization to receive this protected health information.

Client's Signature: _____   Date: _____/_____/_____

Parent/guardian/legal representative (if applicable)

    Signature: _____   Date: _____/_____/_____

Witness (if client is unable to sign)

    Signature: _____   Date: _____/_____/_____

Form 16   Release of Information Consent

Client's Name: _____

Address: _____ City: _____ State: _____ Zip: _____

Phone: _____ DOB: _____

I, _____ , authorize _____ to:

_____ (send) _____ (receive) the following _____ (to) _____ (from)

Name: _____

Address: _____ City: _____ State: _____ Zip: _____

A SEPARATE AUTHORIZATION, AS DEFINED BY HIPAA, IS REQUIRED FOR *PSYCHOTHERAPY NOTES.

_____ Academic testing results   _____ Psychological testing results

_____ Behavior programs   _____ Service plans

_____ Progress reports   _____ Summary reports

_____ Intelligence testing results   _____ Vocational testing results

_____ Medical reports   _____ Entire record, except progress notes

_____ Personality profiles   _____ *Psychotherapy Notes

_____ Psychological reports   _____ Other, specify_____

The above information will be used for the following purposes:

_____ Planning appropriate treatment or program

_____ Continuing appropriate treatment or program

_____ Determining eligibility for benefits or program

_____ Case review   _____ Updating files

_____ Other (specify) _____

I understand that this information may be protected by Title 42 (Code of Federal Rules of Privacy of Individually Identifiable Health Information, Parts 160 and 164) and Title 45 (Federal Rules of Confidentiality of Alcohol and Drug Abuse Patient Records, Chapter 1, Part 2), plus applicable state laws. I further understand the information disclosed to the recipient may not be protected under these guidelines if they are not a health care provider covered by state or federal rules.

I understand that this authorization is voluntary, and I may revoke this consent at any time by providing written notice, and after (some states vary, usually 1 year) this consent automatically expires. I have been informed what information will be given, its purpose, and who will receive the information. I understand that I have a right to receive a copy of this authorization. I understand that I have a right to refuse to sign this authorization.

Your relationship to client: __Self   __Parent/legal guardian   __Personal representative

__Other (describe)_____

If you are the legal guardian or representative appointed by the court for the client, please attach a copy of this authorization to receive this protected health information.

Client's Signature: _____ Date: _____/_____/_____

Parent/guardian/personal representative (if applicable)

Signature: _____ Date: _____/_____/_____

Witness (if client is unable to sign)

Signature: _____ Date: _____/_____/_____

Form 17   Record of Requests for Client Information

Client:_____ DOB:_____

Restrictions requested by client:_____

_____

Requests for release of records from other agencies

Date release signed by client:_____ (expires in one year)

Renewals of release of information:_____

Name of person/agency requesting information	Date	Purpose of use of information	Action taken
_____	_____	_____	_____
_____	_____	_____	_____
_____	_____	_____	_____
_____	_____	_____	_____
_____	_____	_____	_____

Use of information within this agency

Name of person/agency requesting information	Date	Purpose of use of information	Action taken
_____	_____	_____	_____
_____	_____	_____	_____
_____	_____	_____	_____
_____	_____	_____	_____
_____	_____	_____	_____

Form 18   Request for Listing of Disclosures of Client Records

The purpose of this form is to request a listing of disclosures of client records made by
_____(name of clinic)_____ for a client. It does not include routine requests such as billing, treatment, or typical clinic operations. Disclosures prior to 4-14-03 are not available.

Client

Name: _____

Address: _____ City: _____ State: _____ Zip: _____

Phone: _____ DOB: _____

Your relationship to client: __Self   __Parent/legal guardian   __Legal representative
                              __Other (describe)_____

Dates of requests for listing of disclosures you are requesting:

__All

__From _____ to _____

I authorize the above request.

If you are the legal guardian or representative appointed by the court for the client, please attach a copy of this authorization to receive this protected health information.

Client's Signature: _____   Date: _____/_____/_____

Parent/guardian/legal representative (if applicable)

   Signature: _____   Date: _____/_____/_____

Witness (if client is unable to sign)

   Signature: _____   Date: _____/_____/_____

Chapter 3

Assessment Forms

FORMS 19 and 20
Initial Assessment Forms

Two initial assessment forms are provided, adults (Form 19) and children (Form 20). The initial assessment material is gathered during the first session with the client. The goal of the first session is to establish and document a diagnosis, identify functional impairments, and determine respective onsets, frequencies, durations, intensities, and examples of *DSM-IV-TR (Diagnostic and Statistical Manual of Mental Disorders, 4th ed., Text Revisions),* symptoms and impairments. Statements comparing current to previous functioning are also helpful.

The information obtained is tentative and generally based on one session, but many third-party reimbursers require this information prior to the second session. The form allows for the presenting problem, background information, history, biopsychosocial information, mental status, and a rule-in/rule-out procedure for various diagnoses. Client strengths and weaknesses are also assessed to be incorporated into the treatment plan.

The initial assessment is a screening device to help determine the need for services. It is revised as more information is collected in subsequent sessions. The usual time needed to collect the information is one hour. *The Psychotherapy Documentation Primer* (Wiger, 1999, 2005, in press), provides specific training in conducting a diagnostic interview and mental status exam.

Intake information provides necessary information for the treatment plan and validates the diagnosis. Unless the intake material sufficiently supports a diagnosis according to the *DSM-IV-TR,* it is vulnerable to rejection by a third party. The specific functional impairments documented in the intake material may include social, family, occupational, affective, physical, cognitive, sexual, educational, biopsychological, and other areas of impairment that support the diagnosis.

Treatment, according to several third-party criteria, becomes the process of alleviated functional impairments. Documentation is generally requested to be in behavioral terms (usually quantifiable, observable, and measurable). Thus, intake notes should specifically list baseline rates of behavior for later comparisons of progress and setbacks. Baseline rates are also needed to help determine objective discharge criteria.

Judy Doe's (our case example) initial assessment lists both background and current information about the client. Both types of information are necessary for therapy, but observations regarding the current functional impairments are more needed for third-party documentation and accountability procedures. The Initial Assessment Form for Judy Doe (Form 19A) contains the therapist's documentation statements.

Judy Doe's initial assessment statements help to document a diagnosis, describe the client's mental health condition, provide a baseline for certain depressive behaviors, and reflect issues to be dealt with in therapy.

Five Sources of Information Available from the Intake Session(s)

The mental health intake procedure serves several purposes, including rapport building, information gathering, diagnosis, and setting up the treatment plan, each of which is necessary for accurate documentation. Information is available from at least five sources, including:

1. Diagnostic interview and mental status examination (observations by the clinician).

2. Testing (standardized, objective measures).

3. Self-report information (questionnaires filled out by the client).

4. Historical documents (past behaviors).

5. Collateral information (other people involved in the client's life).

1. *The Diagnostic Interview and Mental Status Examination.* The diagnostic interview is subject to limitations of validity and reliability. It is as valid as the diagnostic category. Some diagnoses have clear *DSM-IV-TR* criteria and are more easily identified than others. For example, a major depressive episode is clearly defined in the *DSM-IV-TR;* but several other disorders seem to be less clearly defined, causing the differential diagnosis to be more tentative and less valid.

The interview is as reliable as the clinician's knowledge of psychopathology. A vague knowledge of *DSM-IV-TR* symptomology and differential diagnoses limits specificity, leading to erratic treatment. Mental health professionals can increase the reliability of their diagnoses by increasing their knowledge of psychopathology.

The interview should clearly document the Onset, Frequency, Antecedents, Intensity, and Duration (OFAID procedure) of each symptom. Without this information, there would be problems in differential diagnosis. For example, a diagnosis of dysthymic disorder cannot be given unless an adult has been depressed for at least two years. Without documentation of a history of depression for this time period, dysthymia is not adequately documented. A misdiagnosis could lead to improper treatment. Treatment for dysthymia is not the same as treatment for other types of depression such as single-episode major depression, bipolar disorder, or an adjustment disorder with depressed mood.

2. *Testing.* It is the clinician's responsibility to choose tests that are valid measures of the behaviors in question. That is, the test must measure what it purports to measure. Some clinics have administered the same battery of tests to all clients, whatever the reason for therapy or evaluation. Current contracts with third-party payers stipulate that if a test is administered there must be documented verification that the information derived for the particular test is necessary for accurate treatment. Clients should be informed that services such as testing or other procedures may not be covered by third-party payers. Payment contracts and financial policies should cover such provisions.

Standardized testing may be used as a documentation procedure in at least three ways: norm-referenced, criterion-referenced, and self-referenced. The same test can be used for all three purposes.

In norm-referenced testing, a person's test performance is compared with a normal population or a reference group. Most test distributions follow a normal curve in which the greatest number of people score at the 50th percentile and increasingly fewer people's scores approach the extremes. Scores are generally reported as standard scores. For example, most intelligence tests (e.g., Wechsler Adult Intelligence Scale–4th Edition [WAIS-IV]) have a mean of 100 (i.e., average intelligence quotient [IQ] = 100) and a standard deviation of 15. Approximately 68 percent of test takers score within one standard deviation from the mean (i.e., 68 percent of the population have an IQ between 85 and 115). Increasingly fewer people score higher or lower if the test follows a normal curve.

Criterion-referenced testing involves setting cutoff scores based on diagnostic categories. Referring to the previous example, WAIS-III criterion scores have been set as follows:

Standard Score (IQ)	Category
69 and below	Mentally retarded or mentally deficient
70–79	Borderline
80–89	Low average
90–109	Average
110–119	High average
120–129	Superior
130 and above	Very superior

In self-referenced testing, an individual's test scores are compared over time. For example, some therapists ask clients to fill out a brief test periodically (e.g., Beck Depression Inventory). Scores are charted throughout therapy and progress is measured by affective changes depicted by test scores. Self-referenced testing could be charted as in Figure 3.1.

3. *Self-Report Information.* Additional information may be obtained by asking the client to fill out a biographical information form either prior to the initial interview or after the intake session (and returned prior to the second session). This information is especially helpful because the client is able to spend sufficient time in private delineating various historical, familial, medical, and mental health concerns. Also, using simple graphs such as those depicted in Figure 3.2, the client can furnish examples of impairment involving a wide range of mental health and behavioral symptoms. The information provided converts to treatment plan objectives.

4. *Historical Documents.* Reports and evaluations by other professionals are quite helpful in documenting the client's mental health history. These are generally obtained from other professionals, schools,

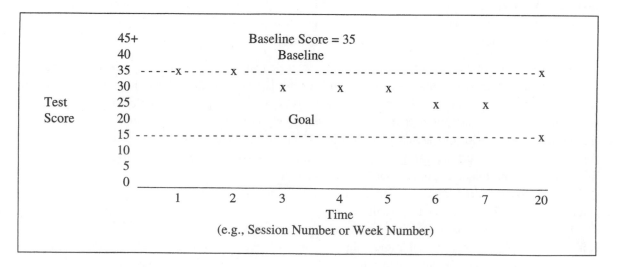

Figure 3.1 Graph of Therapeutic Progress Using Self-Referenced Testing.

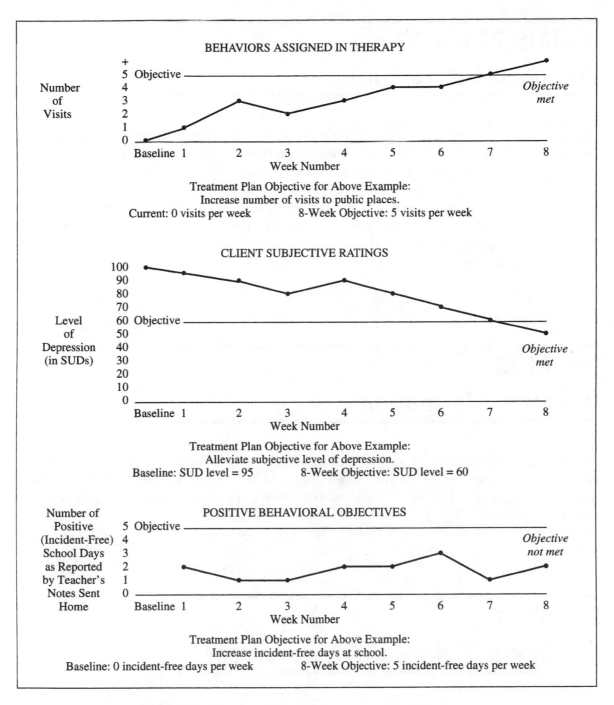

Figure 3.2 Samples of Various Documentation Techniques.

and agencies or, at times, brought in by the client. They must be requested in writing and the request form signed by the client. (See Release of Information Consent form on page 2.13.)

5. *Collateral Information.* Collateral information is data disclosed by others in the assessment session. For example, a parent might supply background information about a child, or a stroke victim's spouse might provide information about functioning before and after the stroke.

FORMS 21 and 22
Personal History Forms

These forms are usually filled out prior to the initial assessment session. The Personal History Form—Adult (Form 21) is filled out by adult clients, while the Personal History Form—Child/Adolescent (Form 22) is filled out by the child's caregiver. Each form is written in the same order as the Initial Assessment and the Biopsychosocial Information Form. Thus, the clinician can quickly reference both the Personal History Form and Initial Assessment Form when completing summary reports or psychological evaluations.

Like the Biographical Information Form, the Personal History Form is designed in conjunction with the *DSM-IV-TR*. The Personal History Forms are specifically designed to fit JCAHO standards for background information.

FORM 23
Couple's Information

This form provides valuable information regarding strengths and weaknesses in the relationship. Each partner's point of view and perspective on their partner's point of view are assessed to help increase clients' understanding of each other. The forms end with a written consent for the therapist to discuss each other's responses.

FORM 24
Emotional/Behavioral Assessment

The Emotional/Behavioral Assessment Form (Form 24) is primarily used for children and people diagnosed with developmental disabilities. It is designed to solicit information about the client's current level of emotional expression, positive behaviors, behaviors targeted for change, and recent stressors. It further helps set treatment plan goals.

FORM 25
Emotional/Behavioral Update

The Emotional/Behavioral Update (Form 25) is filled out by a caregiver of the client. It is used to inform the therapist of specific current emotional/behavioral problems areas that are current. Without knowledge of specific ongoing issues, the therapy could easily be off-track or not relevant to issues that are fresh in the client's memory.

Caution and sound judgment are needed as to whether and how to incorporate the information from this form into therapy. It can work positively when the client (usually a child or low-functioning adult such as mentally retarded) has difficulty relating current issues and welcomes the interventions of trusted others. It may be problematic if the client views the shared information as an alliance between the caregiver and therapist resulting in an unbalanced relationship.

FORM 26
Diagnostic Assessment Report

The Diagnostic Assessment Report (Form 26) is similar to the Biopsychosocial Report, but is based on clinical information and mental status, more than on biopsychosocial information. It is designed to be written after the first or second visit. It tends to satisfy managed care requirements of providing assessment information upfront.

The Diagnostic Assessment Report is designed to summarize the intake and assessment material, providing clear documentation of the client's current mental health condition—presenting problem, history, current functional impairments, and mental status. The report includes specific examples of frequency, duration, and intensity of symptoms.

In the Diagnosis Validation section of the form, the therapist may use diagnostic material such as testing, biographical data, collateral information, and intake material to document the diagnosis. This section may be especially helpful for an adult, for forensics, and in justifying the need for further services.

This form is useful in at least two ways: 1) it helps the therapist to keep on target in documenting the diagnosis and treatment, and 2) it is helpful to send this form in to third-party payers along with their request form for additional service authorization.

The Diagnosis Assessment Report for Judy Doe (Form 26A) provides clear validation of supporting material for a diagnosis of major depression. Information provided in the form is a summary of the previous assessment material.

FORM 27
Diagnostic Assessment—
Lower Functioning

This Diagnostic Assessment form (Form 27) is designed for people with concerns such as mental retardation or delays in adaptive functioning. Many states require periodic evaluations for individuals with delayed adaptive functioning. In many cases, most of the evaluation will involve little or no communication with the client (due to poor insight or lack of comprehension).

The diagnostic information in such cases comes from caregivers, previous records, observations, and testing, when possible. Generally, the higher the level of functioning, the less need there is for this form. The Diagnostic Assessment—Lower Functioning Form is routinely used for clients with mental retardation. Information is divided into eight categories that often serve as an outline for a write up or psychological evaluation which concludes with a summary and recommendations:

Background Information	Observations
Medical Concerns	Previous Testing
Present Behaviors	Present Testing
Emotional Issues	Clinical Diagnosis

FORM 28
Biopsychosocial Report

The Biopsychosocial Report (Form 28) provides background information in several areas of the client's life. Much of the information is obtained in the initial interview, and additions and revisions are made throughout therapy. Information covered includes biological (or physical), psychological, and social. Biological information includes any background material such as information about the client's family, development, education, employment, legal, and other medical history. Psychological information focuses on previous and current psychological status and treatment. Social information includes the client's social relationships and supports. Each area of biopsychosocial information collected should include both strengths and weaknesses.

The order of information in the Biopsychosocial Report is written in the same order as the information in the Personal History Forms. This procedure saves much time and effort when coordinating clinical information and in report writing.

Some therapists choose to collect this information by the first two sessions, while others fill it in as the information unfolds, usually within the first six sessions. Biopsychosocial information is very important for clinics subject to JCAHO guidelines. The report concludes with an integrated summary of information gathered. It is designed to be written after the sixth client visit, rather than after the first or second session. It is strong in following JCAHO guidelines, but weak in providing upfront information as per managed care guidelines.

Form 19   Initial Assessment—Adult

Client's name: _____   Date: _____

Starting time: _____   Ending time: _____   Duration: _____

PART A.   BIOPSYCHOSOCIAL ASSESSMENT

1. Presenting Problem

_____

_____

_____

_____

2. Signs and Symptoms (*DSM-IV-TR* based) . . . Resulting in Impairment(s)

(Include current examples for treatment planning, e.g., social, occupational, affective, cognitive, physical)

_____

_____

_____

_____

3. History of Presenting Problem

Events, precipitating factors or incidents leading to need for services: _____

_____

_____

_____

Frequency/duration/severity/cycling of symptoms: _____

_____

_____

_____

Was there a clear time when Sx worsened? _____

Family mental health history: _____

_____

_____

_____

4. Current Family and Significant Relationships   (See Personal History Form)

Strengths/support: _____

Stressors/problems: _____

Recent changes: _____

Changes desired: _____

Comment on family circumstances: _____

5. **Childhood/Adolescent History**   (See Personal History Form)

(Developmental milestones, past behavioral concerns, environment abuse, school, social, mental health)

_____

_____

_____

_____

6. **Social Relationships**   (See Personal History Form)

Strengths/support: _____

Stressors/problems: _____

Recent changes: _____

Changes desired: _____

7. **Cultural/Ethnic**   (See Personal History Form)

Strengths/support: _____

Stressors/problems: _____

Beliefs/practices to incorporate into therapy: _____

8. **Spiritual/Religious**   (See Personal History Form)

Strengths/support: _____

Stressors/problems: _____

Beliefs/practices to incorporate into therapy: _____

Recent changes: _____

Changes desired: _____

9. **Legal**   (See Personal History Form)

_____

_____

Status/impact/stressors: _____

10. **Education**   (See Personal History Form)

Strengths: _____

Weaknesses: _____

11. **Employment/Vocational**   (See Personal History Form)

Strengths/support: _____

Stressors/problems: _____

12. **Military**   (See Personal History Form)

_____

Current impact: _____

13. **Leisure/Recreational**   (See Personal History Form)

Strengths/support: _____

Recent changes: _____

Changes desired: _____

14. Physical Health   (See Personal History Form)

_____

_____

Physical factors affecting mental condition: _____

_____

15. Chemical Use History   (See Personal History Form)

_____

_____

Patient's perception of problem: _____

_____

16. Counseling/Prior Treatment History   (See Personal History Form)

_____

_____

Benefits of previous treatment: _____

Setbacks of previous treatment: _____

PART B.   DIAGNOSTIC INTERVIEW

Mood

(Rule-in and rule-out signs and symptoms: validate with _DSM-IV-TR_)

Predominant mood during interview: _____

Current Concerns (give examples of impairments (i), severity (s), frequency (f), duration (d))

Adjustment Disorder

(w/in 3 months of identified stressor, Sx persist < 6 months after stressor, marked distressed)

____ Depressed   ____ Anxiety   ____ Mixed anxiety & depression   ____ Conduct

____ Emotions & conduct   ____ Unspecified

Specify disturbance: ____ Acute (<6 months)   ____ Chronic (>6 months) _____

_____

Impairment(s): ____ social ____ occupational/educational ____ affective ____ cognitive __ other

Examples of impairment(s): _____

_____

Major Depression (2 or more wks): ____ Usually depressed or _____ anhedonia. (4+ of following):

____ wght + / (-) 5%/month ____ appetite + / (-) ____ sleep + / (-) __ psychomotor + / (-)

____ fatigue ____ worthlessness/guilt ____ concentration ____ death/suicidal ideation

Other: __ crying spells __ withdrawal ____ add'l. sx _____

_____

Impairment(s): __ social ____ occupational/educational __ affective ____ cognitive __ other

Examples of impairment(s): _____

_____

3.11

Dysthymia (2 or more years): _____depressed most of time. (2+ of following)

____ low/high appetite or eating ____ in/hypersomnia ____ low energy/fatigue ____ low self-esteem

____ low concentration/decisions ____ hopelessness ____ other

_____

Impairment(s): ___ social ___ occupational/educational ____ affective ___ cognitive ____ other

Examples of impairment(s): _____

_____

Mania (3+):

____ grandiosity ____ low sleep ____ talkative ____ flight of ideas ____ distractibility

____ goals/agitation ____ excessive pleasure

_____

Impairment(s): ____ social ____ occupational/educational ____ affective ____ cognitive ___ other

Examples of impairment(s): _____

_____

Panic Attacks (4+, abrupt development of):

____ palpitations ____ sweating ____ trembling ____ shortness of breath ____ feeling of choking

____ chest pain ____ nausea ____dizziness ____ light-headed ____ derealization

____ fear of losing control ____ fear of dying ____ numbness __ chills/hot flashes

_____

Impairment(s): ____ social ___ occupational/educational ____ affective ____ cognitive __ other

Examples of impairment(s): _____

_____

Anxiety (GAD: 3+, most of time, 6 months):

____ restlessness ____ easily fatigued ____ concentration ____ irritability

____ muscle tension ____ sleep disturbance

_____

Impairment(s): ____ social ____ occupational/educational ____ affective ____ cognitive __ other

Examples of impairment(s): _____

_____

Other Diagnostic Concerns or Behavioral Issues

(e.g., ____ dissociation ____ eating ____ sleep ____ impulse control ____ thought disorders ____ anger

____ relationships ____ cognitive __ phobias ____ substance abuse ____ medical conditions

____ somatization ____ phobias ____ sexual ____ PTSD, etc.)

_____

Impairment(s): ____ social ____ occupational/educational ____ affective ____ cognitive __ other

Examples of impairment(s): _____

_____

USE ADDITIONAL PAPER AS NECESSARY

Mental Status
(Check appropriate level of impairment: N/A or OK signifies no known impairment. Comment on significant areas of impairment.)

Appearance	N/A or OK	Slight	Moderate	Severe
Unkempt, disheveled	(__)	(__)	(__)	(__)
Clothing, dirty, atypical	(__)	(__)	(__)	(__)
Odd phys. characteristics	(__)	(__)	(__)	(__)
Body odor	(__)	(__)	(__)	(__)
Appears unhealthy	(__)	(__)	(__)	(__)

Posture	N/A or OK	Slight	Moderate	Severe
Slumped	(__)	(__)	(__)	(__)
Rigid, tense	(__)	(__)	(__)	(__)

Body Movements	N/A or OK	Slight	Moderate	Severe
Accelerated, quick	(__)	(__)	(__)	(__)
Decreased, slowed	(__)	(__)	(__)	(__)
Restlessness, fidgety	(__)	(__)	(__)	(__)
Atypical, unusual	(__)	(__)	(__)	(__)

Speech	N/A or OK	Slight	Moderate	Severe
Rapid	(__)	(__)	(__)	(__)
Slow	(__)	(__)	(__)	(__)
Loud	(__)	(__)	(__)	(__)
Soft	(__)	(__)	(__)	(__)
Mute	(__)	(__)	(__)	(__)
Atypical (e.g., slurring)	(__)	(__)	(__)	(__)

Attitude	N/A or OK	Slight	Moderate	Severe
Domineering, controlling	(__)	(__)	(__)	(__)
Submissive, dependent	(__)	(__)	(__)	(__)
Hostile, challenging	(__)	(__)	(__)	(__)
Guarded, suspicious	(__)	(__)	(__)	(__)
Uncooperative	(__)	(__)	(__)	(__)

Affect	N/A or OK	Slight	Moderate	Severe
Inappropriate to thought	(__)	(__)	(__)	(__)
Increased lability	(__)	(__)	(__)	(__)
Blunted, dull, flat	(__)	(__)	(__)	(__)
Euphoria, elation	(__)	(__)	(__)	(__)
Anger, hostility	(__)	(__)	(__)	(__)
Depression, sadness	(__)	(__)	(__)	(__)
Anxiety	(__)	(__)	(__)	(__)
Irritability	(__)	(__)	(__)	(__)

Perception	N/A or OK	Slight	Moderate	Severe
Illusions	(__)	(__)	(__)	(__)
Auditory hallucinations	(__)	(__)	(__)	(__)
Visual hallucinations	(__)	(__)	(__)	(__)
Other hallucinations	(__)	(__)	(__)	(__)
Cognitive	N/A or OK	Slight	Moderate	Severe
Alertness	(__)	(__)	(__)	(__)
Attn. span, distractibility	(__)	(__)	(__)	(__)
Short-term memory	(__)	(__)	(__)	(__)
Long-term memory	(__)	(__)	(__)	(__)
Judgment	N/A or OK	Slight	Moderate	Severe
Decision making	(__)	(__)	(__)	(__)
Impulsivity	(__)	(__)	(__)	(__)
Thought Content	N/A or OK	Slight	Moderate	Severe
Obsessions/compulsions	(__)	(__)	(__)	(__)
Phobic	(__)	(__)	(__)	(__)
Depersonalization	(__)	(__)	(__)	(__)
Suicidal ideation	(__)	(__)	(__)	(__)
Homicidal ideation	(__)	(__)	(__)	(__)
Delusions	(__)	(__)	(__)	(__)

Estimated level of intelligence: _____

Orientation: ____ Time ____ Place ____ Person

Able to hold normal conversation? ___ Yes ____ No

Eye contact: _____

Level of insight:

    ____ Complete denial   ____ Slight awareness

    ____ Blames others   ____ Blames self

    ____ Intellectual insight, but few changes likely

    ____ Emotional insight, understanding, change can occur

Client's view of actions needed to change: _____

Comments

_____
_____
_____
_____
_____
_____
_____
_____

PART C.   DIAGNOSIS VALIDATION

Diagnosis 1: _____   Code: _____

DSM-IV-TR Criteria

_____
_____
_____

Examples of impairment/dysfunction: _____

_____
_____
_____

Additional validation (e.g., testing, previous records, self-report): _____

_____
_____
_____

Diagnosis 2: _____   Code: _____

DSM-IV-TR Criteria

_____
_____

Examples of impairment/dysfunction: _____

_____
_____

Additional validation (e.g., testing, previous records, self-report): _____

_____
_____
_____

Diagnosis 3: _____   Code: _____

DSM-IV-TR Criteria

_____
_____
_____

Examples of impairment/dysfunction: _____

_____
_____

Additional validation (e.g., testing, previous records, self-report): _____

_____
_____
_____

Diagnosis	Code

Axis I   1: _____   _____

2: _____   _____

3: _____   _____

Axis II   1: _____   _____

2: _____   _____

Axis III   _____   _____

Axis IV   _____

Axis V   Current GAF = _____   Highest past year GAF = _____

Prognosis: ___ Poor   ___ Marginal   ___ Guarded   ___ Moderate   ___ Good   ___ Excellent

Qualifiers to prognosis: ___ Med compliance   ___ Tx compliance   ___ Home environment

___ Activity changes   ___ Behavioral changes   ___ Attitudinal changes   ___ Education/training

___ Other: _____

Treatment Considerations

Is the patient appropriate for treatment? ___ Yes   ___ No

If no, explain and indicate referral made: _____

Tx modality: ___ Indiv.   ___ Conjoint   ___ Family   ___ Collateral   ___ Group

Frequency: _____   _____   _____   _____   _____

If Conjoint, Family or Collateral, specify with whom: _____

Adjunctive Services Needed:

___ Physical exam   ___ School records

___ Laboratory tests (specify): _____

___ Patient records (specify): _____

Therapist's Questions/Concerns/Comments: _____ Psychiatric evaluation   ___ Psychological testing

_____

_____

_____

Therapist's signature/credentials: _____   Date: ____/____/____

Supervisor's Remarks

_____

_____

_____

Supervisor's signature/credentials: _____   Date: ____/____/____

Therapist's Response to Supervisor's Remarks

_____

_____

_____

Therapist's signature/credentials: _____   Date: ____/____/____

Form 19A   Initial Assessment—Adult   (*Completed*)

Client's name: _Judy Doe_   Date: _3/8/2005_

Starting time: _10:00 A.M._   Ending time: _11:30 A.M._   Duration: _90 min._

PART A.   BIOPSYCHOSOCIAL ASSESSMENT

1. Presenting Problem

Missing increasingly more time at work, avoiding friends, marital conflict. "I just can't snap
out of this depression."

2. Signs and Symptoms (*DSM-IV-TR* based) . . . Resulting in Impairment(s)

(Include current examples for treatment planning, e.g., social, occupational, affective, cognitive, physical)

Usually fatigued, depressed and has low motivation to go to work, resulting in occupational
impairment. Avoiding most of her close friends, rarely answers the door or telephone.
Increasing anger outbursts toward spouse, with decreased sexual activity, resulting in marital
relationship problems and possible divorce. Has unintentionally lost 20 lbs. in past 6 months.

3. History of Presenting Problem

Events, precipitating factors or incidents leading to need for services: _Previous history of_
diagnosis of Major Depression in 1973 due to coping with a relationship break-up. Current
relationship issues are exacerbating similar problems.

Frequency/duration/severity/cycling of symptoms: _Feels depressed 3 out of 4 days, most of_
the day, especially in the morning. Symptoms increase when feeling stressed or after a conflict
with spouse or family members.

Was there a clear time when Sx worsened? _One year ago with increased marital conflict._

Family mental health history: _Functional family of origin. No family history of depression._

4. Current Family and Significant Relationships   (See Personal History Form)

Strengths/support: _Very supportive family of origin_

Stressors/problems: _Marital conflict, intrusive mother and older sister_

Recent changes: _Spouse threatening divorce_

Changes desired: _To be less dependent on others, increase assertiveness_

Comment on family circumstances: _Family of origin may interfere with marriage_

5. **Childhood/Adolescent History**   (See Personal History Form)

(Developmental milestones, past behavioral concerns, environment abuse, school, social, mental health)

Normal childhood development, often dependent on others. No history of abuse or neglect.

Above average grades in school.

6. **Social Relationships**   (See Personal History Form)

Strengths/support: _History of social activities_

Stressors/problems: _Avoid all previous friends_

Recent changes: _Has dropped all social activities_

Changes desired: _Return to premorbid functioning_

7. **Cultural/Ethnic**   (See Personal History Form)

Strengths/support: _Mainstream culture_

Stressors/problems: _No_

Beliefs/practices to incorporate into therapy: _No_

8. **Spiritual/Religious**   (See Personal History Form)

Strengths/support: _States that belief in God prevents suicide_

Stressors/problems: _None_

Beliefs/practices to incorporate into therapy: _None_

Recent changes: _None_

Changes desired: _None_

9. **Legal**   (See Personal History Form)

No history of legal issues

Status/impact/stressors: _None_

10. **Education**   (See Personal History Form)

Strengths: _Superior academic achievement when in high school_

Weaknesses: _None_

11. **Employment/Vocational**   (See Personal History Form)

Strengths/support: _Steady employment as teacher, history of good job._

Stressors/problems: _Currently feels "burnt out"_

12. **Military**   (See Personal History Form)

_N/A_

Current impact: _____

13. **Leisure/Recreational**   (See Personal History Form)

Strengths/support: _History of exercising, bowling and being active_

Recent changes: _Has stopped all such activities_

Changes desired: _Return to previous functioning_

3.18

14. Physical Health (See Personal History Form)

History of good health. Currently experiences weight loss, increased headaches, fatigue,
decreased libido, and poor sleep

Physical factors affecting mental condition: *Vegetative symptoms of depression*

15. Chemical Use History (See Personal History Form)

Light social drinking. No history of drug or alcohol abuse. No treatment history, no DWI.
No job loss.

Patient's perception of problem: *Not a problem*

16. Counseling/Prior Treatment History (See Personal History Form)

1973 counseling after relationship break-up. Successful treatment with individual counseling.

Benefits of previous treatment: *Returned to previous functioning*
Setbacks of previous treatment: *None known*

PART B. DIAGNOSTIC INTERVIEW

Mood

(Rule-in and rule-out signs and symptoms: validate with *DSM-IV-TR*)

Predominant mood during interview: *Depressed*

Current Concerns (give examples of impairments (i), severity (s), frequency (f), duration (d))

Adjustment Disorder

(w/in 3 months of identified stressor, Sx persist < 6 months after stressor, marked distressed)

____ Depressed ____ Anxiety ____ Mixed anxiety & depression ____ Conduct

____ Emotions & conduct ____ Unspecified

Specify disturbance: ____ Acute (<6 months) ____ Chronic (>6 months) *Denies*

Impairment(s): ____ social ____ occupational/educational ____ affective ____ cognitive __ other
Examples of impairment(s): _____

Major Depression (2 or more wks): _X_ Usually depressed or _X_ anhedonia. (4+ of following):

_X_ wght + / (-) 5%/month _X_ appetite + / (-) _X_ sleep + / (-) _X_ psychomotor + / (-)

_X_ fatigue _X_ worthlessness/guilt _X_ concentration _X_ death/suicidal ideation

Other: __ crying spells _X_ withdrawal ____ add'l. sx _____

Impairment(s): _X_ social _X_ occupational/educational _X_ affective ___ cognitive ___ other
Examples of impairment(s): *Avoiding and losing friends, impending divorce. Sad most of the time.*
Can't focus on lesson plans (teacher).

3.19

Dysthymia (2 or more years): _____ depressed most of time. (2+ of following)

_____ low/high appetite or eating _____ in/hypersomnia _____ low energy/fatigue _____ low self-esteem

_____ low concentration/decisions _____ hopelessness _____ other

_____ *Denies* _____

Impairment(s): ___ social ___ occupational/educational ___ affective ___ cognitive ___ other

Examples of impairment(s): _____

_____

Mania (3+):

_____ grandiosity _____ low sleep _____ talkative _____ flight of ideas _____ distractibility

_____ goals/agitation _____ excessive pleasure

_____ *Denies* _____

Impairment(s): ___ social ___ occupational/educational ___ affective ___ cognitive ___ other

Examples of impairment(s): _____

_____

Panic Attacks (4+, abrupt development of):

_____ palpitations _____ sweating _____ trembling _____ shortness of breath _____ feeling of choking

_____ chest pain _____ nausea _____ dizziness _____ light-headed _____ derealization

_____ fear of losing control _____ fear of dying _____ numbness __ chills/hot flashes

_____ *Denies* _____

Impairment(s): ___ social ___ occupational/educational ___ affective ___ cognitive __ other

Examples of impairment(s): _____

_____

Anxiety (GAD: 3+, most of time, 6 months):

_____ restlessness _____ easily fatigued _____ concentration _____ irritability

_____ muscle tension _____ sleep disturbance

_____ *Denies* _____

Impairment(s): ___ social ___ occupational/educational ___ affective ___ cognitive __ other

Examples of impairment(s): _____

_____

Other Diagnostic Concerns or Behavioral Issues

(e.g., _____ dissociation _____ eating _____ sleep _____ impulse control _____ thought disorders _____ anger

_____ relationships _____ cognitive __ phobias _____ substance abuse _____ medical conditions

_____ somatization _____ phobias _____ sexual _____ PTSD, etc.)

_____ *Each ruled out* _____

Impairment(s): ___ social ___ occupational/educational ___ affective ___ cognitive __ other

Examples of impairment(s): _____

_____

USE ADDITIONAL PAPER AS NECESSARY

Mental Status

(Check appropriate level of impairment: N/A or OK signifies no known impairment. Comment on significant areas of impairment.)

Appearance	N/A or OK	Slight	Moderate	Severe
Unkempt, disheveled	(__)	(_X_)	(__)	(__)
Clothing, dirty, atypical	(_X_)	(__)	(__)	(__)
Odd phys. characteristics	(_X_)	(__)	(__)	(__)
Body odor	(_X_)	(__)	(__)	(__)
Appears unhealthy	(__)	(_X_)	(__)	(__)

Posture	N/A or OK	Slight	Moderate	Severe
Slumped	(__)	(__)	(_X_)	(__)
Rigid, tense	(__)	(__)	(_X_)	(__)

Body Movements	N/A or OK	Slight	Moderate	Severe
Accelerated, quick	(_X_)	(__)	(__)	(__)
Decreased, slowed	(__)	(__)	(_X_)	(__)
Restlessness, fidgety	(__)	(_X_)	(__)	(__)
Atypical, unusual	(_X_)	(__)	(__)	(__)

Speech	N/A or OK	Slight	Moderate	Severe
Rapid	(_X_)	(__)	(__)	(__)
Slow	(__)	(__)	(_X_)	(__)
Loud	(_X_)	(__)	(__)	(__)
Soft	(__)	(__)	(_X_)	(__)
Mute	(_X_)	(__)	(__)	(__)
Atypical (e.g., slurring)	(_X_)	(__)	(__)	(__)

Attitude	N/A or OK	Slight	Moderate	Severe
Domineering, controlling	(_X_)	(__)	(__)	(__)
Submissive, dependent	(__)	(__)	(_X_)	(__)
Hostile, challenging	(_X_)	(__)	(__)	(__)
Guarded, suspicious	(__)	(_X_)	(__)	(__)
Uncooperative	(_X_)	(__)	(__)	(__)

Affect	N/A or OK	Slight	Moderate	Severe
Inappropriate to thought	(_X_)	(__)	(__)	(__)
Increased lability	(_X_)	(__)	(__)	(__)
Blunted, dull, flat	(__)	(__)	(__)	(_X_)
Euphoria, elation	(_X_)	(__)	(__)	(__)
Anger, hostility	(_X_)	(__)	(__)	(__)
Depression, sadness	(__)	(__)	(__)	(_X_)
Anxiety	(__)	(_X_)	(__)	(__)
Irritability	(__)	(__)	(_X_)	(__)

Perception	N/A or OK	Slight	Moderate	Severe
Illusions	(X)	(__)	(__)	(__)
Auditory hallucinations	(X)	(__)	(__)	(__)
Visual hallucinations	(X)	(__)	(__)	(__)
Other hallucinations	(X)	(__)	(__)	(__)

Cognitive	N/A or OK	Slight	Moderate	Severe
Alertness	(__)	(X)	(__)	(__)
Attn. span, distractibility	(__)	(__)	(X)	(__)
Short-term memory	(__)	(X)	(__)	(__)
Long-term memory	(__)	(X)	(__)	(__)

Judgment	N/A or OK	Slight	Moderate	Severe
Decision making	(__)	(__)	(X)	(__)
Impulsivity	(X)	(__)	(__)	(__)

Thought Content	N/A or OK	Slight	Moderate	Severe
Obsessions/compulsions	(X)	(__)	(__)	(__)
Phobic	(X)	(__)	(__)	(__)
Depersonalization	(X)	(__)	(__)	(__)
Suicidal ideation	(__)	(__)	(X)	(__)
Homicidal ideation	(X)	(__)	(__)	(__)
Delusions	(X)	(__)	(__)	(__)

Estimated level of intelligence: _IQ = (110–120)_

Orientation: _X_ Time _X_ Place _X_ Person

Able to hold normal conversation? _X_ Yes ____ No

Eye contact: _Moderate_

Level of insight:

    ____ Complete denial   ____ Slight awareness

    ____ Blames others   _X_ Blames self

    ____ Intellectual insight, but few changes likely

    ____ Emotional insight, understanding, change can occur

Client's view of actions needed to change: _Meds & counseling_

Comments

Very low energy; often cried; psycho-motor retardation; very low self-concept; cried often during interview; slumped posture entire interview.

PART C.   DIAGNOSIS VALIDATION

Diagnosis 1: _Major depressive disorder recurrent, moderate, w/o psychotic features_   Code: _296.32_

DSM-IV-TR Criteria

Depressed most of the time past year, no pleasure, weight loss, low appetite, sleep disturbance,

fatigue, feels worthless, decreased concentration, suicidal ideation.

_____

Examples of impairment/dysfunction: _Loss of friends, withdrawn. Decreased performance and_

attendance at work.

_____

_____

Additional validation (e.g., testing, previous records, self-report):   _MMPI-2 = (2-4-7 profile)—_

Depressed anxious; BDI score = 32—severe depression

_____

_____

_____

Diagnosis 2: _____   Code: _____

DSM-IV-TR Criteria

_____

_____

Examples of impairment/dysfunction: _____

_____

_____

Additional validation (e.g., testing, previous records, self-report): _____

_____

_____

_____

Diagnosis 3: _____   Code: _____

DSM-IV-TR Criteria

_____

_____

Examples of impairment/dysfunction: _____

_____

_____

Additional validation (e.g., testing, previous records, self-report): _____

_____

_____

_____

	Diagnosis	Code

Axis I   1: _Major depression, recurrent, moderate w/o psychotic features_   _296.32_

          2: _____   _____

          3: _____   _____

Axis II   1: _Deferred_   _V71.09_

          2: _____   _____

Axis III   _Defer to physician_   _____

Axis IV   _Marital discord, occupational social problems_

Axis V   Current GAF = ___55___   Highest past year GAF = ___75___

Prognosis: ___ Poor   ___ Marginal   ___ Guarded   _X_ Moderate   ___ Good   ___ Excellent

Qualifiers to prognosis: _X_ Med compliance   _X_ Tx compliance   _X_ Home environment

_X_ Activity changes   ___ Behavioral changes   ___ Attitudinal changes   ___ Education/training

___ Other: _____

Treatment Considerations

Is the patient appropriate for treatment? _X_ Yes   ___ No

If no, explain and indicate referral made: _____

Tx modality: _X_ Indiv.   ___ Conjoint   ___ Family   ___ Collateral   ___ Group

Frequency: _weekly_   _____   _____   _____   _____

If Conjoint, Family or Collateral, specify with whom: _____

Adjunctive Services Needed:

_X_ Physical exam   ___ School records

___ Laboratory tests (specify): _____

___ Patient records (specify): _____

Therapist's Questions/Concerns/Comments: _X_ Psychiatric evaluation   _X_ Psychological testing

Is marital counseling appropriate?

_____

_____

Therapist's signature/credentials: _Darlene Benton, PhD_   Date: _3_ / _8_ / _2005_

Supervisor's Remarks

First work on stabilizing mood and alleviating depression. Share information with psychiatrist.

Concur with diagnosis.

_____

Supervisor's signature/credentials: _Sharon Bell, PhD_   Date: _3_ / _12_ / _2005_

Therapist's Response to Supervisor's Remarks

None

_____

_____

Therapist's signature/credentials: _Darlene Benton, PhD_   Date: _3_ / _12_ / _2005_

3.24

Form 20   Initial Assessment—Children and Adolescents (< 18)

Client's name: _____   Date: _____

Starting time: _____   Ending time: _____   Duration: _____

PART A.   BIOPSYCHOSOCIAL ASSESSMENT

1. **Presenting Problem**

    (Client's brief statement as to reason for seeking services, in behavioral terms) .

    _____

    _____

    Onset: _____   Frequency: _____

    Duration: _____   Severity: ___ Mild   ___ Moderate   ___ Severe   ___ Remission

2. **Signs and Symptoms (*DSM-IV-TR* based) . . . Resulting in Impairment(s)**

    (e.g., social, occupational, affective, cognitive, physical)

    _____

    _____

    _____

    _____

    _____

    _____

3. **History of Presenting Problem**

    Events, precipitating factors, stressors, and/or incidents leading to need for services: _____

    _____

    _____

    _____

    Was there a clear time when Sx worsened? _____

    Family mental health history: _____

    _____

    _____

    _____

4. **Current Family and Significant Relationships**   (See Personal History Form)

    Strengths/support: _____

    Stressors/problems: _____

    Recent changes: _____

    Changes desired: _____

    Comment on family circumstances: _____

5. **Childhood/Adolescent History** (See Personal History Form)

(Developmental milestones, past behavioral concerns, environment, abuse, school, social, mental health)

_____

_____

_____

6. **Social Relationships** (See Personal History Form)

Strengths/support: _____

Stressors/problems: _____

Recent changes: _____

Changes desired: _____

7. **Cultural/Ethnic** (See Personal History Form)

_____

Strengths/support: _____

Stressors/problems: _____

Beliefs/practices to incorporate into therapy: _____

8. **Spiritual/Religious** (See Personal History Form)

_____

Strengths/support: _____

Stressors/problems: _____

Beliefs/practices to incorporate into therapy: _____

Recent changes: _____

Changes desired: _____

9. **Legal** (See Personal History Form)

_____

Status/impact/stressors: _____

_____

10. **Education** (See Personal History Form)

_____

In special education? __ No _____ Yes (describe): _____

Strengths: _____

Weaknesses: _____

11. **Employment/Vocational** (See Personal History Form)

_____

Strengths/support: _____

Stressors/problems: _____

12. **Leisure/Recreational** (See Personal History Form)

Strengths/support: _____

Recent changes: _____

Changes desired: _____

13. Physical Health   (See Personal History Form)

_____

_____

Physical factors affecting mental condition: _____

_____

14. Chemical Use History   (See Personal History Form)

_____

_____

Patient's perception of problem: _____

_____

15. Counseling/Prior Treatment History   (See Personal History Form)

_____

_____

Benefits of previous treatment: _____
Setbacks of previous treatment: _____

PART B.   DIAGNOSTIC INTERVIEW

Mood

(Rule-in and rule-out signs and symptoms: validate with _DSM-IV-TR_)

Predominant mood during interview: _____

Current Concerns (give examples of impairments (i), severity (s), frequency (f), duration (d))

Adjustment Disorder

(w/in 3 months of identified stressor, Sx persist < 6 months after stressor, marked distress)

____ Depressed   ____ Anxiety   __ Mixed anxiety & depression   ____ Conduct

____ Emotions & conduct   ____ Unspecified

Specify disturbance: ____ Acute (<6 months)   ____ Chronic (>6 months) _____

_____

Impairment(s): ___ social ____ occupational/educational ___ affective __ cognitive __ other
Examples of impairment(s): _____

_____

Major Depression (2 or more wks): ___ Usually depressed or   ____ anhedonia. (4+ of following):
____ wght + / (-) 5%/month   ___ appetite + / (-)   ___ sleep + / (-)   ____ psychomotor + / (-)
____ fatigue   __ worthlessness/guilt   ____ concentration   ___ death/suicidal ideation
Other: ___ crying spells   ____ withdrawal   ____ add'l. sx _____

_____

Impairment(s): ____ social ____ occupational/educational ____ affective ____ cognitive ___ other
Examples of impairment(s): _____

_____

3.27

Dysthymia (2 or more years): _____ depressed most of time. (2+ of following):
_____ low/high appetite or eating _____ in/hypersomnia _____ low energy/fatigue __ low self-esteem
_____ low concentration/decisions _____ hopelessness _____ other

_____

Impairment(s): ___ social ___ occupational/educational ___ affective ___ cognitive __ other
Examples of impairment(s): _____

_____

Anxiety (GAD: 3+, most of time, 6 months):
_____ restlessness _____ easily fatigued _____ concentration _____ irritability
_____ muscle tension _____ sleep disturbance

_____

Impairment(s): ___ social ___ occupational/educational ___ affective ___ cognitive __ other
Examples of impairment(s): _____

_____

ODD (Pattern of negativistic, hostile, and defiant behaviors > 6 months: 4+ of following):
_____ loses temper __ argues with adults _____ actively defies adult's requests _____ deliberately
annoys people __ blames others for own mistakes or misbehavior _____ touchy/easily annoyed
__ angry/resentful ___ spiteful/vindictive. 1+ impairment: _____ social _____ academic ___ occupational

_____

Conduct Repetitive/persistent behavior violating rights of others. 3+ (past 12 mo. 1 in past 6 mos.):
_____ Aggression to people/animals: ___ bullies, threatens, intimidates _____ initiates physical fights
_____ has used harmful weapon. Physically cruel to: ___ people _____ animals ___ stolen while
confronting victim _____ forces sexual activity. Destruction of property: ___ deliberate fire setting
(intended damage) _____ deliberate property destruction. Deceitfulness or theft: ___ broken into
someone's property _____ often lies/cons _____ has stolen without confrontation. Serious violation of
rules: _____ stays out at night against parents' rules before age 13 _____ has run away 2+ or one extended
_____ often truant before age 13. 1+ impairment: ___ social __ academic _____ occupational

_____

ADHD Inattention: 6+ Sx, 6+ months:
_____ poor attn/careless mistakes _____ difficult sustaining attn. __ not listen when spoken to
_____ not follow through _____ difficult organizing, avoids tasks requiring sustained mental effort
_____ loses things _____ easily distracted _____ forgetful and/or Hyperactivity/impulsivity. 6+ hyperactivity
_____ fidgety __ leaves seat often _____ runs/climbs _____ difficult being quiet _____ "on the go"
_____ talks excessively. Impulsivity: ___ blurts out answers _____ difficulty awaiting turn ___ interrupts.
_____ some SX < 7. 1+ impairment: ___ social __ academic _____ occupational

_____

Other Diagnostic Concerns or Behavioral Issues
(e.g., ___ dissociation _____ eating _____ sleep _____ impulse control ___ thought disorders _____ anger
_____ relationships _____ cognitive __ phobias _____ substance abuse _____ medical conditions
_____ somatization _____ sexual _____ PTSD, etc.)

_____

Impairment(s): ___ social ___ occupational/educational ___ affective ___ cognitive __ other
Examples of impairment(s): _____

_____

USE ADDITIONAL PAPER AS NECESSARY

3.28

Mental Status
(Check appropriate level of impairment: N/A or OK signifies no known impairment. Comment on significant areas of impairment.)

Appearance	N/A or OK	Slight	Moderate	Severe
Unkempt, disheveled	(__)	(__)	(__)	(__)
Clothing, dirty, atypical	(__)	(__)	(__)	(__)
Odd phys. characteristics	(__)	(__)	(__)	(__)
Body odor	(__)	(__)	(__)	(__)
Appears unhealthy	(__)	(__)	(__)	(__)

Posture	N/A or OK	Slight	Moderate	Severe
Slumped	(__)	(__)	(__)	(__)
Rigid, tense	(__)	(__)	(__)	(__)

Body Movements	N/A or OK	Slight	Moderate	Severe
Accelerated, quick	(__)	(__)	(__)	(__)
Decreased, slowed	(__)	(__)	(__)	(__)
Restlessness, fidgety	(__)	(__)	(__)	(__)
Atypical, unusual	(__)	(__)	(__)	(__)

Speech	N/A or OK	Slight	Moderate	Severe
Rapid	(__)	(__)	(__)	(__)
Slow	(__)	(__)	(__)	(__)
Loud	(__)	(__)	(__)	(__)
Soft	(__)	(__)	(__)	(__)
Mute	(__)	(__)	(__)	(__)
Atypical (e.g., slurring)	(__)	(__)	(__)	(__)

Attitude	N/A or OK	Slight	Moderate	Severe
Domineering, controlling	(__)	(__)	(__)	(__)
Submissive, dependent	(__)	(__)	(__)	(__)
Hostile, challenging	(__)	(__)	(__)	(__)
Guarded, suspicious	(__)	(__)	(__)	(__)
Uncooperative	(__)	(__)	(__)	(__)

Affect	N/A or OK	Slight	Moderate	Severe
Inappropriate to thought	(__)	(__)	(__)	(__)
Increased lability	(__)	(__)	(__)	(__)
Blunted, dull, flat	(__)	(__)	(__)	(__)
Euphoria, elation	(__)	(__)	(__)	(__)
Anger, hostility	(__)	(__)	(__)	(__)
Depression, sadness	(__)	(__)	(__)	(__)
Anxiety	(__)	(__)	(__)	(__)
Irritability	(__)	(__)	(__)	(__)

Perception	N/A or OK	Slight	Moderate	Severe
Illusions	(__)	(__)	(__)	(__)
Auditory hallucinations	(__)	(__)	(__)	(__)
Visual hallucinations	(__)	(__)	(__)	(__)
Other hallucinations	(__)	(__)	(__)	(__)
Cognitive	N/A or OK	Slight	Moderate	Severe
Alertness	(__)	(__)	(__)	(__)
Attn. span, distractibility	(__)	(__)	(__)	(__)
Short-term memory	(__)	(__)	(__)	(__)
Long-term memory	(__)	(__)	(__)	(__)
Judgment	N/A or OK	Slight	Moderate	Severe
Decision making	(__)	(__)	(__)	(__)
Impulsivity	(__)	(__)	(__)	(__)
Thought Content	N/A or OK	Slight	Moderate	Severe
Obsessions/compulsions	(__)	(__)	(__)	(__)
Phobic	(__)	(__)	(__)	(__)
Depersonalization	(__)	(__)	(__)	(__)
Suicidal ideation	(__)	(__)	(__)	(__)
Homicidal ideation	(__)	(__)	(__)	(__)
Delusions	(__)	(__)	(__)	(__)

Estimated level of intelligence: _____

Orientation: ____ Time ____ Place ____ Person

Able to hold normal conversation? ___ Yes ____ No

Eye contact: _____

Level of insight:

    ____ Complete denial   ____ Slight awareness

    ____ Blames others   ____ Blames self

    ____ Intellectual insight, but few changes likely

    ____ Emotional insight, understanding, change can occur

Client's view of actions needed to change: _____

Comments

_____

_____

_____

_____

_____

_____

_____

PART C.   DIAGNOSIS VALIDATION

Diagnosis 1: _____ Code: _____

DSM-IV-TR Criteria

_____

_____

_____

Examples of impairment/dysfunction: _____

_____

_____

Additional validation (e.g., testing, previous records, self-report): _____

_____

_____

_____

Diagnosis 2: _____ Code: _____

DSM-IV-TR Criteria

_____

_____

_____

Examples of impairment/dysfunction: _____

_____

_____

Additional validation (e.g., testing, previous records, self-report): _____

_____

_____

_____

Diagnosis 3: _____ Code: _____

DSM-IV-TR Criteria

_____

_____

_____

Examples of impairment/dysfunction: _____

_____

_____

Additional validation (e.g., testing, previous records, self-report): _____

_____

_____

_____

	Diagnosis	Code

Axis I   1: _____   _____

             2: _____   _____

             3: _____   _____

Axis II   1: _____   _____

             2: _____   _____

Axis III   _____   _____

Axis IV   _____

Axis V   Current GAF = _____   Highest past year GAF = _____

Prognosis: ___ Poor ____ Marginal ____ Guarded ___ Moderate ___ Good ____ Excellent

Qualifiers to prognosis: ___ Med compliance ___ Tx compliance ___ Home environment

___ Activity changes ___ Behavioral changes ___ Attitudinal changes ___ Education/training

___ Other: _____

Treatment Considerations

Is the patient appropriate for treatment? ___ Yes ___ No

If no, explain and indicate referral made: _____

Tx modality: ____ Indiv. ____ Conjoint ____ Family ____ Collateral ____ Group

Frequency: _____ _____ _____ _____ _____

If Conjoint, Family or Collateral, specify with whom: _____

Adjunctive Services Needed:

____ Physical exam ____ School records

____ Laboratory tests (specify): _____

____ Patient records (specify): _____

Therapist's Questions/Concerns/Comments: ____ Psychiatric evaluation ____ Psychological testing

_____

_____

_____

Therapist's signature/credentials: _____ Date: ____/____/____

Supervisor's Remarks

_____

_____

_____

Supervisor's signature/credentials: _____ Date: ____/____/____

Therapist's Response to Supervisor's Remarks

_____

_____

_____

Therapist's signature/credentials: _____ Date: ____/____/____

Client's name: _William Olden_   Date: _4/4/1999_

Starting time: _3:00 P.M._   Ending time: _3:58 P.M._   Duration: _58 min._

PART A.   BIOPSYCHOSOCIAL ASSESSMENT

1. Presenting Problem

(Client's brief statement as to reason for seeking services, in behavioral terms)

Often suspended from school for "sassing teachers." Disrespectful to parents. Hits and
bullies other children.

Onset: _age 12–13 (2 years ago)_   Frequency: _almost daily_

Duration: _varies_   Severity: ___ Mild _X_ Moderate ___ Severe ___ Remission

2. Signs and Symptoms (*DSM-IV-TR* based) . . . Resulting in Impairment(s)

(e.g., social, occupational, affective, cognitive, physical)

Argues with teacher and aide 2–3x/day resulting in frequent in-school suspensions at least
4x/week. Refuses to do homework or participate in any class assignments, resulting in 3
failing grades last term. Initiates fights in school or in neighborhood at least 3x/week,
resulting in having no friends, thus, increased frustration and anger. "Trashes" room of
sister after disagreements average of 1x/week. Temper tantrums (yelling, swearing, stomping)
at home when told to do chores or anything he doesn't want to do.

3. History of Presenting Problem

Events, precipitating factors, stressors, and/or incidents leading to need for services:

Parents' divorce led to some behavior problems, but dramatic increase in defiance when
mother remarried. Very defiant toward step-father.

Was there a clear time when Sx worsened? _1st time corrected by step-father._

Family mental health history: _No mental health treatment. Biological father has history of_
alcoholism and domestic violence charges toward mother.

4. Current Family and Significant Relationships   (See Personal History Form)

Strengths/support: _Mother, step-father and sister get along. Willing to help._

Stressors/problems: _Occasional visits to father lead to increased violence._

Recent changes: _Mainly mother's remarriage 2 years ago._

Changes desired: _Cooperative in school and at home. Learn to cope._

Comment on family circumstances: _His behaviors causing marital conflict._

5. Childhood/Adolescent History   (See Personal History Form)

(Developmental milestones, past behavioral concerns, environment, abuse, school, social, mental health)

No unusual developmental concerns. Prior to parents' divorce, no behavioral/emotional
incidents. No history of abuse, but observed much verbal and physical abuse from father to
mother. Used to have stable friendships prior to age 13.

6. Social Relationships   (See Personal History Form)

Strengths/support: *Used to have friends; positive memories*

Stressors/problems: *No friends at this time*

Recent changes: *Gradual loss of 3 previous friends*

Changes desired: *Stabilize friendships. Stop bullying peers*

7. Cultural/Ethnic   (See Personal History Form)

Native-American

Strengths/support: *Family practices traditional tribal beliefs/traditions*

Stressors/problems: *Some teasing by peers due to "pow-wows"*

Beliefs/practices to incorporate into therapy: *Tribe as support system*

8. Spiritual/Religious   (See Personal History Form)

Non-organized. Incorporation of nature

Strengths/support: *Family teaching and practices*

Stressors/problems: *Some teasing by peers*

Beliefs/practices to incorporate into therapy: *Respect for all*

Recent changes: *None*

Changes desired: *Ok*

9. Legal   (See Personal History Form)

No formal arrests but brought home by police 4 times in past year for fighting/bullying.

Status/impact/stressors: *Recent warning by school police officer that next incident will*
result in arrest.

10. Education   (See Personal History Form)

In 10th grade, Dalton School mainstreamed, but is being considered for EBD program.

In special education? _X_ No _____ Yes (describe): *But grades have decreased significantly*

Strengths: *Recent intelligence testing: WISC-IV IQ of 115.*

Weaknesses: *Not completing assignments or tests.*

11. Employment/Vocational   (See Personal History Form)

N/A

Strengths/support: _____

Stressors/problems: _____

12. Leisure/Recreational   (See Personal History Form)

Strengths/support: *History of being athletic, good runner, well-conditioned*

Recent changes: *No longer involved in sports or exercising*

Changes desired: *Become involved in cooperative sports*

13. **Physical Health**   (See Personal History Form)

Good health. No significant illnesses. Normal height and weight

Physical factors affecting mental condition: _None known_

14. **Chemical Use History**   (See Personal History Form)

Mother states that she has been missing small amounts of alcohol at times.

Patient's perception of problem: _Denies_

15. **Counseling/Prior Treatment History**   (See Personal History Form)

No formal counseling. A few visits to school counselor as part of suspensions, but would

not talk about issues.

Benefits of previous treatment: _N/A_

Setbacks of previous treatment: _N/A_

PART B.   DIAGNOSTIC INTERVIEW

Mood

(Rule-in and rule-out signs and symptoms: validate with _DSM-IV-TR_)

Predominant mood during interview: _____

Current Concerns (give examples of impairments (i), severity (s), frequency (f), duration (d))

Adjustment Disorder

(w/in 3 months of identified stressor, Sx persist < 6 months after stressor, marked distress)

___ Depressed   ___ Anxiety   ___ Mixed anxiety & depression   _X_ Conduct

___ Emotions & conduct   ___ Unspecified

Specify disturbance: ___ Acute (<6 months)   _X_ Chronic (>6 months) _Parental divorce and_

soon remarriage of mother has led to dramatic increases in conduct problems

Impairment(s): _X_ social _X_ occupational/educational ___ affective ___ cognitive ___ other

Examples of impairment(s): _Behavioral outbursts, defiance, temper tantrums_

Major Depression (2 or more wks): ___ Usually depressed or ___ anhedonia. (4+ of following):

___ wght + / (-) 5%/month   ___ appetite + / (-)   ___ sleep + / (-)   ___ psychomotor + / (-)

___ fatigue   ___ worthlessness/guilt   ___ concentration   ___ death/suicidal ideation

Other: ___ crying spells   ___ withdrawal   ___ add'l. sx _____

Denies

Impairment(s): ___ social ___ occupational/educational ___ affective ___ cognitive ___ other

Examples of impairment(s): _____

Dysthymia (2 or more years): ___ depressed most of time. (2+ of following):
___ low/high appetite or eating ___in/hypersomnia ___low energy/fatigue ___ low self-esteem
___ low concentration/decisions ___ hopelessness ___ other
_____ *Denies* _____
Impairment(s): ___ social ___ occupational/educational ___ affective ___ cognitive ___ other
Examples of impairment(s): _____
_____

Anxiety (GAD: 3+, most of time, 6 months):
___ restlessness ___ easily fatigued ___ concentration ___ irritability
___ muscle tension ___ sleep disturbance
_____ *Denies* _____
Impairment(s): ___ social ___ occupational/educational ___ affective ___ cognitive ___ other
Examples of impairment(s): _____
_____

ODD (Pattern of negativistic, hostile, and defiant behaviors > 6 months: 4+ of following):
_X_ loses temper _X_ argues with adults _X_ actively defies adult's requests ___ deliberately
annoys people _X_ blames others for own mistakes or misbehavior ___ touchy/easily annoyed
_X_ angry/resentful _X_ spiteful/vindictive. 1+ impairment: _X_ social _X_ academic ___ occupational
Onset: 2 years ago. Daily arguing with teachers and family. Refuses to do anything.

Conduct Repetitive/persistent behavior violating rights of others. 3+ (past 12 mo. 1 in past 6 mos.):
___ Aggression to people/animals: _X_ bullies, threatens, intimidates _X_ initiates physical fights
___ has used harmful weapon. Physically cruel to: ___ people ___ animals ___ stolen while
confronting victim ___ forces sexual activity. Destruction of property: ___ deliberate fire setting
(intended damage) ___ deliberate property destruction. Deceitfulness or theft: ___ broken into
someone's property ___ often lies/cons __ has stolen without confrontation. Serious violation of
rules: ___ stays out at night against parents' rules before age 13 ___ has run away 2+ or one extended
___ often truant before age 13. 1+ impairment: ___ social ___ academic ___ occupational
Features—not full diagnosis.

ADHD Inattention: 6+ Sx, 6+ months:
___ poor attn/careless mistakes ___ difficult sustaining attn. ___ not listen when spoken to
___ not follow through ___ difficult organizing, avoids tasks requiring sustained mental effort
___ loses things ___ easily distracted ___ forgetful and/or Hyperactivity/impulsivity. 6+ hyperactivity
___ fidgety ___ leaves seat often ___ runs/climbs ___difficult being quiet ___ "on the go"
___ talks excessively. Impulsivity: ___ blurts out answers ___ difficulty awaiting turn ___ interrupts.
___ some SX < 7. 1+ impairment: ___ social ___ academic ___ occupational
_____ *Denies* _____

Other Diagnostic Concerns or Behavioral Issues
(e.g., ___ dissociation ___ eating ___ sleep ___ impulse control ___ thought disorders ___ anger
___ relationships ___ cognitive ___ phobias ___ substance abuse ___ medical conditions
___ somatization ___ sexual ___ PTSD, etc.)
_____
Impairment(s): ___ social ___ occupational/educational ___ affective ___ cognitive ___ other
Examples of impairment(s): _____
_____

USE ADDITIONAL PAPER AS NECESSARY

3.36

Mental Status

(Check appropriate level of impairment: N/A or OK signifies no known impairment. Comment on significant areas of impairment.)

Appearance	N/A or OK	Slight	Moderate	Severe
Unkempt, disheveled	(__)	(_X_)	(__)	(__)
Clothing, dirty, atypical	(__)	(_X_)	(__)	(__)
Odd phys. characteristics	(_X_)	(__)	(__)	(__)
Body odor	(_X_)	(__)	(__)	(__)
Appears unhealthy	(_X_)	(__)	(__)	(__)

Posture	N/A or OK	Slight	Moderate	Severe
Slumped	(_X_)	(__)	(__)	(__)
Rigid, tense	(__)	(_X_)	(__)	(__)

Body Movements	N/A or OK	Slight	Moderate	Severe
Accelerated, quick	(__)	(_X_)	(__)	(__)
Decreased, slowed	(__)	(_X_)	(__)	(__)
Restlessness, fidgety	(__)	(__)	(_X_)	(__)
Atypical, unusual	(_X_)	(__)	(__)	(__)

Speech	N/A or OK	Slight	Moderate	Severe
Rapid	(_X_)	(__)	(__)	(__)
Slow	(_X_)	(__)	(__)	(__)
Loud	(__)	(__)	(_X_)	(__)
Soft	(__)	(__)	(__)	(__)
Mute	(_X_)	(__)	(__)	(__)
Atypical (e.g., slurring)	(_X_)	(__)	(__)	(__)

Attitude	N/A or OK	Slight	Moderate	Severe
Domineering, controlling	(__)	(__)	(_X_)	(__)
Submissive, dependent	(_X_)	(__)	(__)	(__)
Hostile, challenging	(__)	(__)	(_X_)	(__)
Guarded, suspicious	(__)	(__)	(_X_)	(__)
Uncooperative	(__)	(__)	(__)	(_X_)

Affect	N/A or OK	Slight	Moderate	Severe
Inappropriate to thought	(_X_)	(__)	(__)	(__)
Increased lability	(__)	(__)	(_X_)	(__)
Blunted, dull, flat	(_X_)	(__)	(__)	(__)
Euphoria, elation	(_X_)	(__)	(__)	(__)
Anger, hostility	(__)	(__)	(_X_)	(__)
Depression, sadness	(_X_)	(__)	(__)	(__)
Anxiety	(_X_)	(__)	(__)	(__)
Irritability	(__)	(__)	(__)	(_X_)

Perception	N/A or OK	Slight	Moderate	Severe
Illusions	(X)	(__)	(__)	(__)
Auditory hallucinations	(X)	(__)	(__)	(__)
Visual hallucinations	(X)	(__)	(__)	(__)
Other hallucinations	(X)	(__)	(__)	(__)

Cognitive	N/A or OK	Slight	Moderate	Severe
Alertness	(X)	(__)	(__)	(__)
Attn. span, distractibility	(__)	(X)	(__)	(__)
Short-term memory	(X)	(__)	(__)	(__)
Long-term memory	(X)	(__)	(__)	(__)

Judgment Issues	N/A or OK	Slight	Moderate	Severe
Decision making	(__)	(X)	(__)	(__)
Impulsivity	(__)	(__)	(X)	(__)

Thought Content	N/A or OK	Slight	Moderate	Severe
Obsessions/compulsions	(X)	(__)	(__)	(__)
Phobic	(X)	(__)	(__)	(__)
Depersonalization	(X)	(__)	(__)	(__)
Suicidal ideation	(X)	(__)	(__)	(__)
Homicidal ideation	(X)	(__)	(__)	(__)
Delusions	(X)	(__)	(__)	(__)

Estimated level of intelligence: _average_

Orientation: _X_ Time _X_ Place _X_ Person

Able to hold normal conversation? _X_ Yes ___ No

Eye contact: _Poor_

Level of insight:

    ___ Complete denial   ___ Slight awareness

    _X_ Blames others   ___ Blames self

    ___ Intellectual insight, but few changes likely

    ___ Emotional insight, understanding, change can occur

Client's view of actions needed to change: _"Nothing, except have dad back"_

Comments

Very loud in waiting room with threats to walk home. Several statements about desire to get out

of his "stupid family." Seemed to smile when mother discussed current behavioral issues.

Threatened to leave session three times. Appeared angry, frustrated and agitated. Very persistent.

PART C. DIAGNOSIS VALIDATION

Diagnosis 1: _Oppositional Defiant Disorder_   Code: _313.81_

DSM-IV-TR Criteria

Loses temper easily and often, daily arguing with adults, very defiant toward adults when simple requests made. Usually blames others for own mistakes, usually angry and spiteful toward family.

Examples of impairment/dysfunction: _No friends, failing in school._

Additional validation (e.g., testing, previous records, self-report): _School reports indicate 17 in-school suspensions in past month._

Diagnosis 2: _Adjustment Disorder: conduct, chronic_   Code: _309.3_

DSM-IV-TR Criteria

Stressor: parental divorce and remarriage of mother. During past 2 years increased stressors which compound each other. Since that time dramatic conduct problems.

Examples of impairment/dysfunction: _Behavioral outbursts, bullying, fighting._

Additional validation (e.g., testing, previous records, self-report): _School reports indicate being sent home 2 times in past month for bullying._

Diagnosis 3: _____   Code: _____

DSM-IV-TR Criteria

Examples of impairment/dysfunction: _____

Additional validation (e.g., testing, previous records, self-report): _____

3.39

	Diagnosis	Code

Axis I   1:   _Oppositional Defiant Disorder_   _313.81_

               2:   _Adj. Disorder: conduct, chronic_   _309.3_

               3: _____

Axis II   1:   _No diagnosis_   _V71.09_

               2: _____

Axis III   _Defer to physician_ _____

Axis IV   _Social, family, and academic problems_ _____

Axis V   Current GAF = ___58___   Highest past year GAF = ___65___

Prognosis: ___ Poor   ___ Marginal   ___ Guarded   _X_ Moderate   ___ Good   ___ Excellent

Qualifiers to prognosis: ___ Med compliance   _X_ Tx compliance   _X_ Home environment

___ Activity changes   _X_ Behavioral changes   _X_ Attitudinal changes   ___ Education/training

___ Other: _____

Treatment Considerations

Is the patient appropriate for treatment? _X_ Yes   ___ No

If no, explain and indicate referral made: _____

Tx modality: _X_ Indiv.   ___ Conjoint   _X_ Family   ___ Collateral   ___ Group

Frequency: _weekly_   _2x/mo_

If Conjoint, Family or Collateral, specify with whom: _mother, step-father, sister_ _____

Adjunctive Services Needed:

   _X_ Physical exam   _X_ School records

___ Laboratory tests (specify): _____

___ Patient records (specify): _____

Therapist's Questions/Concerns/Comments: _____ Psychiatric evaluation   _X_ Psychological testing

   (1) Would in-home family counseling be helpful? _____

   (2) What about our anger management group? _____

_____

Therapist's signature/credentials: _Charles W. Wollat, MSW_   Date: _4_ / _4_ / _2005_

Supervisor's Remarks

   (1) Yes, perhaps after a few family sessions here _____

   (2) Probably helpful _____

_____

Supervisor's signature/credentials: _Samuel Jones, LICSW_   Date: _4_ / _4_ / _2005_

Therapist's Response to Supervisor's Remarks

   None _____

_____

_____

Therapist's signature/credentials: _Charles W. Wollat, MSW_   Date: _4_ / _12_/ _2005_

Form 21   Personal History—Adult (18+)

Client's name: _____   Date: _____

Gender: ____ F   ____ M   Date of birth: _____   Age: _____

Form completed by (if someone other than client): _____

Address: _____ City: _____ State: _____ Zip: _____

Phone (home): _____   (work): _____   ext: _____

If you need any more space for any of the questions please use the back of the sheet.

Primary reason(s) for seeking services:

___ Anger management   ____ Anxiety   ____ Coping   ____ Depression

___ Eating disorder   ____ Fear/phobias   ____ Mental confusion   ____ Sexual concerns

___ Sleeping problems   ____ Addictive behaviors   ____ Alcohol/drugs

___ Other mental health concerns (specify): _____

Family Information

Relationship	Name	Age	Living Yes	Living No	Living with you Yes	Living with you No
Mother	_____	_____	____	____	____	____
Father	_____	_____	____	____	____	____
Spouse	_____	_____	____	____	____	____
Children	_____	_____	____	____	____	____
	_____	_____	____	____	____	____
	_____	_____	____	____	____	____

Significant others (e.g., brothers, sisters, grandparents, step-relatives, half-relatives. Please specify relationship.)

Relationship	Name	Age	Living Yes	Living No	Living with you Yes	Living with you No
_____	_____	_____	____	____	____	____
_____	_____	_____	____	____	____	____
_____	_____	_____	____	____	____	____
_____	_____	_____	____	____	____	____
_____	_____	_____	____	____	____	____
_____	_____	_____	____	____	____	____

Marital Status (more than one answer may apply)

___ Single   ___ Divorce in process   ___ Unmarried, living together

                                Length of time: _____   Length of time: _____

___ Legally married   ___ Separated   ___ Divorced

Length of time: _____   Length of time: _____   Length of time: _____

___ Widowed   ___ Annulment

Length of time: _____   Length of time: _____   Total number of marriages: __

Assessment of current relationship (if applicable): ___ Good ___ Fair ___ Poor

Parental Information

___ Parents legally married   ___ Mother remarried: Number of times: _____

___ Parents have ever been separated   ___ Father remarried: Number of times: _____

___ Parents ever divorced

Special circumstances (e.g., raised by person other than parents, information about spouse/children not living with you, etc.): _____

Development

Are there special, unusual, or traumatic circumstances that affected your development? ___ Yes ___ No

If Yes, please describe: _____

Has there been history of child abuse? ____ Yes ____ No

If Yes, which type(s)? ____ Sexual ____ Physical ____ Verbal

If Yes, the abuse was as a: ____ Victim ____ Perpetrator

Other childhood issues: ____ Neglect ____ Inadequate nutrition ____ Other (please specify): _____

Comments re: childhood development: _____

_____

Social Relationships

Check how you generally get along with other people: (check all that apply)

___ Affectionate   ___ Aggressive   ___ Avoidant   ___ Fight/argue often   ___ Follower

___ Friendly   ___ Leader   ___ Outgoing   ___ Shy/withdrawn   ___ Submissive

___ Other (specify): _____

Sexual orientation: _____   Comments: _____

Sexual dysfunctions? ____ Yes ____ No

If Yes, describe: _____

Any current or history of being as sexual perpetrator? ____ Yes ____ No

If Yes, describe: _____

Cultural/Ethnic

To which cultural or ethnic group, if any, do you belong? _____

Are you experiencing any problems due to cultural or ethnic issues? ____ Yes ____ No

If Yes, describe: _____

Other cultural/ethnic information: _____

Spiritual/Religious

How important to you are spiritual matters? ____ Not ____ Little ___ Moderate ____ Much

Are you affiliated with a spiritual or religious group? ____ Yes ____ No

If Yes, describe: _____

Were you raised within a spiritual or religious group? ____ Yes ____ No

If Yes, describe: _____

Would you like your spiritual/religious beliefs incorporated into the counseling? ____ Yes ____ No

If Yes, describe: _____

Legal

Current Status

Are you involved in any active cases (traffic, civil, criminal)? ____ Yes ____ No

If Yes, please describe and indicate the court and hearing/trial dates and charges: _____

_____

Are you presently on probation or parole? ____ Yes ____ No

If Yes, please describe: _____

Past History

Traffic violations: ____ Yes ___ No		DWI, DUI, etc.: ____ Yes ____ No		
Criminal involvement: ____ Yes ___ No		Civil involvement: ___ Yes ____ No		

If you responded Yes to any of the above, please fill in the following information. _____

Charges	Date	Where (city)	Results
_____	_____	_____	_____
_____	_____	_____	_____
_____	_____	_____	_____
_____	_____	_____	_____

Education

Fill in all that apply: Years of education: _____   Currently enrolled in school? ___ Yes ____ No

__ High school grad/GED

__ Vocational: Number of years: ___   Graduated: ___ Yes ___ No Major: _____

__ College: Number of years: ___   Graduated: ___ Yes ___ No Major: _____

__ Graduate: Number of years: ___   Graduated: ___ Yes ___ No Major: _____

Other training: _____

Special circumstances (e.g., learning disabilities, gifted): _____

Employment

Begin with most recent job, list job history: _____

Employer	Dates	Title	Reason left the job	How often miss work?
_____	_____	_____	_____	_____
_____	_____	_____	_____	_____
_____	_____	_____	_____	_____
_____	_____	_____	_____	_____

Currently: ____ FT ____ PT ____ Temp __ Laid-off ____ Disabled ____ Retired
__ Social Security ____ Student ____ Other (describe): _____

Military

Military experience? ____ Yes ____ No   Combat experience? ___ Yes ____ No

Where: _____

Branch: _____ Discharge date: _____

Date drafted: _____ Type of discharge: _____

Date enlisted: _____ Rank at discharge: _____

Leisure/Recreational

Describe special areas of interest or hobbies (e.g., art, books, crafts, physical fitness, sports, outdoor activities, church activities, walking, exercising, diet/health, hunting, fishing, bowling, traveling, etc.)

Activity	How often now?	How often in the past?
_____	_____	_____
_____	_____	_____
_____	_____	_____
_____	_____	_____

Medical/Physical Health

___ AIDS	___ Dizziness	____ Nose bleeds
___ Alcoholism	___ Drug abuse	____ Pneumonia
___ Abdominal pain	___ Epilepsy	____ Rheumatic Fever
___ Abortion	___ Ear infections	____ Sexually transmitted diseases
___ Allergies	___ Eating problems	____ Sleeping disorders
___ Anemia	___ Fainting	____ Sore throat
___ Appendicitis	___ Fatigue	____ Scarlet Fever
___ Arthritis	___ Frequent urination	____ Sinusitis
___ Asthma	___ Headaches	____ Smallpox
___ Bronchitis	___ Hearing problems	____ Stroke
___ Bed wetting	___ Hepatitis	____ Sexual problems
___ Cancer	___ High blood pressure	____ Tonsillitis
___ Chest pain	___ Kidney problems	____ Tuberculosis
___ Chronic pain	___ Measles	____ Toothache
___ Colds/Coughs	___ Mononucleosis	____ Thyroid problems
___ Constipation	___ Mumps	____ Vision problems
___ Chicken Pox	___ Menstrual pain	____ Vomiting
___ Dental problems	___ Miscarriages	____ Whooping cough
___ Diabetes	___ Neurological disorders	____ Other (describe): _____
___ Diarrhea	___ Nausea	_____

List any current health concerns: _____

List any recent health or physical changes: _____

_____

Nutrition

Meal	How often (times per week)	Typical foods eaten	Typical amount eaten
Breakfast	____ / week	_____	___ No __ Low ___ Med ___ High
Lunch	____ / week	_____	___ No __ Low ___ Med ___ High
Dinner	____ / week	_____	___ No __ Low ___ Med ___ High
Snacks	____ / week	_____	___ No __ Low ___ Med ___ High

Comments: _____

Current prescribed medications	Dose	Dates	Purpose	Side effects
_____	_____	_____	_____	_____
_____	_____	_____	_____	_____
_____	_____	_____	_____	_____
_____	_____	_____	_____	_____

Current over-the-counter meds	Dose	Dates	Purpose	Side effects
_____	_____	_____	_____	_____
_____	_____	_____	_____	_____
_____	_____	_____	_____	_____
_____	_____	_____	_____	_____

Are you allergic to any medications or drugs? ____ Yes ____ No

If Yes, describe: _____

_____

	Date	Reason	Results
Last physical exam	_____	_____	_____
Last doctor's visit	_____	_____	_____
Last dental exam	_____	_____	_____
Most recent surgery	_____	_____	_____
Other surgery	_____	_____	_____
Upcoming surgery	_____	_____	_____

Family history of medical problems: _____

_____

Please check if there have been any recent changes in the following:

___ Sleep patterns   ____ Eating patterns   ____ Behavior   ____ Energy level

___ Physical activity level   ____ General disposition   ____ Weight   ____ Nervousness/tension

Describe changes in areas in which you checked above: _____

_____

Chemical Use History

	Method of use and amount	Frequency of use	Age of first use	Age of last use	Used in last 48 hours		Used in last 30 days	
					Yes	No	Yes	No
Alcohol	_____	_____	_____	_____	___	___	___	___
Barbiturates	_____	_____	_____	_____	___	___	___	___
Valium/Librium	_____	_____	_____	_____	___	___	___	___
Cocaine/Crack	_____	_____	_____	_____	___	___	___	___
Heroin/Opiates	_____	_____	_____	_____	___	___	___	___
Marijuana	_____	_____	_____	_____	___	___	___	___
PCP/LSD/Mescaline	_____	_____	_____	_____	___	___	___	___
Inhalants	_____	_____	_____	_____	___	___	___	___
Caffeine	_____	_____	_____	_____	___	___	___	___
Nicotine	_____	_____	_____	_____	___	___	___	___
Over the counter	_____	_____	_____	_____	___	___	___	___
Prescription drugs	_____	_____	_____	_____	___	___	___	___
Other drugs	_____	_____	_____	_____	___	___	___	___

Substance of preference

1. _____   3. _____
2. _____   4. _____

Substance Abuse Questions

Describe when and where you typically use substances: _____
_____

Describe any changes in your use patterns: _____
_____

Describe how your use has affected your family or friends (include their perceptions of your use): ____
_____

Reason(s) for use:

__ Addicted   ____ Build confidence   ____ Escape   ____ Self-medication

__ Socialization   ____ Taste   ____ Other (specify): _____

How do you believe your substance use affects your life? _____

Who or what has helped you in stopping or limiting your use? _____

Does/Has someone in your family present/past have/had a problem with drugs or alcohol?

__ Yes ___ No   If Yes, describe: _____

Have you had withdrawal symptoms when trying to stop using drugs or alcohol? ____ Yes ___ No

If Yes, describe: _____

Have you had adverse reactions or overdose to drugs or alcohol? (describe):_____
_____

Does your body temperature change when you drink? ___ Yes ___ No

If Yes, describe: _____

Have drugs or alcohol created a problem for your job? ___ Yes ___ No

If Yes, describe: _____

Counseling/Prior Treatment History

Information about client (past and present):

	Yes	No	When	Where	Your reaction to overall experience
Counseling/Psychiatric treatment	___	___	_____	_____	_____
Suicidal thoughts/attempts	___	___	_____	_____	_____
Drug/alcohol treatment	___	___	_____	_____	_____
Hospitalizations	___	___	_____	_____	_____
Involvement with self-help groups (e.g., AA, Al-Anon, NA, Overeaters Anonymous)	___	___	_____	_____	_____

Information about family/significant others (past and present):

	Yes	No	When	Where	Your reaction to overall experience
Counseling/Psychiatric treatment	___	___	_____	_____	_____
Suicidal thoughts/attempts	___	___	_____	_____	_____
Drug/alcohol treatment	___	___	_____	_____	_____
Hospitalizations	___	___	_____	_____	_____
Involvement with self-help groups (e.g., AA, Al-Anon, NA, Overeaters Anonymous)	___	___	_____	_____	_____

Please check behaviors and symptoms that occur to you more often than you would like them to take place:

___ Aggression	___ Elevated mood	___ Phobias/fears
___ Alcohol dependence	___ Fatigue	___ Recurring thoughts
___ Anger	___ Gambling	___ Sexual addiction
___ Antisocial behavior	___ Hallucinations	___ Sexual difficulties
___ Anxiety	___ Heart palpitations	___ Sick often
___ Avoiding people	___ High blood pressure	___ Sleeping problems
___ Chest pain	___ Hopelessness	___ Speech problems
___ Cyber addiction	___ Impulsivity	___ Suicidal thoughts
___ Depression	___ Irritability	___ Thoughts disorganized
___ Disorientation	___ Judgment errors	___ Trembling
___ Distractibility	___ Loneliness	___ Withdrawing
___ Dizziness	___ Memory impairment	___ Worrying
___ Drug dependence	___ Mood shifts	___ Other (specify): _____
___ Eating disorder	___ Panic attacks	_____

Briefly discuss how the above symptoms impair your ability to function effectively: _____

_____

_____

_____

_____

_____

_____

_____

_____

Any additional information that would assist us in understanding your concerns or problems: _____

_____

_____

_____

_____

_____

_____

_____

What are your goals for therapy? _____

_____

_____

_____

_____

_____

_____

Do you feel suicidal at this time? ___ Yes   ___ No

If Yes, explain: _____

_____

_____

_____

For Staff Use

Therapist's signature/credentials: _____   Date: ____/____/_____

Supervisor's comments: _____

_____

_____   Physical exam: ___ Required   ___ Not required

Supervisor's signature/credentials: _____   Date: ____/____/_____

(Certifies case assignment, level of care and need for exam)

Client's name: _Judy Doe_   Date: _3/8/2005_

Gender: _X_ F ___ M   Date of birth: _7/6/1954_   Age: _50_

Form completed by (if someone other than client): ___ _same_

Address: _1234 Main St._   City: _Pleasantville_   State: _NJ_ Zip: _99998_

Phone (home): _201-555-5555_   (work): _201-555-5554_   ext: _281_

If you need any more space for any of the questions please use the back of the sheet.

Primary reason(s) for seeking services:

_X_ Anger management   ___ Anxiety   _X_ Coping   _X_ Depression

___ Eating disorder   ___ Fear/phobias   ___ Mental confusion   ___ Sexual concerns

___ Sleeping problems   ___ Addictive behaviors   ___ Alcohol/drugs

___ Other mental health concerns (specify): _____

Family Information

Relationship	Name	Age	Living Yes	Living No	Living with you Yes	Living with you No
Mother	Reana Sims	73	X			X
Father	Roger Sims			X		
Spouse	Bill Doe	51	X		X	
Children	Sally Doe	24	X			X
	James Doe	16	X		X	
	Julie Doe	12	X		X	

Significant others (e.g., brothers, sisters, grandparents, step-relatives, half-relatives. Please specify relationship.)

Relationship	Name	Age	Living Yes	Living No	Living with you Yes	Living with you No
Brother	Steven Doe	51	X			X
Sister	Holly Lockery	46	X			X
Sister	Sheila Kropp	44	X			X
Brother	Raymond Doe	42	X			X

Marital Status (more than one answer may apply)

___ Single   ___ Divorce in process   ___ Unmarried, living together

                 Length of time: _____   Length of time: _____

_X_ Legally married   ___ Separated   ___ Divorced

Length of time: ___*22 years*___   Length of time: _____   Length of time: _____

___ Widowed   ___ Annulment

Length of time: _____   Length of time: _____   Total number of marriages: _*1*_

Assessment of current relationship (if applicable): ___ Good   ___ Fair _X_ Poor

Parental Information

_X_ Parents legally married   ___ Mother remarried: Number of times: _____

___ Parents have ever been separated   ___ Father remarried: Number of times: _____

___ Parents ever divorced

Special circumstances (e.g., raised by person other than parents, information about spouse/children not living with you, etc.): _*None*_____

Development

Are there special, unusual, or traumatic circumstances that affected your development? ___ Yes _X_ No

If Yes, please describe: _____

Has there been history of child abuse? ___ Yes _X_ No

If Yes, which type(s)? ___ Sexual   ___ Physical ___ Verbal

If Yes, the abuse was as a: ___ Victim   ___ Perpetrator

Other childhood issues: ___ Neglect ___ Inadequate nutrition ___ Other (please specify): _____

Comments re: childhood development: _*My mother and older sister seemed to think that they could*_ _*make all of my decisions. It goes on today!*_____

Social Relationships

Check how you generally get along with other people: (check all that apply)

___ Affectionate   ___ Aggressive   ___ Avoidant   ___ Fight/argue often   ___ Follower

_X_ Friendly   ___ Leader   _X_ Outgoing   ___ Shy/withdrawn   ___ Submissive

___ Other (specify): _*But now I'm withdrawn*_____

Sexual orientation: _*Heterosexual*___   Comments: _____

Sexual dysfunctions? ___ Yes _X_ No

If Yes, describe: _____

Any current or history of being as sexual perpetrator? ___ Yes _X_ No

If Yes, describe: _____

Cultural/Ethnic

To which cultural or ethnic group, if any, do you belong? ____*White, middle class*_____

Are you experiencing any problems due to cultural or ethnic issues? ___ Yes _X_ No

If Yes, describe: _____

Other cultural/ethnic information: _*None*_____

Spiritual/Religious

How important to you are spiritual matters? ____ Not ____ Little _X_ Moderate ____ Much

Are you affiliated with a spiritual or religious group? ____ Yes _X_ No

If Yes, describe: _____

Were you raised within a spiritual or religious group? _X_ Yes ____ No

If Yes, describe: _Catholic, strict_ _____

Would you like your spiritual/religious beliefs incorporated into the counseling? ____ Yes _X_ No

If Yes, describe: _____

Legal

Current Status

Are you involved in any active cases (traffic, civil, criminal)? ____ Yes _X_ No

If Yes, please describe and indicate the court and hearing/trial dates and charges: _____

_____

Are you presently on probation or parole? ____ Yes _X_ No

If Yes, please describe: _____

Past History

Traffic violations: _X_ Yes ____ No		DWI, DUI, etc.: ____ Yes _X_ No
Criminal involvement: ____ Yes _X_ No		Civil involvement: ____ Yes _X_ No

If you responded Yes to any of the above, please fill in the following information.

Charges	Date	Where (city)	Results
Speeding ticket	1998	Baneville	$80 fine

Education

Fill in all that apply: Years of education: _16_ Currently enrolled in school? ____ Yes _X_ No

__ High school grad/GED

__ Vocational: Number of years: ___ Graduated: ___ Yes ___ No Major: _____

_X_ College: Number of years: _4_ Graduated: ___ Yes ___ No Major: _____

__ Graduate: Number of years: ___ Graduated: ___ Yes ___ No Major: _____

Other training: _____

Special circumstances (e.g., learning disabilities, gifted): _____ _None_ _____

Employment

Begin with most recent job, list job history: _____

Employer	Dates	Title	Reason left the job	How often miss work?
Empire School	1986–present	Teacher		2–4/month
Bently School	1974–1986	Teacher	Moved	Seldom

Currently: _X_ FT ___ PT ___ Temp ___ Laid-off ___ Disabled ___ Retired
___ Social Security ___ Student ___ Other (describe): _____

Military

Military experience? ___ Yes ___ No   Combat experience? ___ Yes ___ No

Where: _____

Branch: _____   Discharge date: _____

Date drafted: _____   Type of discharge: _____

Date enlisted: _____   Rank at discharge: _____

Leisure/Recreational

Describe special areas of interest or hobbies (e.g., art, books, crafts, physical fitness, sports, outdoor activities, church activities, walking, exercising, diet/health, hunting, fishing, bowling, traveling, etc.)

Activity	How often now?	How often in the past?
Bowling	_None_	_3x/month_
Exercising	_None_	_Daily_
Reading	_1 hr/wk_	_2 hr/day_

Medical/Physical Health

___ AIDS	___ Dizziness	___ Nose bleeds
___ Alcoholism	___ Drug abuse	___ Pneumonia
___ Abdominal pain	___ Epilepsy	___ Rheumatic Fever
___ Abortion	___ Ear infections	___ Sexually transmitted diseases
___ Allergies	___ Eating problems	_X_ Sleeping disorders
___ Anemia	___ Fainting	___ Sore throat
___ Appendicitis	_X_ Fatigue	___ Scarlet Fever
___ Arthritis	___ Frequent urination	___ Sinusitis
___ Asthma	_X_ Headaches	___ Smallpox
___ Bronchitis	___ Hearing problems	___ Stroke
___ Bed wetting	___ Hepatitis	_X_ Sexual problems
___ Cancer	___ High blood pressure	___ Tonsillitis
___ Chest pain	___ Kidney problems	___ Tuberculosis
___ Chronic pain	___ Measles	___ Toothache
___ Colds/Coughs	___ Mononucleosis	___ Thyroid problems
___ Constipation	___ Mumps	___ Vision problems
___ Chicken Pox	___ Menstrual pain	___ Vomiting
___ Dental problems	___ Miscarriages	___ Whooping cough
___ Diabetes	___ Neurological disorders	___ Other (describe): _____
___ Diarrhea	___ Nausea	_____

List any current health concerns: _Usually in good health_ _____

List any recent health or physical changes: _Increasing headaches, fatigue and poor sleep. Have_ _____
lost 20 pounds in past year. _____

Nutrition

Meal	How often (times per week)	Typical foods eaten	Typical amount eaten				
Breakfast	3 / week	Cereal or toast	___ No	__ Low	_X_ Med	___ High
Lunch	5 / week	Sandwich or soup	___ No	__ Low	_X_ Med	___ High
Dinner	7 / week	Meat, potato, veg.	___ No	_X_ Low	___ Med	___ High
Snacks	7 / week	Candy bar	___ No	__ Low	_X_ Med	___ High

Comments: _Some days I have no appetite._

Current prescribed medications	Dose	Dates	Purpose	Side effects
None				

Current over-the-counter meds	Dose	Dates	Purpose	Side effects
Aspirin	2 tabs	past year	headache	None

Are you allergic to any medications or drugs? ____ Yes _X_ No

If Yes, describe: _____

	Date	Reason	Results
Last physical exam	1994	Routine physical	Good health
Last doctor's visit	1998	Headache	None
Last dental exam	1997	Check-up	2 cavities filled
Most recent surgery	None		
Other surgery			
Upcoming surgery	None		

Family history of medical problems: _No family history of medical problems in family_

Please check if there have been any recent changes in the following:

_X_ Sleep patterns   _X_ Eating patterns   _X_ Behavior   _X_ Energy level

_X_ Physical activity level   _X_ General disposition   ___ Weight   ___ Nervousness/tension

Describe changes in areas in which you checked above: _I want to be motivated to teach like I used to, I want to be happy again._

Chemical Use History

	Method of use and amount	Frequency of use	Age of first use	Age of last use	Used in last 48 hours		Used in last 30 days	
					Yes	No	Yes	No
Alcohol	_Wine–1 glass_	_Holidays_	_24_	_present_	___	_X_	_X_	___
Barbiturates					___	___	___	___
Valium/Librium					___	___	___	___
Cocaine/Crack					___	___	___	___
Heroin/Opiates					___	___	___	___
Marijuana					___	___	___	___
PCP/LSD/Mescaline					___	___	___	___
Inhalants					___	___	___	___
Caffeine					___	___	___	___
Nicotine					___	___	___	___
Over the counter	_Aspirin–2 tabs_	_3x/week_	_teen_	_present_	_X_	___	_X_	___
Prescription drugs					___	___	___	___
Other drugs					___	___	___	___

Substance of preference

1. _____   3. _____

2. _____   4. _____

Substance Abuse Questions

Describe when and where you typically use substances: ___ _No substance abuse issues_ ___

_____

Describe any changes in your use patterns: _____

_____

Describe how your use has affected your family or friends (include their perceptions of your use): ___
_____ _No effect_ _____

Reason(s) for use:

___ Addicted   ___ Build confidence   ___ Escape   ___ Self-medication

_X_ Socialization   ___ Taste   ___ Other (specify): _____

How do you believe your substance use affects your life? _Not_ _____

Who or what has helped you in stopping or limiting your use? _____

Does/Has someone in your family present/past have/had a problem with drugs or alcohol?

_X_ Yes ___ No   If Yes, describe: ___ _Sometimes my father drank too much._ ___

Have you had withdrawal symptoms when trying to stop using drugs or alcohol? ___ Yes _X_ No

If Yes, describe: _____

Have you had adverse reactions or overdose to drugs or alcohol? (describe): _____

_____

Does your body temperature change when you drink? _____ Yes __X__ No

If Yes, describe: _____

Have drugs or alcohol created a problem for your job? _____ Yes __X__ No

If Yes, describe: _____

Counseling/Prior Treatment History

Information about client (past and present):

	Yes	No	When	Where	Your reaction to overall experience
Counseling/Psychiatric treatment	X	___	*1973*	*Lowe Clinic Building*	*Very helpful*
Suicidal thoughts/attempts	X	___	*1968 and now*		*Scared because my kids are older now*
Drug/alcohol treatment	___	X			
Hospitalizations	___	X			
Involvement with self-help groups (e.g., AA, Al-Anon, NA, Overeaters Anonymous)	___	X			

Information about family/significant others (past and present):

	Yes	No	When	Where	Your reaction to overall experience
Counseling/Psychiatric treatment	___	X			
Suicidal thoughts/attempts	___	X			
Drug/alcohol treatment	___	X			
Hospitalizations	___	X			
Involvement with self-help groups (e.g., AA, Al-Anon, NA, Overeaters Anonymous)	___	X			

Please check behaviors and symptoms that occur to you more often than you would like them to take place:

___ Aggression	___ Elevated mood	___ Phobias/fears
___ Alcohol dependence	X Fatigue	___ Recurring thoughts
X Anger	___ Gambling	___ Sexual addiction
___ Antisocial behavior	___ Hallucinations	X Sexual difficulties
___ Anxiety	___ Heart palpitations	___ Sick often
X Avoiding people	___ High blood pressure	X Sleeping problems
___ Chest pain	X Hopelessness	___ Speech problems
___ Cyber addiction	___ Impulsivity	X Suicidal thoughts
X Depression	X Irritability	___ Thoughts disorganized
___ Disorientation	___ Judgment errors	___ Trembling
___ Distractibility	X Loneliness	X Withdrawing
___ Dizziness	___ Memory impairment	___ Worrying
___ Drug dependence	___ Mood shifts	___ Other (specify): _____
___ Eating disorder	___ Panic attacks	_____

Briefly discuss how the above symptoms impair your ability to function effectively: _____ *I just don't care about anything. I don't want to be around people, go to work or even get up in the morning. I'm a loser. I feel like quitting teaching. I am empty inside and just don't care most of the time.*

Any additional information that would assist us in understanding your concerns or problems: _____ *What good am I? I'm a poor wife and a poor teacher.*

What are your goals for therapy? _____ *Feel alive again.*

Do you feel suicidal at this time? __X__ Yes _____ No

If Yes, explain: _*But, I won't do it.*_

For Staff Use

Therapist's signature/credentials: _____ *Darlene Benton, PhD* _____   Date: __3__ / __8__ / __2005__

Supervisor's comments: _____ *Fully assess suicide potential. Consider leave at work. Schedule medical evaluation immediately.*

_____   Physical exam: __X__ Required _____ Not required

Supervisor's signature/credentials: _____ *Sharon Bell, PhD* _____   Date: __3__ / __12__ / __2005__

(Certifies case assignment, level of care and need for exam)

Form 22 Personal History—Children and Adolescents (< 18)

Client's name: _____   Date: _____

Gender: ___ F ___ M   Date of birth: _____   Age: _____   Grade in school: _____

Form completed by (if someone other than client): _____

Address: _____   City: _____   State: _____   Zip: _____

Phone (home): _____   (work): _____   Ext: _____

If you need any more space for any of the following questions please use the back of the sheet.

Primary reason(s) for seeking services:

___ Anger management   _____ Anxiety   _____ Coping   _____ Depression

___ Eating disorder   _____ Fear/phobias   _____ Mental confusion _____ Sexual concerns

___ Sleeping problems   _____ Addictive behaviors _____ Alcohol/drugs   _____ Hyperactivity

___ Other mental health concerns (specify): _____

_____

Family History

Parents

With whom does the child live at this time? _____

Are parent's divorced or separated? _____

If Yes, who has legal custody? _____

Were the child's parents ever married? ___ Yes ___ No

Is there any significant information about the parents' relationship or treatment toward the child which might be beneficial in counseling? ___ Yes ___ No

If Yes, describe: _____

Client's Mother

Name: _____   Age: _____   Occupation: _____   ___ FT ___ PT

Where employed: _____   Work phone: _____

Mother's education: _____

Is the child currently living with mother? ___ Yes ___ No

___ Natural parent ___ Step-parent ___ Adoptive parent ___ Foster home ___ Other (specify): _____

Is there anything notable, unusual or stressful about the child's relationship with the mother?

___ Yes ___ No   If Yes, please explain: _____

_____

How is the child disciplined by the mother? _____

For what reasons is the child disciplined by the mother? _____

Client's Father

Name: _____ Age: _____ Occupation: _____ ____ FT ____ PT

Where employed: _____ Work phone: _____

Father's education: _____

Is the child currently living with father? __ Yes ____ No

___ Natural parent ____ Step-parent ____ Adoptive parent __ Foster home ___ Other (specify): _____

Is there anything notable, unusual or stressful about the child's relationship with the father?

___ Yes ____ No   If Yes, please explain: _____

_____

How is the child disciplined by the father? _____

For what reasons is the child disciplined by the father? _____

Client's Siblings and Others Who Live in the Household

Names of Siblings	Age	Gender	Lives	Quality of relationship with the client
_____	___	___ F ___ M	___ home ___ away	___ poor ___ average ___ good
_____	___	___ F ___ M	___ home ___ away	___ poor ___ average ___ good
_____	___	___ F ___ M	___ home ___ away	___ poor ___ average ___ good
_____	___	___ F ___ M	___ home ___ away	___ poor ___ average ___ good

Others living in the household		Gender	Relationship (e.g., cousin, foster child)	
_____	___	___ F ___ M	_____	___ poor ___ average ___ good
_____	___	___ F ___ M	_____	___ poor ___ average ___ good
_____	___	___ F ___ M	_____	___ poor ___ average ___ good
_____	___	___ F ___ M	_____	___ poor ___ average ___ good

Comments: _____

_____

_____

Family Health History

Have any of the following diseases occurred among the child's blood relatives? (parents, siblings, aunts, uncles or grandparents) Check those which apply:

___ Allergies   ___ Deafness   ___ Muscular Dystrophy

___ Anemia   ___ Diabetes   ___ Nervousness

___ Asthma   ___ Glandular problems   ___ Perceptual motor disorder

___ Bleeding tendency   ___ Heart diseases   ___ Mental Retardation

___ Blindness   ___ High blood pressure   ___ Seizures

___ Cancer   ___ Kidney disease   ___ Spinal Bifida

___ Cerebral Palsy   ___ Mental illness   ___ Suicide

___ Cleft lips   ___ Migraines   ___ Other (specify): _____

___ Cleft palate   ___ Multiple sclerosis   _____

Comments re: Family Health: _____

_____

Childhood/Adolescent History

Pregnancy/Birth

Has the child's mother had any occurances of miscarriages or stillborns? ____ Yes ____ No

If Yes, describe: _____

Was the pregnancy with child planned? ____ Yes ____ No   Length of pregnancy: _____

Mother's age at child's birth: _____   Father's age at child's birth: _____

Child number ____ of __ total children.

How many pounds did the mother gain during the pregnancy? _____

While pregnant did the mother smoke? ____ Yes ____ No   If Yes, what amount: _____ _____

Did the mother use drugs of alcohol? ____ Yes ____ No   If Yes, type/amount: _____

While pregnant, did the mother have any medical or emotional difficulties? (e.g., surgery, hypertension, medication) ____ Yes ____ No

If Yes, describe: _____

Length of labor: _____   Induced: __ Yes ____ No   Caesarean? ____ Yes ____ No

Baby's birth weight: _____   Baby's birth length: _____

Describe any physical or emotional complications with the delivery: _____

_____

Describe any complications for the mother or the baby after the birth: _____

_____

Length of hospitalization: Mother: _____   Baby: _____

Infancy/Toddlerhood Check all which apply:

__ Breast fed	____ Milk allergies	____ Vomiting	____ Diarrhea
__ Bottle fed	____ Rashes	____ Colic	____ Constipation
__ Not cuddly	____ Cried often	____ Rarely cried	____ Overactive
__ Resisted solid food	____ Trouble sleeping	____ Irritable when awakened	____ Lethargic

Developmental History Please note the age at which the following behaviors took place:

Sat alone: _____   Dressed self: _____

Took 1st steps: _____   Tied shoelaces: _____

Spoke words: _____   Rode two-wheeled bike: _____

Spoke sentences: _____   Toilet trained: _____

Weaned: _____   Dry during day: _____

Fed self: _____   Dry during night: _____

Compared with others in the family, child's development was: ____ slow __ average ____ fast

Age for following developments (fill in where applicable)

Began puberty: _____   Menstruation: _____

Voice change: _____   Convulsions: _____

Breast development: _____   Injuries or hospitalization: _____

Issues that affected child's development (e.g., physical/sexual abuse, inadequate nutrition, neglect, etc.)

_____

_____

Education

Current school: _____ School phone number: _____

Type of school: ___ Public ___ Private ___ Home schooled ___ Other (specify): _____

Grade: _____ Teacher: _____ School Counselor: _____

In special education? ___ Yes ___ No If Yes, describe: _____

In gifted program? ___ Yes ___ No If Yes, describe: _____

Has child ever been held back in school? ___ Yes ___ No If Yes, describe: _____

Which subjects does the child enjoy in school? _____

Which subjects does the child dislike in school? _____

What grades does the child usually receive in school? _____

Have there been any recent changes in the child's grades? ___ Yes ___ No

If Yes, describe: _____

Has the child been tested psychologically? ___ Yes ___ No

If Yes, describe: _____

Check the descriptions which specifically relate to your child.

Feelings about School Work:

___ Anxious   ___ Passive   ___ Enthusiastic   ___ Fearful

___ Eager   ___ No expression   ___ Bored   ___ Rebellious

___ Other (describe): _____

Approach to School Work:

___ Organized   ___ Industrious   ___ Responsible   ___ Interested

___ Self-directed   ___ No initiative   ___ Refuses   ___ Does only what is expected

___ Sloppy   ___ Disorganized   ___ Cooperative   ___ Doesn't complete assignments

___ Other (describe): _____

Performance in School (Parent's Opinion):

___ Satisfactory   ___ Underachiever   ___ Overachiever

___ Other (describe): _____

Child's Peer Relationships:

___ Spontaneous   ___ Follower   ___ Leader   ___ Difficulty making friends

___ Makes friends easily   ___ Long-time friends   ___ Shares easily

___ Other (describe): _____

Who handles responsibility for your child in the following areas?

    School: ___ Mother ___ Father ___ Shared ___ Other (specify): _____

    Health: ___ Mother ___ Father ___ Shared ___ Other (specify): _____

    Problem behavior: ___ Mother ___ Father ___ Shared ___ Other (specify): _____

If the child is involved in a vocational program or works a job, please fill in the following:

What is the child's attitude toward work? ___ Poor ___ Average ___ Good ___ Excellent

Current employer: _____ Position: _____ Hours per week: _____

How have the child's grades in school been affected since working? ___ Lower ___ Same ___ Higher

How many previous jobs or placements has the child had? _____

Usual length of employment: _____ Usual reason for leaving: _____

Leisure/Recreational

Describe special areas of interest or hobbies (e.g., art, books, crafts, physical fitness, sports, outdoor activities, church activities, walking, exercising, diet/health, hunting, fishing, bowling, school activities, scouts, etc.)

Activity	How often now?	How often in the past?
_____	_____	_____
_____	_____	_____
_____	_____	_____
_____	_____	_____

Medical/Physical Health

___ Abortion	___ Hayfever	___ Pneumonia
___ Asthma	___ Heart trouble	___ Polio
___ Blackouts	___ Hepatitis	___ Pregnancy
___ Bronchitis	___ Hives	___ Rheumatic Fever
___ Cerebral Palsy	___ Influenza	___ Scarlet Fever
___ Chicken Pox	___ Lead poisoning	___ Seizures
___ Congenital problems	___ Measles	___ Severe colds
___ Croup	___ Meningitis	___ Severe head injury
___ Diabetes	___ Miscarriage	___ Sexually transmitted disease
___ Diphtheria	___ Multiple sclerosis	___ Thyroid disorders
___ Dizziness	___ Mumps	___ Vision problems
___ Ear aches	___ Muscular Dystrophy	___ Wearing glasses
___ Ear infections	___ Nose bleeds	___ Whooping cough
___ Eczema	___ Other skin rashes	___ Other
___ Encephalitis	___ Paralysis	_____
___ Fevers	___ Pleurisy	

List any current health concerns: _____

_____

List any recent health or physical changes: _____

_____

Nutrition

Meal	How often (times per week)	Typical foods eaten	Typical amount eaten
Breakfast	___ / week	_____	___ No ___ Low ___ Med ___ High
Lunch	___ / week	_____	___ No ___ Low ___ Med ___ High
Dinner	___ / week	_____	___ No ___ Low ___ Med ___ High
Snacks	___ / week	_____	___ No ___ Low ___ Med ___ High

Comments: _____

Most recent examinations

Type of examination	Date of most recent visit	Results
Physical examination	_____	_____
Dental examination	_____	_____
Vision examination	_____	_____
Hearing examination	_____	_____

Current prescribed medications	Dose	Dates	Purpose	Side effects
_____	_____	_____	_____	_____
_____	_____	_____	_____	_____
_____	_____	_____	_____	_____
_____	_____	_____	_____	_____

Current over-the-counter meds	Dose	Dates	Purpose	Side effects
_____	_____	_____	_____	_____
_____	_____	_____	_____	_____
_____	_____	_____	_____	_____
_____	_____	_____	_____	_____

Immunization record (check immunizations the child/adolescent has received):

	DPT	Polio
2 months	___	___
4 months	___	___
6 months	___	___
18 months	___	___
4–5 years	___	___

15 months ___ MMR (Measles, Mumps, Rubella)

24 months ___ HBPV (Hib)

Prior to school ___ HepB

Chemical Use History

Does the child/adolescent use or have a problem with alcohol or drugs? ___ Yes ___ No

If Yes, describe: _____

_____

Counseling/Prior Treatment History

Information about child/adolescent (past and present):

	Yes	No	When	Where	Reaction or overall experience
Counseling/Psychiatric treatment	___	___	_____	_____	_____
Suicidal thoughts/attempts	___	___	_____	_____	_____
Drug/alcohol treatment	___	___	_____	_____	_____
Hospitalizations	___	___	_____	_____	_____

Behavioral/Emotional

Please check any of the following that are typical for your child:

___ Affectionate	___ Frustrated easily	___ Sad
___ Aggressive	___ Gambling	___ Selfish
___ Alcohol problems	___ Generous	___ Separation anxiety
___ Angry	___ Hallucinations	___ Sets fires
___ Anxiety	___ Head banging	___ Sexual addiction
___ Attachment to dolls	___ Heart problems	___ Sexual acting out
___ Avoids adults	___ Hopelessness	___ Shares
___ Bedwetting	___ Hurts animals	___ Sick often
___ Blinking, jerking	___ Imaginary friends	___ Short attention span
___ Bizarre behavior	___ Impulsive	___ Shy, timid
___ Bullies, threatens	___ Irritable	___ Sleeping problems
___ Careless, reckless	___ Lazy	___ Slow moving
___ Chest pains	___ Learning problems	___ Soiling
___ Clumsy	___ Lies frequently	___ Speech problems
___ Confident	___ Listens to reason	___ Steals
___ Cooperative	___ Loner	___ Stomach aches
___ Cyber addiction	___ Low self-esteem	___ Suicidal threats
___ Defiant	___ Messy	___ Suicidal attempts
___ Depression	___ Moody	___ Talks back
___ Destructive	___ Nightmares	___ Teeth grinding
___ Difficulty speaking	___ Obedient	___ Thumb sucking
___ Dizziness	___ Often sick	___ Tics or twitching
___ Drugs dependence	___ Oppositional	___ Unsafe behaviors
___ Eating disorder	___ Over active	___ Unusual thinking
___ Enthusiastic	___ Overweight	___ Weight loss
___ Excessive masturbation	___ Panic attacks	___ Withdrawn
___ Expects failure	___ Phobias	___ Worries excessively
___ Fatigue	___ Poor appetite	___ Other:
___ Fearful	___ Psychiatric problems	_____
___ Frequent injuries	___ Quarrels	_____

Please describe any of the above (or other) concerns: _____
_____

How are problem behaviors generally handled? _____
_____

What are the family's favorite activities? _____
_____

What does the child/adolescent do with unstructured time? _____
_____

Has the child/adolescent experienced death? (friends, family pets, other) ___ Yes ___ No

At what age? ____ If Yes, describe the child's/adolescent's reaction: _____

_____

Have there been any other significant changes or events in your child's life? (family, moving, fire, etc.)

___ Yes ___ No If Yes, describe: _____

_____

Any additional information that you believe would assist us in understanding your child/adolescent?

_____

_____

_____

Any additional information that would assist us in understanding current concerns or problems?

_____

_____

_____

What are your goals for the child's therapy? _____

_____

What family involvement would you like to see in the therapy? _____

_____

Do you believe the child is suicidal at this time? ___ Yes ___ No

If Yes, explain: _____

_____

For Staff Use

Therapist's comments: _____

_____

_____

_____

_____

Therapist's signature/credentials: _____ Date: ____/____/____

Supervisor's comments: _____

_____

_____

_____

_____ Physical exam: ___ Required ___ Not required

Supervisor's signature/credentials: _____ Date: ____/____/____

(Certifies case assignment, level of care and need for exam)

Form 22A   Personal History—Children and Adolescents (< 18)   (*Completed*)

Client's name: _William Olden_   Date: _4/4/2005_

Gender: ___ F _X_ M   Date of birth: _3/7/1990_   Age: _15_   Grade in school: _10_

Form completed by (if someone other than client): _Mother: Lanna Olden_

Address: _3257 Brooks Ave #316_   City: _Provo_   State: _ND_   Zip: _02511_

Phone (home): _555-3742_   (work): _____   Ext: _____

If you need any more space for any of the following questions please use the back of the sheet.

Primary reason(s) for seeking services:

_X_ Anger management   ____ Anxiety   _X_ Coping   _X_ Depression

___ Eating disorder   ____ Fear/phobias   ____ Mental confusion   ____ Sexual concerns

___ Sleeping problems   ____ Addictive behaviors   ____ Alcohol/drugs   ____ Hyperactivity

___ Other mental health concerns (specify): _____

_____

Family History

Parents

With whom does the child live at this time? _Mother_

Are parent's divorced or separated? _Divorced 2 years_

If Yes, who has legal custody? _Mother_

Were the child's parents ever married? _X_ Yes ____ No

Is there any significant information about the parents' relationship or treatment toward the child which might be beneficial in counseling? _X_ Yes ____ No

If Yes, describe: _Dysfunctional, violent relationship_

Client's Mother

Name: _Lanna Olden_   Age: _35_   Occupation: _Billing clerk_   _X_ FT ____ PT

Where employed: _Century Clinic_   Work phone: _555-3373_

Mother's education: _H.S. graduate_

Is the child currently living with mother? _X_ Yes ____ No

_X_ Natural parent ____ Step-parent ____ Adoptive parent ____ Foster home ____ Other (specify): _____

Is there anything notable, unusual or stressful about the child's relationship with the mother?

_X_ Yes ____ No   If Yes, please explain: _Very defiant toward me since I remarried._

_____

How is the child disciplined by the mother? _Time-out_

For what reasons is the child disciplined by the mother? _Sassing, not doing school work._

Client's Father

Name: _Reno Olden_   Age: _38_   Occupation: _Furnace repair_   _X_ FT   ___ PT

Where employed: _Century Furnace_   Work phone: _555-7337_

Father's education: _H.S. graduate + 2 yrs voc. tech_

Is the child currently living with father? __ Yes _X_ No

_X_ Natural parent ____ Step-parent ____Adoptive parent __Foster home ___ Other (specify): _____

Is there anything notable, unusual or stressful about the child's relationship with the father?

_X_ Yes   ___ No   If Yes, please explain: _He idolizes his father, but father seldom phones_

  or visits.

How is the child disciplined by the father? _____Spanking, I believe_

For what reasons is the child disciplined by the father? _____

Client's Siblings and Others Who Live in the Household

Names of Siblings	Age	Gender	Lives	Quality of relationship with the client
Marsha Olden	12	_X_ F ___ M	_X_ home ___ away	_X_ poor ___ average ___ good
_____	___	___ F ___ M	___ home ___ away	___ poor ___ average ___ good
_____	___	___ F ___ M	___ home ___ away	___ poor ___ average ___ good
_____	___	___ F ___ M	___ home ___ away	___ poor ___ average ___ good

Others living in the household   Relationship (e.g., cousin, foster child)

_____	___	___ F ___ M	_____	___ poor ___ average ___ good
_____	___	___ F ___ M	_____	___ poor ___ average ___ good
_____	___	___ F ___ M	_____	___ poor ___ average ___ good
_____	___	___ F ___ M	_____	___ poor ___ average ___ good

Comments: _He is increasingly annoying his sister. Sometimes he hits her or trashes her room._
  Often teases her.

Family Health History

Have any of the following diseases occurred among the child's blood relatives? (parents, siblings, aunts, uncles or grandparents) Check those which apply:

___ Allergies	___ Deafness	___ Muscular Dystrophy
___ Anemia	___ Diabetes	___ Nervousness
___ Asthma	___ Glandular problems	___ Perceptual motor disorder
___ Bleeding tendency	___ Heart diseases	___ Mental Retardation
___ Blindness	___ High blood pressure	___ Seizures
___ Cancer	___ Kidney disease	___ Spinal Bifida
___ Cerebral Palsy	___ Mental illness	___ Suicide
___ Cleft lips	___ Migraines	___ Other (specify): _____
___ Cleft palate	___ Multiple sclerosis	

Comments re: Family Health: _____Good health_

Childhood/Adolescent History

Pregnancy/Birth

Has the child's mother had any occurances of miscarriages or stillborns? ___ Yes _X_ No

If Yes, describe: _____

Was the pregnancy with child planned? ___ Yes _X_ No   Length of pregnancy: _Full term_

Mother's age at child's birth: _20_   Father's age at child's birth: _23_

Child number _1_ of _2_ total children.

How many pounds did the mother gain during the pregnancy? _32_

While pregnant did the mother smoke? ___ Yes _X_ No   If Yes, what amount: _____

Did the mother use drugs of alcohol?   ___ Yes _X_ No   If Yes, type/amount: _____

While pregnant, did the mother have any medical or emotional difficulties? (e.g., surgery, hypertension, medication) _X_ Yes ___ No

If Yes, describe: _Ongoing physical abuse and stress_

Length of labor: _6 hrs_   Induced? ___ Yes _X_ No   Caesarean? ___ Yes _X_ No

Baby's birth weight: _9lb 1 oz_   Baby's birth length: _average_

Describe any physical or emotional complications with the delivery: _None_

_____

Describe any complications for the mother or the baby after the birth: _None_

_____

Length of hospitalization: Mother: _3 days_   Baby: _3 days_

Infancy/Toddlerhood Check all which apply:

___ Breast fed	___ Milk allergies	___ Vomiting	___ Diarrhea
_X_ Bottle fed	___ Rashes	___ Colic	___ Constipation
___ Not cuddly	_X_ Cried often	___ Rarely cried	___ Overactive
___ Resisted solid food	___ Trouble sleeping	_X_ Irritable when awakened	___ Lethargic

Developmental History Please note the age at which the following behaviors took place:

Sat alone: _6–7m_	Dressed self: _28m_
Took 1st steps: _11m_	Tied shoelaces: _4 1/2y_
Spoke words: _11m_	Rode two-wheeled bike: _5y_
Spoke sentences: _18m_	Toilet trained: _2 1/2y_
Weaned: _14m_	Dry during day: _18m_
Fed self: _16m_	Dry during night: _3y_

Compared with others in the family, child's development was: ___ slow _X_ average ___ fast

Age for following developments (fill in where applicable)

Began puberty: _12–13_	Menstruation: _____
Voice change: _12–13_	Convulsions: _____
Breast development: _____	Injuries or hospitalization: _____

Issues that affected child's development (e.g., physical/sexual abuse, inadequate nutrition, neglect, etc.)

Observed abuse from father to mother

_____

Education

Current school: ___*Dalton*___   School phone number: ___*555-2253*___

Type of school: _X_ Public ___ Private ___ Home schooled ___ Other (specify): _____

Grade: ___*10*___   Teacher: ___*Several*___   School Counselor: ___*Mrs. Keenan*___

In special education? _X_ Yes ___ No   If Yes, describe: _____

In gifted program? ___ Yes ___ No   If Yes, describe: _____

Has child ever been held back in school? ___ Yes _X_ No   If Yes, describe: _____

Which subjects does the child enjoy in school? ___*None*_____

Which subjects does the child dislike in school? ___*All*_____

What grades does the child usually receive in school? ___*C–D–F*_____

Have there been any recent changes in the child's grades? _X_ Yes ___ No

If Yes, describe: ___*Decreasing past 2 years*_____

Has the child been tested psychologically? ___ Yes _X_ No

If Yes, describe: ___*Except IQ testing (WISC-IV FSIQ = 115)*_____

Check the descriptions which specifically relate to your child.

Feelings about School Work:

___ Anxious   ___ Passive   ___ Enthusiastic   ___ Fearful

___ Eager   ___ No expression   ___ Bored   ___ Rebellious

___ Other (describe): _____

Approach to School Work:

___ Organized   ___ Industrious   ___ Responsible   ___ Interested

___ Self-directed   _X_ No initiative   _X_ Refuses   ___ Does only what is expected

___ Sloppy   ___ Disorganized   ___ Cooperative   _X_ Doesn't complete assignments

___ Other (describe): _____

Performance in School (Parent's Opinion):

___ Satisfactory   _X_ Underachiever   ___ Overachiever

___ Other (describe): ___*Refuses to do work*_____

Child's Peer Relationships:

___ Spontaneous   ___ Follower   ___ Leader   _X_ Difficulty making friends

___ Makes friends easily   ___ Long-time friends   ___ Shares easily

_X_ Other (describe): ___*Bullies peers*_____

Who handles responsibility for your child in the following areas?

   School: _X_ Mother ___ Father ___ Shared ___ Other (specify): _____

   Health: _X_ Mother ___ Father ___ Shared ___ Other (specify): _____

   Problem behavior: _X_ Mother ___ Father ___ Shared ___ Other (specify): _____

If the child is involved in a vocational program or works a job, please fill in the following:

What is the child's attitude toward work? ___ Poor ___ Average ___ Good ___ Excellent

Current employer: _____ Position: _____ Hours per week: _____

How have the child's grades in school been affected since working? ___ Lower ___ Same ___ Higher

How many previous jobs or placements has the child had? _____

Usual length of employment: _____ Usual reason for leaving: _____

Leisure/Recreational

Describe special areas of interest or hobbies (e.g., art, books, crafts, physical fitness, sports, outdoor activities, church activities, walking, exercising, diet/health, hunting, fishing, bowling, school activities, scouts, etc.)

Activity	How often now?	How often in the past?
Baseball team	*None*	*2x/wk*
Exercising	*None*	*Daily*
School activities	*None*	*1x/wk*

Medical/Physical Health

___ Abortion	___ Hayfever	___ Pneumonia
___ Asthma	___ Heart trouble	___ Polio
___ Blackouts	___ Hepatitis	___ Pregnancy
___ Bronchitis	___ Hives	___ Rheumatic Fever
___ Cerebral Palsy	___ Influenza	___ Scarlet Fever
_X_ Chicken Pox	___ Lead poisoning	___ Seizures
___ Congenital problems	_X_ Measles	___ Severe colds
___ Croup	___ Meningitis	___ Severe head injury
___ Diabetes	___ Miscarriage	___ Sexually transmitted disease
___ Diphtheria	___ Multiple sclerosis	___ Thyroid disorders
___ Dizziness	___ Mumps	___ Vision problems
___ Ear aches	___ Muscular Dystrophy	___ Wearing glasses
___ Ear infections	___ Nose bleeds	___ Whooping cough
___ Eczema	___ Other skin rashes	___ Other
___ Encephalitis	___ Paralysis	
___ Fevers	___ Pleurisy	

List any current health concerns: *None*

List any recent health or physical changes: *None*

Nutrition

Meal	How often (times per week)	Typical foods eaten	Typical amount eaten				
Breakfast	_7_ / week	*Cereal*	___ No	___ Low	_X_ Med	___ High
Lunch	_7_ / week	*Soup or sandwich*	___ No	___ Low	_X_ Med	___ High
Dinner	_7_ / week	*Hot meal*	___ No	___ Low	_X_ Med	___ High
Snacks	_7_ / week		___ No	___ Low	_X_ Med	___ High

Comments: *No eating problems*

Most recent examinations

Type of examination	Date of most recent visit	Results
Physical examination	*8/04*	*School physical: no problems*
Dental examination	*8/04*	*1 cavity*
Vision examination	*5/02*	*Good vision*
Hearing examination	*OK*	

Current prescribed medications	Dose	Dates	Purpose	Side effects
None				

Current over-the-counter meds	Dose	Dates	Purpose	Side effects
None				

Immunization record (check immunizations the child/adolescent has received):

	DPT	Polio
2 months	*X*	*X*
4 months	*X*	*X*
6 months	*X*	*X*
18 months	*X*	*X*
4–5 years	*X*	*X*

15 months *X* MMR (Measles, Mumps, Rubella)

24 months *X* HBPV (Hib)

Prior to school *X* HepB

Chemical Use History

Does the child/adolescent use or have a problem with alcohol or drugs? _____ Yes *X* No

If Yes, describe: _____

Counseling/Prior Treatment History

Information about child/adolescent (past and present):

	Yes	No	When	Where	Reaction or overall experience
Counseling/Psychiatric treatment		*X*			
Suicidal thoughts/attempts		*X*			
Drug/alcohol treatment		*X*			
Hospitalizations		*X*			

Behavioral/Emotional

Please check any of the following that are typical for your child:

___ Affectionate	_X_ Frustrated easily	___ Sad
_X_ Aggressive	___ Gambling	___ Selfish
___ Alcohol problems	___ Generous	___ Separation anxiety
_X_ Angry	___ Hallucinations	___ Sets fires
___ Anxiety	___ Head banging	___ Sexual addiction
___ Attachment to dolls	___ Heart problems	___ Sexual acting out
___ Avoids adults	___ Hopelessness	___ Shares
___ Bedwetting	___ Hurts animals	___ Sick often
___ Blinking, jerking	___ Imaginary friends	___ Short attention span
___ Bizarre behavior	___ Impulsive	___ Shy, timid
_X_ Bullies, threatens	_X_ Irritable	___ Sleeping problems
___ Careless, reckless	___ Lazy	___ Slow moving
___ Chest pains	___ Learning problems	___ Soiling
___ Clumsy	___ Lies frequently	___ Speech problems
___ Confident	___ Listens to reason	___ Steals
___ Cooperative	___ Loner	___ Stomach aches
___ Cyber addiction	_?_ Low self-esteem	___ Suicidal threats
_X_ Defiant	___ Messy	___ Suicidal attempts
___ Depression	_X_ Moody	_X_ Talks back
___ Destructive	___ Nightmares	___ Teeth grinding
___ Difficulty speaking	___ Obedient	___ Thumb sucking
___ Dizziness	___ Often sick	___ Tics or twitching
___ Drugs dependence	_X_ Oppositional	___ Unsafe behaviors
___ Eating disorder	___ Over active	___ Unusual thinking
___ Enthusiastic	___ Overweight	___ Weight loss
___ Excessive masturbation	___ Panic attacks	___ Withdrawn
___ Expects failure	___ Phobias	___ Worries excessively
___ Fatigue	___ Poor appetite	___ Other:
___ Fearful	___ Psychiatric problems	_____
___ Frequent injuries	_X_ Quarrels	_____

Please describe any of the above (or other) concerns: ___The problem is his attitude and the way he___ ___treats people. No criminal behaviors. He used to be good.___

How are problem behaviors generally handled? ___Time out, discussion, sometimes yells or___ ___threatens him.___

What are the family's favorite activities? ___Picnics, movies, go to mall, visit zoo.___

What does the child/adolescent do with unstructured time? ___TV or agitate sister___

Has the child/adolescent experienced death? (friends, family pets, other) ____ Yes __X__ No

At what age? _____ If Yes, describe the child's/adolescent's reaction: _____

_____

Have there been any other significant changes or events in your child's life? (family, moving, fire, etc.)

__X__ Yes ____ No If Yes, describe: _My divorce and soon remarriage._ _____

_____

Any additional information that you believe would assist us in understanding your child/adolescent?

Since I remarried he has been uncontrollable. I believe that he saw his father bully me, and he

wants to be like his father. His step-father isn't that way. _____

_____

Any additional information that would assist us in understanding current concerns or problems?

His behavior is now causing marriage problems for me _____

_____

_____

What are your goals for the child's therapy? _____ _Calm down—respect adults, make friends,_ _____

be cooperative. _____

What family involvement would you like to see in the therapy? _____ _We are willing to do anything!_ ___

_____

Do you believe the child is suicidal at this time? ____ Yes __X__ No

If Yes, explain: _____

_____

For Staff Use

Therapist's comments: _____ _R/O ODD, conduct, ADHD, Adjustment Disorder, Dysthymic Disorder_ _____

_____

_____

_____

_____

Therapist's signature/credentials: _____ _Charles W. Wollat, MSW_ _____ Date: _4_ / _8_ / _2005_

Supervisor's comments: _____ _Suggest individual and family counseling. Seems like O.D.D. secondary_ _____

to Adjustment Disorder. _____

_____

_____

_____ Physical exam: ____ Required __X__ Not required

Supervisor's signature/credentials: _Samuel Jones, LICSW_ _____ Date: _4_ / _8_ / _2005_

(Certifies case assignment, level of care and need for exam)

Form 23   Couple's Information Form

---

1) Name: _____   2) Age: _____   3) Date: _____

4) Address: _____   City: _____   State: _____   Zip: _____

5) Briefly, what is your main purpose in coming to couple's counseling? _____
_____

Instructions: To assist us in helping you, please fill out this form as fully and openly as possible. Your answers will help plan a course of couple's therapy that is most suitable for you and your partner. Do not exchange this information with your partner at this time.

Several of your answers on this form may be shared later with your partner during joint therapy sessions if you give us permission to share this information. For this reason you are advised to respond honestly and carefully to each item. If certain questions do not apply to you or you do not want to share this information, please leave them blank.

6) Have you been married before? ___ Yes   ___ No

   If Yes, how many previous marriages have you had?   1   2   3   4   5+

7) How long have you and your partner been in this relationship? _____

8) Are you and your partner presently living together? ___ Yes   ___ No

9) Are you and your partner engaged to be married? ___ Yes When? _____   ___ No

10) Fill out the following information for each child of whom the natural parent is both you and your partner, children from previous relationships, and adopted children.

   ___ Neither of us has children (go to next page)   ___ One or each of us has children (continue)

   *"Whose child?" answering options: B = Both of ours, natural child

                                                BA = Both of ours, adopted (or taken on)

                                                M = My natural child

                                              MA = My child, adopted (or taken on)

                                                P = Partner's natural child

                                              PA = Partner's child, adopted (or taken on)

	Child's name	Age	Sex	*Whose child?	Lives with whom?
1)	_____	_____	F M	_____	___ Yes ___ No
2)	_____	_____	F M	_____	___ Yes ___ No
3)	_____	_____	F M	_____	___ Yes ___ No
4)	_____	_____	F M	_____	___ Yes ___ No
5)	_____	_____	F M	_____	___ Yes ___ No
6)	_____	_____	F M	_____	___ Yes ___ No
7)	_____	_____	F M	_____	___ Yes ___ No
8)	_____	_____	F M	_____	___ Yes ___ No

11) List five qualities that initially attracted you to your partner:

Does your partner still possess this trait?

1) _____ ___ Yes ___ No
2) _____ ___ Yes ___ No
3) _____ ___ Yes ___ No
4) _____ ___ Yes ___ No
5) _____ ___ Yes ___ No

12) List four negative concerns that you initially had in the relationship:

Does your partner still possess this trait?

1) _____ ___ Yes ___ No
2) _____ ___ Yes ___ No
3) _____ ___ Yes ___ No
4) _____ ___ Yes ___ No

13) List five present positive attributes of your partner:

Do you often praise your partner for this trait?

1) _____ ___ Yes ___ No
2) _____ ___ Yes ___ No
3) _____ ___ Yes ___ No
4) _____ ___ Yes ___ No
5) _____ ___ Yes ___ No

14) List five present negative attributes of your partner:

Do you nag your partner about this trait?

1) _____ ___ Yes ___ No
2) _____ ___ Yes ___ No
3) _____ ___ Yes ___ No
4) _____ ___ Yes ___ No
5) _____ ___ Yes ___ No

15) List five things you do (or could do) to make the marriage more fulfilling for your partner:

Do you often implement this behavior?

1) _____ ___ Yes ___ No
2) _____ ___ Yes ___ No
3) _____ ___ Yes ___ No
4) _____ ___ Yes ___ No
5) _____ ___ Yes ___ No

16) List five things that your partner does (or could do) to make the marriage more fulfilling for you:

Does your partner often implement this behavior?

1) _____ ___ Yes ___ No
2) _____ ___ Yes ___ No
3) _____ ___ Yes ___ No
4) _____ ___ Yes ___ No
5) _____ ___ Yes ___ No

17) List five expectations or dreams you had about   Has this been
relationships before you met your partner: fulfilled?

1) _____   ___ Yes ___ No

2) _____   ___ Yes ___ No

3) _____   ___ Yes ___ No

4) _____   ___ Yes ___ No

5) _____   ___ Yes ___ No

18) On a scale of 1 to 5 rate the following items as they pertain to:

1) The present state of the relationship

2) Your need or desire for it

3) Your partner's need or desire for it

Circle the Appropriate Response for Each (If not applicable, leave blank.)

	Present state of the relationship	Your need or desire	Partner's need or desire
	Poor Great	Low High	Low High
1) Affection	1 2 3 4 5	1 2 3 4 5	1 2 3 4 5
2) Childrearing rules	1 2 3 4 5	1 2 3 4 5	1 2 3 4 5
3) Commitment together	1 2 3 4 5	1 2 3 4 5	1 2 3 4 5
4) Communication	1 2 3 4 5	1 2 3 4 5	1 2 3 4 5
5) Emotional closeness	1 2 3 4 5	1 2 3 4 5	1 2 3 4 5
6) Financial security	1 2 3 4 5	1 2 3 4 5	1 2 3 4 5
7) Honesty	1 2 3 4 5	1 2 3 4 5	1 2 3 4 5
8) Housework sharing	1 2 3 4 5	1 2 3 4 5	1 2 3 4 5
9) Love	1 2 3 4 5	1 2 3 4 5	1 2 3 4 5
10) Physical attraction	1 2 3 4 5	1 2 3 4 5	1 2 3 4 5
11) Religious commitment	1 2 3 4 5	1 2 3 4 5	1 2 3 4 5
12) Respect	1 2 3 4 5	1 2 3 4 5	1 2 3 4 5
13) Sexual fulfillment	1 2 3 4 5	1 2 3 4 5	1 2 3 4 5
14) Social life together	1 2 3 4 5	1 2 3 4 5	1 2 3 4 5
15) Time together	1 2 3 4 5	1 2 3 4 5	1 2 3 4 5
16) Trust	1 2 3 4 5	1 2 3 4 5	1 2 3 4 5
Other (specify)			
17) _____	1 2 3 4 5	1 2 3 4 5	1 2 3 4 5
18) _____	1 2 3 4 5	1 2 3 4 5	1 2 3 4 5
19) _____	1 2 3 4 5	1 2 3 4 5	1 2 3 4 5
20) _____	1 2 3 4 5	1 2 3 4 5	1 2 3 4 5

19) For couples living together. Which partner spends more time conducting the following activities?

Circle the Appropriate Response for Each (If not applicable, leave blank.)

(M = Me   P = Partner   E = Equal time)

		Is this equitable (fair)?	Comments
1) Auto repairs	M P E	___ Yes ___ No	_____
2) Child care	M P E	___ Yes ___ No	_____
3) Child discipline	M P E	___ Yes ___ No	_____
4) Cleaning bathrooms	M P E	___ Yes ___ No	_____
5) Cooking	M P E	___ Yes ___ No	_____
6) Employment	M P E	___ Yes ___ No	_____
7) Grocery shopping	M P E	___ Yes ___ No	_____

3.75

8) House cleaning	M	P	E	___ Yes	___ No	_____
9) Inside repairs	M	P	E	___ Yes	___ No	_____
10) Laundry	M	P	E	___ Yes	___ No	_____
11) Making bed	M	P	E	___ Yes	___ No	_____
12) Outside repairs	M	P	E	___ Yes	___ No	_____
13) Recreational events	M	P	E	___ Yes	___ No	_____
14) Social activities	M	P	E	___ Yes	___ No	_____
15) Sweeping kitchen	M	P	E	___ Yes	___ No	_____
16) Taking out garbage	M	P	E	___ Yes	___ No	_____
17) Washing dishes	M	P	E	___ Yes	___ No	_____
18) Yard work	M	P	E	___ Yes	___ No	_____
19) Other: _____	M	P	E	___ Yes	___ No	_____
20) Other: _____	M	S	E	___ Yes	___ No	_____

20) If some of the following behaviors take place only during MILD arguments circle an "M" in the appropriate blanks. If they take place only during SEVERE arguments, circle an "S." If they take place during ALL arguments circle an "A." Fill this out for you and your impression of your partner. If certain behaviors do not take place, leave them blank.

Circle the Appropriate Response for Each

(M = Mild arguments only   S = Severe arguments only   A = All arguments)

Behavior	By me	By partner	Should this change?
1) Apologize	M S A	M S A	___ Yes ___ No
2) Become silent	M S A	M S A	___ Yes ___ No
3) Bring up the past	M S A	M S A	___ Yes ___ No
4) Criticize	M S A	M S A	___ Yes ___ No
5) Cruel accusations	M S A	M S A	___ Yes ___ No
6) Cry	M S A	M S A	___ Yes ___ No
7) Destroy property	M S A	M S A	___ Yes ___ No
8) Leave the house	M S A	M S A	___ Yes ___ No
9) Make peace	M S A	M S A	___ Yes ___ No
10) Moodiness	M S A	M S A	___ Yes ___ No
11) Not listen	M S A	M S A	___ Yes ___ No
12) Physical abuse	M S A	M S A	___ Yes ___ No
13) Physical threats	M S A	M S A	___ Yes ___ No
14) Sarcasm	M S A	M S A	___ Yes ___ No
15) Scream	M S A	M S A	___ Yes ___ No
16) Slam doors	M S A	M S A	___ Yes ___ No
17) Speak irrationally	M S A	M S A	___ Yes ___ No
18) Speak rationally	M S A	M S A	___ Yes ___ No
19) Sulk	M S A	M S A	___ Yes ___ No
20) Swear	M S A	M S A	___ Yes ___ No
21) Threaten breaking up	M S A	M S A	___ Yes ___ No
22) Threaten to take kids	M S A	M S A	___ Yes ___ No
23) Throw things	M S A	M S A	___ Yes ___ No
24) Verbal abuse	M S A	M S A	___ Yes ___ No
25) Yell	M S A	M S A	___ Yes ___ No
26) _____	M S A	M S A	___ Yes ___ No
27) _____	M S A	M S A	___ Yes ___ No
28) _____	M S A	M S A	___ Yes ___ No

21) How often do you have: Mild arguments? _____

    Severe arguments? _____

22) When a MILD argument is over
    how do you usually feel?

    Check Appropriate Responses

    ___ Angry   ___ Lonely
    ___ Anxious   ___ Nauseous
    ___ Childish   ___ Numb
    ___ Defeated   ___ Regretful
    ___ Depressed   ___ Relieved
    ___ Guilty   ___ Stupid
    ___ Happy   ___ Victimized
    ___ Hopeless   ___ Worthless
    ___ Irritable

23) When a SEVERE argument is over
    how do you usually feel?

    Check Appropriate Responses

    ___ Angry   ___ Lonely
    ___ Anxious   ___ Nauseous
    ___ Childish   ___ Numb
    ___ Defeated   ___ Regretful
    ___ Depressed   ___ Relieved
    ___ Guilty   ___ Stupid
    ___ Happy   ___ Victimized
    ___ Hopeless   ___ Worthless
    ___ Irritable

24)   Which of the following issues or behaviors of you and/or your partner may be attributable to your relationship or personal conflicts? If an item does not apply, leave it blank.

Circle the Appropriate Responses

(M = My behavior   P = Partner's behavior   B = Both)

Alcohol consumption	M P B		Perfectionist	M P B
Childishness	M P B		Possessive	M P B
Controlling	M P B		Spends too much	M P B
Defensiveness	M P B		Steals	M P B
Degrading	M P B		Stubbornness	M P B
Demanding	M P B		Uncaring	M P B
Drugs	M P B		Unstable	M P B
Flirts with others	M P B		Violent	M P B
Gambling	M P B		Withdrawn	M P B
Irresponsibility	M P B		Works too much	M P B
Lies	M P B		Other (specify)	
Past marriage(s)/relationship(s)	M P B		_____	M P B
Other's advice	M P B		_____	M P B
Outside interests	M P B		_____	M P B
Past failures	M P B		_____	M P B

25) In the remaining space please provide additional information that would be helpful:

_____

_____

_____

I, _____ , hereby give my permission for this clinic to share the information that I provide on this form to _____ (partner) when it is deemed appropriate by an agreement between me, my partner, and our therapist. This sharing of information may take place only during a joint counseling session (both partners present).

Client's signature: _____   Date: ____ / ___/_____

PLEASE RETURN THIS AND OTHER ASSESSMENT MATERIALS TO THIS
OFFICE AT LEAST TWO DAYS BEFORE YOUR NEXT APPOINTMENT.

Name (answers apply to): _____   Date: _____

Residence: _____   DOB: _____   Age: _____

Address: _____   City: _____   State: _____   Zip: _____

Respondent's name: _____   Relationship: _____

Please use the back of any sheet of more space if needed.

1. Check the following behaviors or skills that describe positive characteristics of the client. (Add others that apply.)

____ Accepts praise	____ Friendly	____ Polite
____ Affectionate	____ Gregarious	____ Reading/writing
____ Apologizes	____ Grooming/hygiene	____ Respects others
____ Assertive	____ Helpful	____ Responsible
____ Cleanliness (household)	____ Hobbies/crafts	____ Safety skills
____ Community skills	____ Honesty	____ Sense of humor
____ Cooperative	____ Independent	____ Shares
____ Courteous	____ Insightful	____ Survival skills
____ Daily living skills	____ Listening skills	____ Verbal expression
____ Dependable	____ Money management skills	____ Works hard
____ Emotional	____ Motivated	____ _____
____ Eye contact	____ Organized	____ _____
____ _____	____ _____	____ _____

   Comments on any of the above: _____

   _____

2. Which of the following normal emotions or responses do you recognize as at least sometimes taking place with the client? (Add others that apply.)

____ Anger	____ Embarrassment	____ Grief
____ Anxiety	____ Envy	____ Happiness
____ Boredom	____ Fear	____ Loneliness
____ Depression	____ Frustration	____ Stress
____ _____	____ _____	____ _____

3. List any concerns you have regarding any of the above emotions or responses. _____

   _____

   _____

   _____

4. How does s/he express (verbally and nonverbally) the following emotions?

   Happiness: _____

   _____

   Sadness: _____

   _____

   Anger: _____

   _____

   Frustration: _____

   _____

5. Briefly describe any self-injurious behaviors (SIBs) and/or inappropriate self-stimulation behaviors (SSBs).

   Behavior: (describe the problem behavior)
   Antecedents: (describe what usually takes place before the behavior occurs)
   Consequences: (describe what actions are taken after the behavior occurs)
   Frequency/duration: (describe how often and for how long it occurs)

   Behavior: _____
   Antecedents: _____
   Consequences: _____
   Frequency/duration: _____

   Behavior: _____
   Antecedents: _____
   Consequences: _____
   Frequency/duration: _____

   Behavior: _____
   Antecedents: _____
   Consequences: _____
   Frequency/duration: _____

6. Briefly describe aggressive acts (to people or property).

   Behavior: _____
   Antecedents: _____
   Consequences: _____
   Frequency/duration: _____

   Behavior: _____
   Antecedents: _____
   Consequences: _____
   Frequency/duration: _____

   Behavior: _____
   Antecedents: _____
   Consequences: _____
   Frequency/duration: _____

7. Describe any inappropriate sexual behavior. ___ None known

_____

_____

_____

8. Describe any inappropriate social behaviors. ___ None known

_____

_____

_____

9. How would you rate his/her listening skills?

Low		Average		High	___ NA
1	2	3	4	5	

Comments: _____

10. How would you rate his/her ability to cope with problems?

Low		Average		High	___ NA
1	2	3	4	5	

Comments: _____

11. How would you rate his/her respect for other people?

Low		Average		High	___ NA
1	2	3	4	5	

Comments: _____

12. How would you rate his/her ability to manage anger?

Low		Average		High	___ NA
1	2	3	4	5	

Comments: _____

13. How would you rate his/her motivation to change negative behaviors?

Low		Average		High	___ NA
1	2	3	4	5	

Comments: _____

14. How would you rate his/her ability to accept constructive criticism?

Low		Average		High	___ NA
1	2	3	4	5	

Comments: _____

15. How would you rate his/her potential for increased independent living?

Low		Average		High	___ NA
1	2	3	4	5	

Comments: _____

16. Please list any significant stressful events or major changes in his/her life in the past six months (e.g., loss of loved one, significant others moving, change in residence, new roommate or housemate, new sibling, major illness, etc.). ___ None known

_____

_____

_____

If applicable, what behavioral/emotional effects may this have had? ___ None known

_____

_____

_____

17. Check any of the following which apply to him/her. (Add others that apply.)

___ Anxiety	___ Explosive behaviors	___ Schizophrenia
___ Auditory hallucinations	___ Impulse control concerns	___ Sexual concerns
___ Chemical dependency	___ Mood shifts	___ Social withdrawal
___ Conduct problems	___ Obsessive/compulsive	___ Suicidal threats
___ Depression	___ Paranoid	___ Thought disorder
___ Eating disorder	___ Phobias/fears	___ Visual hallucinations
___ _____	___ _____	___ _____

Describe behavioral effects or incidents of each of the above items.

_____

_____

_____

_____

_____

_____

_____

_____

18. Briefly describe any past events that may be difficult for him/her to handle at this time (e.g., abuse, injuries).

_____

_____

_____

19. Briefly describe any past events that were particularly encouraging or led to positive life changes for him/her.

_____

_____

_____

20. Please list any other information about him/her (e.g., important background information, special strengths/weaknesses, concerns with other people, problems on the job).

_____

_____

_____

Form 24A   Emotional/Behavioral Assessment   (*Completed*)

Name (answers apply to): _____*Christine Watters*_____   Date: _____*4/6/2005*_____

Residence: _*(family residence)*_   DOB: _*3/6/1999*_   Age: __*6*__

Address: __*45678 Hayward St.*__   City: __*Tacoma*__   State: _*WA*_   Zip: _*99889*_

Respondent's name: __*Lisa Watters*__   Relationship: _____*Mother*_____

Please use the back of any sheet of more space if needed.

1. Check the following behaviors or skills that describe positive characteristics of the client. (Add others that apply.)

_X_ Accepts praise	___ Friendly	___ Polite
_X_ Affectionate	___ Gregarious	___ Reading/writing
___ Apologizes	_X_ Grooming/hygiene	___ Respects others
_X_ Assertive	___ Helpful	___ Responsible
___ Cleanliness (household)	_X_ Hobbies/crafts	___ Safety skills
___ Community skills	___ Honesty	_X_ Sense of humor
___ Cooperative	_X_ Independent	___ Shares
_X_ Courteous	___ Insightful	___ Survival skills
_X_ Daily living skills	___ Listening skills	___ Verbal expression
___ Dependable	___ Money management skills	___ Works hard
___ Emotional	___ Motivated	___ _____
___ Eye contact	___ Organized	___ _____
___ _____	___ _____	___ _____

Comments on any of the above: ___*She is a good girl, but just can't stay with any one activity*___ ___*for very long. She tries to be helpful, but goes on to something else.*___

2. Which of the following normal emotions or responses do you recognize as at least sometimes taking place with the client? (Add others that apply.)

_X_ Anger	_X_ Embarrassment	___ Grief
_X_ Anxiety	___ Envy	_X_ Happiness
_X_ Boredom	___ Fear	___ Loneliness
___ Depression	_X_ Frustration	_X_ Stress
___ _____	___ _____	___ _____

3. List any concerns you have regarding any of the above emotions or responses. __*She gets*__ ___*angry and frustrated too easily. This makes her more hyperactive.*___

3.82

4. How does s/he express (verbally and nonverbally) the following emotions?

Happiness: _*When Christine is happy she is much more helpful around the house. She smiles and might sing. She doesn't directly say she is happy.*_

Sadness: _*She initially will be mopey and withdrawn. After a while she might act like she is mad at everybody. She cries very easily, but doesn't seem to recognize depression.*_

Anger: _*Temper tantrums. It doesn't take much for her to hit people or throw things in her room. At times she will verbally abuse others.*_

Frustration: _*Same as anger.*_

_____

5. Briefly describe any self-injurious behaviors (SIBs) and/or inappropriate self-stimulation behaviors (SSBs).

Behavior: (describe the problem behavior)
Antecedents: (describe what usually takes place before the behavior occurs)
Consequences: (describe what actions are taken after the behavior occurs)
Frequency/duration: (describe how often and for how long it occurs)

Behavior: _*None*_
Antecedents: _____
Consequences: _____
Frequency/duration: _____

Behavior: _____
Antecedents: _____
Consequences: _____
Frequency/duration: _____

Behavior: _____
Antecedents: _____
Consequences: _____
Frequency/duration: _____

6. Briefly describe aggressive acts (to people or property).

Behavior: _*Temper tantrums*_
Antecedents: _*When she does not get her way*_
Consequences: _*Time out in her room, lose upcoming privileges*_
Frequency/duration: _*4–5 times per week/15–30 minutes*_

Behavior: _*Inappropriate yelling at family members*_
Antecedents: _*When she is frustrated or not able to get things immediately*_
Consequences: _*Time out, lose privileges*_
Frequency/duration: _*3–4 times per week/varies*_

Behavior: _*Throw toys against wall*_
Antecedents: _*When she is mad at her sister*_
Consequences: _*Must apologize, time out*_
Frequency/duration: _*1 time per week*_

7. Describe any inappropriate sexual behavior. _X_ None known

_____

_____

_____

8. Describe any inappropriate social behaviors. ___ None known
   Children at school tease her because of her hyperactivity and immaturity. She then acts even
   more immature and may cry and receive more teasing. She is beginning to lash out
   physically at her classmates.

9. How would you rate his/her listening skills?

Low		Average		High	___ NA
1	(2)	3	4	5	

   Comments: _She hears but rarely listens. She is too active to have time for listening._

10. How would you rate his/her ability to cope with problems?

Low		Average		High	___ NA
(1)	2	3	4	5	

    Comments: _Very poor_

11. How would you rate his/her respect for other people?

Low		Average		High	___ NA
1	(2)	3	4	5	

    Comments: _____

12. How would you rate his/her ability to manage anger?

Low		Average		High	___ NA
(1)	2	3	4	5	

    Comments: _____

13. How would you rate his/her motivation to change negative behaviors?

Low		Average		High	___ NA
1	(2)	3	4	5	

    Comments: _____

14. How would you rate his/her ability to accept constructive criticism?

Low		Average		High	___ NA
1	2	(3)	4	5	

    Comments: _____

15. How would you rate his/her potential for increased independent living?

Low		Average		High	___ NA
1	2	(3)	4	5	

    Comments: _____

3.84

16. Please list any significant stressful events or major changes in his/her life in the past six months (e.g., loss of loved one, significant others moving, change in residence, new roommate or housemate, new sibling, major illness, etc.). ___ None known

Her grandmother died about four months ago.

If applicable, what behavioral/emotional effects may this have had? ___ None known

She spent every Saturday at her grandmother's home. They were very close. Although Christine was hyperactive before her grandmother died, she has been much more defiant in the past few months.

17. Check any of the following which apply to him/her. (Add others that apply.)

___ Anxiety	_X_ Explosive behaviors	___ Schizophrenia
___ Auditory hallucinations	_X_ Impulse control concerns	___ Sexual concerns
___ Chemical dependency	___ Mood shifts	___ Social withdrawal
_X_ Conduct problems	___ Obsessive/compulsive	___ Suicidal threats
___ Depression	___ Paranoid	___ Thought disorder
___ Eating disorder	___ Phobias/fears	___ Visual hallucinations

Describe behavioral effects or incidents of each of the above items.

Conduct problems and explosive behaviors: When she does not get her way she gets very frustrated and, at times, will lash out at anything or anyone in her way. It does not take much to set her off. She has never hurt anyone. She usually has a tantrum, then cools off after about 1/2 hour, especially if she gets no attention for the tantrum.

Impulse control: She can't wait for anything. She often gets into trouble at school for cutting in line. She always wants things before it is the right time. She gets edgy when she has to wait.

18. Briefly describe any past events that may be difficult for him/her to handle at this time (e.g., abuse, injuries).

None known

19. Briefly describe any past events that were particularly encouraging or led to positive life changes for him/her.

20. Please list any other information about him/her (e.g., important background information, special strengths/weaknesses, concerns with other people, problems on the job).

Form 25   Emotional/Behavioral Update

Client's name: _____   Date: _____

Describe any stressful events in the client's life which have taken place recently (e.g., friend moved away, sickness): _____

_____

_____

_____

_____

_____

Describe any positive events in the client's life which have taken place recently (e.g., vacation, earned an award): _____

_____

_____

_____

_____

_____

Positive behaviors since last session (emotional, behavioral, social, etc.)

Date(s)	Behavior	How was it reinforced or rewarded?
_____	_____	_____
_____	_____	_____
_____	_____	_____

Problem areas since last session (emotional, behavioral, social, etc.)

Date(s)	Behavior	What were the consequences?
_____	_____	_____
_____	_____	_____
_____	_____	_____

Caregiver's comments: _____

_____

_____

Caregiver's signature: _____   Date: ____/____/_____

Form 25A   Emotional/Behavioral Update   (*Completed*)

Client's name: _William Olden_   Date: _6/10/2005_

Describe any stressful events in the client's life which have taken place recently (e.g., friend moved away, sickness): _Had argument with the friend he met last month. Has not talked to him in_ _four days._

Describe any positive events in the client's life which have taken place recently (e.g., vacation, earned an award): _____

Positive behaviors since last session (emotional, behavioral, social, etc.)

Date(s)	Behavior	How was it reinforced or rewarded?
6/4/2005	Did homework as per plan	Choice of weekend activity
6/8/2005	Discussed his anger without verbal abuse	Later bedtime on weekend
6/9/2005	Apologized to teacher for past behaviors	Allowed extensions on late homework

Problem areas since last session (emotional, behavioral, social, etc.)

Date(s)	Behavior	What were the consequences?
6/3/2005	Started argument with friend, bullied him	Written apology
6/7/2005	Temper tantrum	Discussion

Caregiver's comments: _He continues to struggle but there are improvements, family counseling_ _helps him get along with step-father._

Caregiver's signature: _Lanna Olden_   Date: _6 / 10 / 2005_

Form 26   Diagnostic Assessment Report

Name: _____   Therapist: _____

Intake/Assessment date(s): _____   Report date: _____

1. **Purpose of Visit/Current Life Situation** (Include duration/frequency of symptoms.)

   _____
   _____
   _____
   _____
   _____
   _____
   _____
   _____
   _____
   _____

2. **History of Current Problem/Developmental Incidents/Treatment History/Medications, etc.**

   _____
   _____
   _____
   _____
   _____
   _____
   _____
   _____
   _____
   _____

3. **Current Functioning, Symptoms, and Impairments** (e.g., occupational, social, emotional)

   _____
   _____
   _____
   _____
   _____
   _____
   _____

   Strengths: _____
   Weaknesses: _____

4. Family Mental Health History

_____
_____
_____
_____
_____
_____
_____
_____
_____
_____

5. Other (substance abuse, suicidal ideations, court referral, etc.)

_____
_____
_____
_____
_____
_____
_____
_____
_____
_____
_____

Mental Status Exam

	Normal	Slight		Moderate			Severe
	0	1	2	3	4	5	6

Appearance

Unkempt, unclean, disheveled	(__)	(__)	(__)	(__)	(__)	(__)	(__)
Clothing and/or grooming atypical	(__)	(__)	(__)	(__)	(__)	(__)	(__)
Unusual physical characteristics	(__)	(__)	(__)	(__)	(__)	(__)	(__)

Comments re: Appearance: _____
_____
_____

	Normal	Slight		Moderate			Severe
	0	1	2	3	4	5	6

Posture

Slumped	(__)	(__)	(__)	(__)	(__)	(__)	(__)
Rigid, tense	(__)	(__)	(__)	(__)	(__)	(__)	(__)

	Normal	Slight		Moderate			Severe
	0	1	2	3	4	5	6

Facial Expressions Suggest

Anxiety	(__)	(__)	(__)	(__)	(__)	(__)	(__)
Depression, sadness	(__)	(__)	(__)	(__)	(__)	(__)	(__)
Absence of feeling, blandness	(__)	(__)	(__)	(__)	(__)	(__)	(__)
Atypical, unusual	(__)	(__)	(__)	(__)	(__)	(__)	(__)

	Normal	Slight		Moderate			Severe
	0	1	2	3	4	5	6

General Body Movements

	0	1	2	3	4	5	6
Accelerated, increased speed	(__)	(__)	(__)	(__)	(__)	(__)	(__)
Decreased, slowed	(__)	(__)	(__)	(__)	(__)	(__)	(__)
Atypical, unusual	(__)	(__)	(__)	(__)	(__)	(__)	(__)
Restless, fidgety	(__)	(__)	(__)	(__)	(__)	(__)	(__)

	Normal	Slight		Moderate			Severe
	0	1	2	3	4	5	6

Speech

	0	1	2	3	4	5	6
Rapid speech	(__)	(__)	(__)	(__)	(__)	(__)	(__)
Slowed speech	(__)	(__)	(__)	(__)	(__)	(__)	(__)
Loud speech	(__)	(__)	(__)	(__)	(__)	(__)	(__)
Soft speech	(__)	(__)	(__)	(__)	(__)	(__)	(__)
Mute	(__)	(__)	(__)	(__)	(__)	(__)	(__)
Atypical quality (e.g., slurring)	(__)	(__)	(__)	(__)	(__)	(__)	(__)

	Normal	Slight		Moderate			Severe
	0	1	2	3	4	5	6

Therapist/Client Relationship

	0	1	2	3	4	5	6
Domineering, controlling	(__)	(__)	(__)	(__)	(__)	(__)	(__)
Submissive, compliant, dependent	(__)	(__)	(__)	(__)	(__)	(__)	(__)
Provocative, hostile, challenging	(__)	(__)	(__)	(__)	(__)	(__)	(__)
Suspicious, guarded, evasive	(__)	(__)	(__)	(__)	(__)	(__)	(__)
Uncooperative, noncompliant	(__)	(__)	(__)	(__)	(__)	(__)	(__)

Comments re: Behavior: _____

_____

_____

	Normal	Slight		Moderate			Severe
	0	1	2	3	4	5	6

Affect/Mood

	0	1	2	3	4	5	6
Inappropriate to thought content	(__)	(__)	(__)	(__)	(__)	(__)	(__)
Increased liability of affect	(__)	(__)	(__)	(__)	(__)	(__)	(__)
Blunted, dulled, bland	(__)	(__)	(__)	(__)	(__)	(__)	(__)
Euphoria, elation	(__)	(__)	(__)	(__)	(__)	(__)	(__)
Anger, hostility	(__)	(__)	(__)	(__)	(__)	(__)	(__)
Anxiety, fear, apprehension	(__)	(__)	(__)	(__)	(__)	(__)	(__)
Depression, sadness	(__)	(__)	(__)	(__)	(__)	(__)	(__)

Comments re: Affect: _____

_____

_____

	Normal	Slight		Moderate			Severe
	0	1	2	3	4	5	6

Perception

	Normal	Slight		Moderate			Severe
Illusions	(__)	(__)	(__)	(__)	(__)	(__)	(__)
Auditory hallucinations	(__)	(__)	(__)	(__)	(__)	(__)	(__)
Visual hallucinations	(__)	(__)	(__)	(__)	(__)	(__)	(__)
Other hallucinations	(__)	(__)	(__)	(__)	(__)	(__)	(__)

Comments re: Perception: _____

_____

	Normal	Slight		Moderate			Severe
	0	1	2	3	4	5	6

Intellectual Functioning Impairments

Level of consciousness	(__)	(__)	(__)	(__)	(__)	(__)	(__)
Attention span, distractible	(__)	(__)	(__)	(__)	(__)	(__)	(__)
Abstract thinking	(__)	(__)	(__)	(__)	(__)	(__)	(__)
Calculation ability	(__)	(__)	(__)	(__)	(__)	(__)	(__)
Intelligence	(__)	(__)	(__)	(__)	(__)	(__)	(__)

	Normal	Slight		Moderate			Severe
	0	1	2	3	4	5	6

Orientation

Time	(__)	(__)	(__)	(__)	(__)	(__)	(__)
Place	(__)	(__)	(__)	(__)	(__)	(__)	(__)
Person	(__)	(__)	(__)	(__)	(__)	(__)	(__)

	Normal	Slight		Moderate			Severe
	0	1	2	3	4	5	6

Memory Impairment

Recent	(__)	(__)	(__)	(__)	(__)	(__)	(__)
Remote	(__)	(__)	(__)	(__)	(__)	(__)	(__)

	Normal	Slight		Moderate			Severe
	0	1	2	3	4	5	6

Insight

Denies psych problems	(__)	(__)	(__)	(__)	(__)	(__)	(__)
Blames others	(__)	(__)	(__)	(__)	(__)	(__)	(__)

	Normal	Slight		Moderate			Severe
	0	1	2	3	4	5	6

Judgment Impairments

Decision making	(__)	(__)	(__)	(__)	(__)	(__)	(__)
Impulse control	(__)	(__)	(__)	(__)	(__)	(__)	(__)

	Normal	Slight		Moderate			Severe
	0	1	2	3	4	5	6

Thought Content

Obsessions   (__) (__) (__) (__) (__) (__) (__)
Compulsions   (__) (__) (__) (__) (__) (__) (__)
Phobias   (__) (__) (__) (__) (__) (__) (__)
Depersonalization   (__) (__) (__) (__) (__) (__) (__)
Suicidal ideation   (__) (__) (__) (__) (__) (__) (__)
Homicidal ideation (__) (__) (__) (__) (__) (__) (__)
Delusions   (__) (__) (__) (__) (__) (__) (__)

Comments re: Thinking: _____

_____

_____

Diagnosis Validation

Primary diagnosis: _____

Name of test	Results
_____	_____
_____	_____
_____	_____
_____	_____
_____	_____

Biographical Information (specific BIF references)

_____

_____

_____

_____

_____

Collateral Information

_____

_____

_____

_____

_____

Case/Intake Notes, MSE References (Include brief descriptions, dates, and line numbers.)

_____

_____

_____

_____

_____

Diagnosis 2: _____   (Make copies for additional Dx's)

Name of test   Results

_____   _____
_____   _____
_____   _____
_____   _____
_____   _____

Biographical Information (specific BIF references)

_____
_____
_____
_____
_____

Case/Intake Notes, MSE References (Include brief descriptions, dates, and line numbers.)

_____
_____
_____
_____
_____

Diagnostic Impressions

Axis I   _____
Axis II   _____
Axis III   _____
Axis IV   _____
Axis V   _____

Needed Mental Health Services

___ Further assessment (specify): _____

___ Individual ___ Group ____ Family ____ Other (specify): _____

Other Needed Services

___ Psychiatric consultation   ____ Physical exam   ____ Neurological consultation

___ CD evaluation   ____ Other (specify): _____

Did client/guardian sign the treatment plan? ___ No ____ Yes

Was Dx explained to client? ____ No ____ Yes

Therapist's signature: _____   Date: ____/____/____

Supervisor's signature: _____   Date: ____/____/____

Form 26A   Diagnostic Assessment Report   (*Completed*)

Name: _____*Judy Doe*_____   Therapist: _____*DLB*_____

Intake/Assessment date(s): ___*3/8/2005 & 3/15/2005*___   Report date: _____*3/16/2005*_____

1. **Purpose of Visit/Current Life Situation** (Include duration/frequency of symptoms.)

   Self-referred. Has felt increasingly sad for past year (average 3 of 4 days). Usually fatigued.
   Increased withdrawal has led to loss of two friends (with whom she used to be close) in past
   month. Now avoids them. Spouse threatening to leave soon due to her anger outbursts and
   lack of sexual activity. Describes marriage as "on the rocks." May desire marital counseling
   at a later date. Quite dissatisfied with teaching career, home life, and self. Little/no
   motivation to "get things done." Missed 2–4 days of work per month in past year due to
   "boredom/frustration with job." Currently finds no pleasures in life.

2. **History of Current Problem/Developmental Incidents/Treatment History/ Medications, etc.**

   Prior counseling for depression in 1967–1968 due to depression after breaking up with a
   college boyfriend. Does not remember the focus of the sessions, but believes that depression
   was alleviated until approximately the last year or so. Now feeling "depressed, like when
   in college." No meds at that time. Increased marital conflict developing, little time spent
   together; generally shouting, blaming, no sex or intimacy. Markedly decreased satisfaction
   as a schoolteacher. Several self-deprecating statements regarding teaching and parenting
   effectiveness. Past two years insomnia. Wakes up 3–4x/night. No mania. Past year lost 20 lbs.
   Views life as "monotonous, uneventful, boring." Exercises 3x/week, but not fun. Wants to
   "start feeling human again."

3. **Current Functioning, Symptoms, and Impairments** (e.g., occupational, social, emotional)

   1) Impaired social functioning (previously spent 1–2 evenings per week with friends, now is
   rarely with others). Has lost friends, initiates little/no social interactions. 2) Marital
   conflict leading to increased anxiety level. Avoiding family/friends. 3) Occupational
   impairment; missing 2–4 days/month (1 year ago rarely missed work), views teaching
   performance as poor at this time. 4) Emotional impairment; sad most of time, fatigued,
   anhedonia, low ego strength.

   Strengths: _____*Moderately motivated to change. Religious reasons vs. suicidality.*_____
   Weaknesses: _____*Seems to blame others for past failures. Level of insight.*_____

4. Family Mental Health History

Describes family of origin as functional. 2nd of 5 children. Left home at age 18 (college). No known family Hx of depression or other mental health concerns. Historically good communication with family. Hx of mother and older sibling helping/making several of her decisions. Family generally provides positive social support, but often viewed as intrusive by client.

5. Other (substance abuse, suicidal ideations, court referral, etc.)

Does not view self as chemically dependent. No suicide plan; ideations when stressed. Signed Limits of Confidentiality. Contracted for actions to be taken when experiencing suicidal thoughts: given phone numbers for Therapist, Crisis Hotline, and Mental Health Intake.

Mental Status Exam

	Normal 0	Slight 1	2	Moderate 3	4	Severe 5	6
Appearance							
Unkempt, unclean, disheveled	(__)	(__)	(__)	(_X_)	(__)	(__)	(__)
Clothing and/or grooming atypical	(_X_)	(__)	(__)	(__)	(__)	(__)	(__)
Unusual physical characteristics	(_X_)	(__)	(__)	(__)	(__)	(__)	(__)

Comments re: Appearance: *T-shirt and jogging pants, moderately groomed, hair somewhat disheveled.*

	Normal 0	Slight 1	2	Moderate 3	4	Severe 5	6
Posture							
Slumped	(__)	(__)	(__)	(__)	(_X_)	(__)	(__)
Rigid, tense	(__)	(__)	(__)	(_X_)	(__)	(__)	(__)

	Normal 0	Slight 1	2	Moderate 3	4	Severe 5	6
Facial Expressions Suggest							
Anxiety	(__)	(_X_)	(__)	(__)	(__)	(__)	(__)
Depression, sadness	(__)	(__)	(__)	(__)	(__)	(_X_)	(__)
Absence of feeling, blandness	(__)	(__)	(__)	(__)	(_X_)	(__)	(__)
Atypical, unusual	(_X_)	(__)	(__)	(__)	(__)	(__)	(__)

	Normal 0	Slight 1	2	Moderate 3	4	5	Severe 6
General Body Movements							
Accelerated, increased speed	(X)	(_)	(_)	(_)	(_)	(_)	(_)
Decreased, slowed	(_)	(_)	(_)	(_)	(X)	(_)	(_)
Atypical, unusual	(X)	(_)	(_)	(_)	(_)	(_)	(_)
Restless, fidgety	(_)	(X)	(_)	(_)	(_)	(_)	(_)

	Normal 0	Slight 1	2	Moderate 3	4	5	Severe 6
Speech							
Rapid speech	(X)	(_)	(_)	(_)	(_)	(_)	(_)
Slowed speech	(_)	(_)	(_)	(_)	(X)	(_)	(_)
Loud speech	(X)	(_)	(_)	(_)	(_)	(_)	(_)
Soft speech	(_)	(_)	(_)	(X)	(_)	(_)	(_)
Mute	(X)	(_)	(_)	(_)	(_)	(_)	(_)
Atypical quality (e.g., slurring)	(_)	(X)	(_)	(_)	(_)	(_)	(_)

	Normal 0	Slight 1	2	Moderate 3	4	5	Severe 6
Therapist/Client Relationship							
Domineering, controlling	(X)	(_)	(_)	(_)	(_)	(_)	(_)
Submissive, compliant, dependent	(_)	(_)	(_)	(_)	(X)	(_)	(_)
Provocative, hostile, challenging	(X)	(_)	(_)	(_)	(_)	(_)	(_)
Suspicious, guarded, evasive	(X)	(_)	(_)	(_)	(_)	(_)	(_)
Uncooperative, noncompliant	(X)	(_)	(_)	(_)	(_)	(_)	(_)

Comments re: Behavior: _Low eye contact_

	Normal 0	Slight 1	2	Moderate 3	4	5	Severe 6
Affect/Mood							
Inappropriate to thought content	(X)	(_)	(_)	(_)	(_)	(_)	(_)
Increased liability of affect	(X)	(_)	(_)	(_)	(_)	(_)	(_)
Blunted, dulled, bland	(_)	(_)	(_)	(X)	(_)	(_)	(_)
Euphoria, elation	(X)	(_)	(_)	(_)	(_)	(_)	(_)
Anger, hostility	(_)	(_)	(X)	(_)	(_)	(_)	(_)
Anxiety, fear, apprehension	(_)	(X)	(_)	(_)	(_)	(_)	(_)
Depression, sadness	(_)	(_)	(_)	(_)	(X)	(_)	(_)

Comments re: Affect: _Behavior, speech, and affect concordant. Onset of most recent episode of depression in past year. Depressed 3 or 4 days, most of day. Daily crying spells, cries when alone. Easily annoyed, but does not express frustration._

	Normal	Slight		Moderate			Severe
	0	1	2	3	4	5	6
Perception							
Illusions	(_X_)	(__)	(__)	(__)	(__)	(__)	(__)
Auditory hallucinations	(_X_)	(__)	(__)	(__)	(__)	(__)	(__)
Visual hallucinations	(_X_)	(__)	(__)	(__)	(__)	(__)	(__)
Other hallucinations	(_X_)	(__)	(__)	(__)	(__)	(__)	(__)

Comments re: Perception: _None_

_____

_____

	Normal	Slight		Moderate			Severe
	0	1	2	3	4	5	6
Intellectual Functioning Impairments							
Level of consciousness	(_X_)	(__)	(__)	(__)	(__)	(__)	(__)
Attention span, distractible	(__)	(__)	(_X_)	(__)	(__)	(__)	(__)
Abstract thinking	(_X_)	(__)	(__)	(__)	(__)	(__)	(__)
Calculation ability	(_X_)	(__)	(__)	(__)	(__)	(__)	(__)
Intelligence	(_X_)	(__)	(__)	(__)	(__)	(__)	(__)

	Normal	Slight		Moderate			Severe
	0	1	2	3	4	5	6
Orientation							
Time	(_X_)	(__)	(__)	(__)	(__)	(__)	(__)
Place	(_X_)	(__)	(__)	(__)	(__)	(__)	(__)
Person	(_X_)	(__)	(__)	(__)	(__)	(__)	(__)

	Normal	Slight		Moderate			Severe
	0	1	2	3	4	5	6
Memory Impairment							
Recent	(__)	(_X_)	(__)	(__)	(__)	(__)	(__)
Remote	(_X_)	(__)	(__)	(__)	(__)	(__)	(__)

	Normal	Slight		Moderate			Severe
	0	1	2	3	4	5	6
Insight							
Denies psych problems	(__)	(__)	(_X_)	(__)	(__)	(__)	(__)
Blames others	(__)	(_X_)	(__)	(__)	(__)	(__)	(__)

	Normal	Slight		Moderate			Severe
	0	1	2	3	4	5	6
Judgment Impairments							
Decision making	(__)	(__)	(__)	(_X_)	(__)	(__)	(__)
Impulse control	(__)	(__)	(__)	(__)	(_X_)	(__)	(__)

	Normal	Slight		Moderate			Severe
	0	1	2	3	4	5	6

Thought Content

Obsessions	(X)	(__)	(__)	(__)	(__)	(__)	(__)
Compulsions	(X)	(__)	(__)	(__)	(__)	(__)	(__)
Phobias	(X)	(__)	(__)	(__)	(__)	(__)	(__)
Depersonalization	(X)	(__)	(__)	(__)	(__)	(__)	(__)
Suicidal ideation	(__)	(__)	(__)	(X)	(__)	(__)	(__)
Homicidal ideation	(X)	(__)	(__)	(__)	(__)	(__)	(__)
Delusions	(X)	(__)	(__)	(__)	(__)	(__)	(__)

Comments re: Thinking: _Historical incidents of poor judgment and impulsivity with subsequent depression. At times will withdraw or miss work when frustrated. Denies suicidal attempts. Ideations at times. Blames self for not motivating spouse, children, and students._

Diagnosis Validation

Primary diagnosis: _296.32 Major depression, recurrent, moderate, w/o psychotic features_

Name of test	Results
Minnesota Multiphasic	_Elevated 2–4–7 Depression, anxiety, CD potential_
Personality Inventory—2	_Profile typical of cycles of acting out, guilt, depression_
(MMPI–2)	_Raw score 32—Severe_
Beck Depression	
Inventory (BDI)	

Biographical Information (specific BIF references)

Frequent feelings of hopelessness, loneliness, no one caring, failure, disappointment, can't do anything right, difficulties concentrating, depression, and having no emotions. Unwanted Sx of avoiding people, depression, fatigue, hopelessness, loneliness, loss of sexual interest, frequent sickness, sleeping difficulties, suicidal thoughts, withdrawal, and worrying. Experiences little/no pleasure.

Collateral Information

Have requested records from previous therapist.

Case/Intake Notes, MSE References (Include brief descriptions, dates, and line numbers.)

3/8/1997, Intake Notes. Section 8; poor appetite; 13: Crying spells daily, fatigued, low ego strength, social withdrawal increasing; 14: psychomotor retardation, blunted affect, difficulty making decisions, suicidal ideation, appeared depressed; 15: usually feels depressed guilt feelings, insomnia.

Diagnosis 2: _Deferred 799.9_ _____ (Make copies for additional Dx's)

Name of test   Results

_____   _____

_____   _____

_____   _____

_____   _____

_____   _____

Biographical Information (specific BIF references)

_____

_____

_____

_____

_____

Case/Intake Notes, MSE References (Include brief descriptions, dates, and line numbers.)

_____

_____

_____

_____

_____

_____

Diagnostic Impressions

Axis I   _296.32 Major depressive disorder, recurrent, moderate, w/o psychotic features_

Axis II   _Deferred_

Axis III   _Defer to physician_

Axis IV   _Spousal discord, loss of friends_

Axis V   _Global Assessment of Functioning (GAF): Current: 58   Past year: 78_

Needed Mental Health Services

___ Further assessment (specify): _____

_X_ Individual ___ Group _____ Family ____ Other (specify): _____

Other Needed Services

_X_ Psychiatric consultation   _X_ Physical exam   ____ Neurological consultation

___ CD evaluation   ____ Other (specify): _____

Did client/guardian sign the treatment plan? ___ No _X_ Yes

Was Dx explained to client? ____ No _X_ Yes

Therapist's signature: _____ _Darlene L. Benton, PhD_ _____ Date: _3_ / _16_ / _2005_

Supervisor's signature: _____ _Sharon Bell, PhD_ _____ Date: _3_ / _16_ / _2005_

Form 27   Diagnostic Assessment—Lower Functioning

Name: _____   Date: _____

Gender: ____ F ____ M Race: _____   DOB: _____ Age: _____

Residence: _____   Contact person(s):

_____   _____

_____   Phone: _____

Date entered residence: _____

Employment: _____   Contact person(s):

_____   _____

_____   Phone: _____

Day program: _____   Contact person(s):

_____   _____

_____   Phone: _____

County case manager: _____   Phone: _____

Guardianship: _____   Comments: _____

Guardian's name and address if not client or case manager: _____

Address: _____ City: _____ State: _____ Zip: _____

SS number: _____

Insurance company: _____

Address: _____ City: _____ State: _____ Zip: _____

Policy number: _____ Group number: _____

Purpose of evaluation: _____

Referred by: _____ Title: _____

Family member to contact: _____

Address: _____ City: _____ State: _____ Zip: _____

1. **Background Information**

    Place of birth: _____ Complications: _____

    Intellectual development: _____

    _____

    Social development: _____

    _____

    Emotional development: _____

    _____

    Schooling: _____

    _____

3.100

Employment/Vocational history: _____

_____

Residential history:

          Name of residence   From   To

_____   _____   _____

_____   _____   _____

_____   _____   _____

Mother: _____

Father: _____

Siblings: Number _____ of _____ siblings. Their ages, sex, comments: _____

_____

Sexual concerns: _____

_____

2. Medical Concerns

Present physical concerns: _____

_____

Behavioral/emotional effects of physical concerns: _____

_____

Past physical concerns: _____

_____

Past suicidal attempts? ___ No   ___ Yes

If Yes, explain: _____

_____

Medications: _____

_____

Currently under physician's care? ___ No   ___ Yes

If Yes, for what purpose(s): _____

_____

Currently in psychological therapy? ___ No   ___ Yes

If Yes, explain: _____

_____

3. Present Behaviors

From staff (oral interview): Positive: _____

_____

Negative: _____

_____

From written sources: Positive: _____

_____

Negative: _____

_____

Observations/Interview: _____

_____

4. Emotional Issues

From staff (oral interview): _____

_____

From written sources: _____

_____

Observations/Interview: _____

_____

Comments: _____

_____

5. Observations

_____

_____

Appearance: _____

Gestures/Mannerisms: _____

Attention span: _____

Level of interest: _____

Speech: _____

Level of conversation: _____

Affect: _____

Eye contact: _____

Cooperation: _____

Understanding of why being interviewed: _____

6. Adaptive Functioning

_____

_____

_____

_____

_____

_____

_____

7. Previous Testing

By whom: _____ Purpose: _____ Date: _____

Results: _____

_____

8. **Present Testing** (list below, plus see test profiles)

_____
_____
_____
_____

9. **Clinical Diagnosis**

Axis I: _____

Axis II: _____

Axis III: _____

Axis IV: _____

Axis V: _____

Comments: _____
_____

10. **Recommendations**

Appropriateness of residential services: _____
_____

Appropriateness of day program/employment: _____
_____

Guardianship: _____
_____

Current/Future mental health/behavioral services: _____
_____

Strategies for caregivers: _____
_____
_____

Additional information needed: _____
_____

11. **Summary**

_____
_____
_____
_____
_____
_____
_____
_____

Therapist's signature: _____ Date: ____/____/_____

Form 27A   Diagnostic Assessment—
Lower Functioning   (*Completed*)

Name: _Peter Fowler_   Date: _3/17/2005_

Gender: ___ F _X_ M Race: _African-Amer._   DOB: _8/12/1979_ Age: _26_

Residence: _Alternatives_   Contact person(s):
          3001 10th Ave N   _Rod Collins_
          Miami, ME 71111   Phone: _555-1778_

Date entered residence: _4/7/1994_

Employment: _Sullivan's Market_   Contact person(s):
           108 Hagar Rd   _Jan Wente_
           Miami, ME 71112   Phone: _555-2841_

Day program: _DAC_   Contact person(s):
            400 8th Ave S   _Pat O'Brien_
            Miami, ME 71113   Phone: _555-9426_

County case manager: _Ron Bolton_   Phone: _555-8522_

Guardianship: _State_   Comments: _____

Guardian's name and address if not client or case manager: _Joseph Fowler_

Address: _4126 'J' Street_   City: _Miami_   State: _ME_ Zip: _71112_

SS number: _987-65-4321_

Insurance company: _State Insurance Fund_

Address: _1418 Capitol Blvd_   City: _Miami_   State: _ME_ Zip: _71115_

Policy number: _987-65-4321-F_   Group number: _N/A_

Purpose of evaluation: _Periodic psychological update_

Referred by: _Ron Bolton_   Title: _County Social Worker_

Family member to contact: _Same as guardian_

Address: _____ City: _____ State: _____ Zip: _____

1. **Background Information**

    Place of birth: _Miami, ME_   Complications: _Oxygen deprived_

    Intellectual development: _Diagnosis of MR at birth. Developmental delays in all areas._

    Social development: _History of no close friendships. Very intrusive in other's personal space. Friendly._

    Emotional development: _Life-long issues in anger management when stressed with environmental changes._

    Schooling: _State Hospital age 3–12 in Myer Program. Special education while in foster care age 13–19. No mainstreaming._

Employment/Vocational history: *No history of competitive employment. Always in supervised setting with minimal tasks.*

Residential history:

Name of residence	From	To
State Hospital	*Birth*	*1984*
Hanna Foster Home	*1984*	*1994*
Alternatives Group Home	*1994*	*Present*

Mother: *Gave up to state custody at birth. No contact since birth.*

Father: *Unknown*

Siblings: Number *DK* of _____ siblings. Their ages, sex, comments: _____

Sexual concerns: *No issues. Expresses interest in nude photos in magazines. No history of relationships.*

2. Medical Concerns

Present physical concerns: *Tires easily, frequent respiratory problems*

Behavioral/emotional effects of physical concerns: *Frustrated when he cannot keep up with others.*

Past physical concerns: *Several operations as child (no records available, though). Seizures until age 8.*

Past suicidal attempts? *X* No ___ Yes

If Yes, explain: _____

Medications: *None—Previous Tegretol–dose unknown*

Currently under physician's care? ___ No *X* Yes

If Yes, for what purpose(s): *Monitor respiratory concerns*

Currently in psychological therapy? *X* No ___ Yes

If Yes, explain: _____

3. Present Behaviors

From staff (oral interview): Positive: *Helpful when praised. Always on time. Keeps room very clean.*

Negative: *Behavioral outbursts when frustrated. Will aggress verbally and physically toward staff average 1x/week.*

From written sources: Positive: *Staff records indicate 85% compliance in behavioral programming.*

Negative: _Staff records indicate sporadic anger outbursts. Property damage 3x last month._

Observations/Interview: _He spoke only a few words during interview. He cooperates with all staff requests._

4. Emotional Issues

From staff (oral interview): _Staff report that he is usually happy but, changes in environment lead to much frustration and poor coping strategies._

From written sources: _Staff records indicate no behavioral issues._

Observations/Interview: _Neutral affect. Did not appear to be depressed, anxious, irritable, or angry._

Comments: _Very little affective expression._

5. Observations

Sat still during entire interview. Did not appear to be stressed. No unusual mannerisms. Laughed at appropriate times. Interrupted staff 4x during staff interview.

Appearance: _Neatly dressed, but 2 buttons undone_

Gestures/Mannerisms: _At times rocked back and forth_

Attention span: _Stared into space a few times. Moderate_

Level of interest: _Seemed interested when his name was mentioned_

Speech: _Spoke very little, 3–4 word sentences. 85% understandable_

Level of conversation: _Poor_

Affect: _Neutral_

Eye contact: _Poor most of the time_

Cooperation: _Moderate_

Understanding of why being interviewed: _No_

6. Adaptive Functioning

Staff report that he requires 24 hour staffing. Never left in home alone. Is able to dress self, perform personal hygiene, and help with household chores. Not able to cook, shop, or use phone independently. History of being vulnerable to strangers. Does not seem to understand the function of money.

7. Previous Testing

By whom: _Jill Cheng, MS_   Purpose: _Periodic Eval_   Date: _3/10/2005_

Results: _Full-scale IQ = 51   Adaptive functioning score = 54   Does not read or perform any math.   Axis I = No diagnosis   Axis II = Moderate MR_

8. **Present Testing** (list below, plus see test profiles)

Full-scale IQ = 50   Adaptive functioning score = 55

9. **Clinical Diagnosis**

Axis I: _No diagnosis   V71.09_

Axis II: _Moderate MR   318_

Axis III: _Records indicate respiratory problems_

Axis IV: _Social problems_

Axis V: _SD_

Comments: _No significant differences in test scores or adaptive functioning._

10. **Recommendations**

Appropriateness of residential services: _Current services are appropriate and in his best interest at this time._

Appropriateness of day program/employment: _Suggest continuing present services_

Guardianship: _Not able to be own guardian. Suggest state remain as guardian._

Current/Future mental health/behavioral services: _No counseling suggested. Consider behavioral programming dealing with rewarding constructive coping mechanisms._

Strategies for caregivers: _Reinforce adaptive behaviors by providing increased choices. Do not give any attention to attention seeking behaviors. Visibly chart his progress and praise him for it._

Additional information needed: _Reports from day program and job placement regarding any behavioral issues._

11. **Summary**

Peter Fowler was referred for a periodic psychological evaluation as required by the state. He was quiet and calm during the entire interview. Staff report no significant emotional issues except temper outbursts when stressed. At times he will hit staff members. Intellectual and adaptive functioning indicates moderate MR. He is not able to function independently. Adaptive functioning is similar to a person approximately age 8. No changes in functioning are noted since his previous evaluation. Suggest keeping present residence, day program, employment and state guardianship.

Therapist's signature: _Sarah Bloom, PhD_   Date: _3 / 12 / 2005_

Form 28   Biopsychosocial Report

Client's name: _____   Case number: _____   Date: _____

Age: _____   Gender: ____ F ____ M   Race: _____   Marital status: _____

1. Current Family and Significant Relationships   (See Personal History Form)
(Include strengths, stressors, problems, recent changes, changes desired and comments on family and relationship circumstances.)

_____

_____

_____

2. Childhood/Adolescent History   (See Personal History Form)
(developmental milestones, past behavioral concerns, environment, abuse, school, social, mental health)

_____

_____

_____

3. Social Relationships   (See Personal History Form)
(Include strengths, stressors, problems, recent changes, changes desired and comments on current circumstances.)

_____

_____

_____

4. Cultural/Ethnic   (See Personal History Form)
(Include strengths, stressors, problems, recent changes, changes desired and beliefs/practices to incorporate into therapy.)

_____

_____

_____

5. Spiritual/Religious   (See Personal History Form)
(Include strengths, stressors, problems, recent changes, changes desired and beliefs/practices to incorporate into therapy.)

_____

_____

_____

6. Legal   (See Personal History Form)
(Include current and previous legal concerns and their impact on behavior, affect and relationship.)

_____

_____

_____

7. **Education** (See Personal History Form)
(Include strengths, stressors, problems, recent changes, changes desired and comments on current circumstances.)

_____

_____

_____

8. **Employment/Vocational** (See Personal History Form)
(Include strengths, stressors, problems, recent changes, changes desired and comments on current circumstances.)

_____

_____

_____

9. **Military** (See Personal History Form)
(Include current impact on affect and behavior.)

_____

_____

_____

10. **Leisure/Recreational** (See Personal History Form)
(Include strengths, stressors, problems, recent changes, changes desired.)

_____

_____

_____

11. **Medical/Physical Health** (See Personal History Form)
(Include speech, language and hearing, visual impairment, sensorimotor dysfunctions, immunization status for children and physical factors affecting medical condition and/or medical factors affecting physical condition.)

_____

_____

_____

12. **Chemical Use History** (See Personal History Form)
(When relevant, include information such as previous and current use patterns, impact on functioning, drugs of choice, last use, relapse dynamics, motivation to recover, overdose history, and patient's perception of the problem.)

_____

_____

_____

13. **Counseling/Psychiatric History** (See Personal History Form)
(Include benefits and setbacks of previous treatment, reasons for admission, termination, and cycles.)

_____

_____

_____

Integrated Summary

Clinical Assessment/Diagnostic Summary

(Evaluate, integrate and summarize the following information: Background, medical, social, presenting problem, signs and symptoms and impairments. Tie these in with the patient's strengths and needs. Integration of data is more important than specific details.)

_____
_____
_____
_____
_____
_____
_____
_____
_____
_____
_____
_____
_____
_____
_____
_____
_____
_____
_____
_____
_____
_____
_____
_____
_____
_____

	Diagnosis	Code
Axis I	_____	_____
Axis II	_____	_____
Axis III	_____	_____
Axis IV	_____	
Axis V	Current GAF = _____	

Therapist's signature/credentials: _____ Date: ____/____/_____

Form 28A   Biopsychosocial Report   (*Completed*)

Client's name: *Judy Doe*   Case number: *DJ030899*   Date: *5/3/2005*

Age: *50*   Gender: *X* F _____ M   Race: *Caucasian*   Marital status: *Married*

1. Current Family and Significant Relationships   (See Personal History Form)
(Include strengths, stressors, problems, recent changes, changes desired and comments on family and relationship circumstances.)

Supportive family of origin, but intrusive. Able to vent feelings with Mother. Avoiding other relatives. High marital conflict, possible divorce. Seldom asserts self to spouse, child, or family of origin.

2. Childhood/Adolescent History   (See Personal History Form)
(developmental milestones, past behavioral concerns, environment, abuse, school, social, mental health)

History of usually being a follower. Did well in school academically, but considered self as "homely and unpopular." Viewed self as being in "shadow of older sister."
No developmental delays physically. No counseling as a child.

3. Social Relationships   (See Personal History Form)
(Include strengths, stressors, problems, recent changes, changes desired and comments on current circumstances.)

Has had a few close friends since adolescence, but has turned down their invitations. Now no contact in several months. Feels rejected about it. Not initiating any social interactions.

4. Cultural/Ethnic   (See Personal History Form)
(Include strengths, stressors, problems, recent changes, changes desired and beliefs/practices to incorporate into therapy.)

Mainstream, middle class values/beliefs, no changes or unusual circumstances

5. Spiritual/Religious   (See Personal History Form)
(Include strengths, stressors, problems, recent changes, changes desired and beliefs/practices to incorporate into therapy.)

History of strong religious convictions. Went to church "religiously" until past year. Feels guilty. Will not consider suicide due to "hell." Misses singing in church but can't get herself to go.

6. Legal   (See Personal History Form)
(Include current and previous legal concerns and their impact on behavior, affect and relationship.)

No legal history

3.111

7. **Education** (See Personal History Form)

(Include strengths, stressors, problems, recent changes, changes desired and comments on current circumstances.)

Did well in high school academically. Always on honor roll. Didn't feel challenged.

College was more competitive but earned GPA of 2.9. Earned teaching certificate.

8. **Employment/Vocational** (See Personal History Form)

(Include strengths, stressors, problems, recent changes, changes desired and comments on current circumstances.)

Very stable work history. But lately "no motivation" to teach or oversee students. Views

students as demanding. Used to believe teaching is rewarding. Gets along "neutrally"

with other teachers. Tries to hide depression at school.

9. **Military** (See Personal History Form)

(Include current impact on affect and behavior.)

N/A

10. **Leisure/Recreational** (See Personal History Form)

(Include strengths, stressors, problems, recent changes, changes desired.)

No current activities. Used to enjoy relaxing, exercising, and various sports; feels "too

tired and worn out." Wants to resume activities some day.

11. **Medical/Physical Health** (See Personal History Form)

(Include speech, language and hearing, visual impairment, sensorimotor dysfunctions, immunization status for children and physical factors affecting medical condition and/or medical factors affecting physical condition.)

No physical problems in the past. Over past year experiencing weight loss, headaches,

fatigue, low libido, poor sleep. "Feels like 100 years old," symptoms concordant with

depression.

12. **Chemical Use History** (See Personal History Form)

(When relevant, include information such as previous and current use patterns, impact on functioning, drugs of choice, last use, relapse dynamics, motivation to recover, overdose history, and patient's perception of the problem.)

Rare, light social drinking. No history of drunkenness, drug abuse or any negative

consequences.

13. **Counseling/Psychiatric History** (See Personal History Form)

(Include benefits and setbacks of previous treatment, reasons for admission, termination, and cycles.)

Relationship break-up in college led to diagnosis of depression. Counseling was successful,

learned coping skills, set goals, and increased pleasurable activities. Has had a few minor

bouts of depression since then but it was manageable. No psychiatric hospitalizations.

Integrated Summary

Clinical Assessment/Diagnostic Summary

(Evaluate, integrate and summarize the following information: Background, medical, social, presenting problem, signs and symptoms and impairments. Tie these in with the patient's strengths and needs. Integration of data is more important than specific details.)

Judy Doe presents with significant depression and marital conflict. She was treated previously for depression 20 years ago due to relationship issues. Counseling was successful. She describes herself as always being in good health, but currently several signs of depression are endorsed. She appears dysphoric and makes several self-depricating statements. She views her family of origin as her only support system. She has a history of academic achievement, and graduated teacher's college. Her employment history is remarkably stable. Increased marital conflict over the past year has coincided with a relapse of Major Depressive Disorder. Divorce threats exacerbate her symptoms. Major concerns at this time are occupational affective, and social impairment. She is considering taking a leave of absence from work due to inability to concentrate adequately on teaching and formulating lesson plans. She states that she wants to "get better again" but "needs direction," as in her previous counseling.

	Diagnosis	Code
Axis I	*Major Depressive Disorder, recurrent moderate*	*296.32*
Axis II	*Deferred*	
Axis III	*Defer to physician*	
Axis IV	*Marital Discord, social and occupational problems*	
Axis V	Current GAF = *55*	

Therapist's signature/credentials: *Darlene Benton, PhD* Date: *5 / 3 / 2005*

Chapter 4

Psychological Evaluations

Generally much more information is needed when a psychological evaluation has been requested, compared to the information required for a client entering a few sessions of therapy. But the following psychological evaluation forms may also be used prior to therapy when needed.

Although the examples of psychological evaluation forms for adults and children are similar, several differences exist, such as the use of collateral information provided by parents, developmental issues, diagnostic categories, and the Mental Status Exam. Each may be used for general purposes and formal evaluations such as Social Security Disability evaluations. A structured interview format is employed from which the final report may be easily dictated. A sample of both an adult and child evaluation are included.

FORMS 29 and 30
Adult and Child
Psychological Evaluations

The psychological evaluation is a structured interview designed to provide symptoms, history, daily activities, ability to relate to others, substance abuse, and an extensive mental status evaluation. The form is also designed to help evaluate thought, affective, personality, and somatoform disorders, plus memory and concentration.

These forms are not ends in themselves; rather, they provide structure for an interview and subsequent data for a psychological report or treatment plan. The requested information in each section is self-explanatory for those trained in diagnostic interviewing and mental status evaluations.

The psychological evaluation forms cover several areas of functioning in the client's life. Information such as a typical daily schedule is useful when conducting the evaluation for assessing mental and physical disabilities. The *Clinical Documentation Primer* (Wiger, 1999, 2005, in Opress) provides detailed explanations as to how to conduct a psychological evaluation.

Form 29   Psychological Evaluation—Adult

Client's name: _____

Phone (home): _____   ID#: _____   Date: _____

Address: _____   City: _____   State: ____   Zip: _____

Transportation to interview: _____   ____ Alone ____ With others   ____ Drove ____ Driven

Collateral information by: _____   Relationship: _____

Physical Description

Identification given: _____   Race: _____   Gender: ____ F ____ M

Age: _____   Height: _____   Weight: _____   Eyes: _____   Hair: _____

Clothing: _____   Hygiene: _____   Other: _____

History

1. **Signs and Symptoms** Client's statement of problem and impairments (e.g., social, occupational, affective, cognitive, memory, physical)

Symptoms or disability(ies)	Resulting impairment(s)
_____	_____
_____	_____
_____	_____
_____	_____
_____	_____
_____	_____

As seen by professional: _____
_____

2. **History of Present Illness**

Events or incidents leading to need for services/benefits: _____
_____
_____

Family Hx of Sx's: _____

Onset/Frequency/Duration/Intensity/Cycling of symptoms: _____
_____
_____

Was there a clear time when Sx's worsened? _____

Previous diagnosis (include by whom): _____

Course of illness: ____ Improving   ____ Stable   ____ Deteriorating   ____ Varies

Current status of past diagnoses? _____

Precipitating factors/events (e.g., emotional, environmental, social): _____
_____

4.3

E = Employment   V = Volunteering

Currently: ___ Yes ___ No   Hours: _____   (Describe below. Include longest position)

	Positions	Dates	FT/PT/Temp	Problems?	Reason left
___ E ___ V	_____	_____	_____	_____	_____
___ E ___ V	_____	_____	_____	_____	_____

Usual length of employment: _____   Usual reason(s) for leaving: _____

Usual reasons for missing work or leaving early: _____   Frequency: _____

Military: ___ N ___ Y   Dates: _____   Branch: _____

Highest rank: _____   Discharge: _____

Problems in military: _____

Medications   C = Current   P = Previous   (attempt to obtain at least 5 years history)

1. ___ C ___ P   Name: _____   Purpose: _____
   Dr. _____ of _____
   Dose: ___ mg X ___ /day   Dates: _____   Compliance: _____
   Last taken: _____   Effectiveness: _____
   Side effects: _____   Effect without the med: _____

2. ___ C ___ P   Name: _____   Purpose: _____
   Dr. _____ of _____
   Dose: ___ mg X ___ /day   Dates: _____   Compliance: _____
   Last taken: _____   Effectiveness: _____
   Side effects: _____   Effect without the med: _____

3. ___ C ___ P   Name: _____   Purpose: _____
   Dr. _____ of _____
   Dose: ___ mg X ___ /day   Dates: _____   Compliance: _____
   Last taken: _____   Effectiveness: _____
   Side effects: _____   Effect without the med: _____

4. ___ C ___ P   Name: _____   Purpose: _____
   Dr. _____ of _____
   Dose: ___ mg X ___ /day   Dates: _____   Compliance: _____
   Last taken: _____   Effectiveness: _____
   Side effects: _____   Effect without the med: _____

Mental Health Treatment History ___ Currently in Tx   (attempt to obtain at least 5 years history)

Dates	Purpose	In/Out pt.	Response to Tx	Professional
_____	_____	___ I ___ O	_____	_____
_____	_____	___ I ___ O	_____	_____

___ Check if continued on back

History of suicidality (___ ideations, ___ threats, ___ gestures, ___ plan, ___ attempts): _____

Physical Health Treatment History   (attempt to obtain at least 5 years history)

Primary physician: _____ of _____ since _____ frequency _____

Dates	Purpose	In/Out pt.	Response to Tx	Professional
_____	_____	___ I ___ O	_____	_____
_____	_____	___ I ___ O	_____	_____

___ Check if continued on back

Current special services (___ social, ___ educational, ___ legal, ___ physical): _____

Note and resolve any discrepancies between stated information and records: _____

4.4

BEGIN 5/30 MINUTE MEMORY CHECK

Current Level of Daily Functioning

1. **Current Hobbies, Interests and Activities**

   Hobby/interest (How persistently is it followed?)   Frequency   Duration

   _____   _____   _____

   _____   _____   _____

   _____   _____   _____

   _____   _____   _____

   _____   _____   _____

   Realistic, appropriate, compare to previous functioning: _____

   _____

2. **Activities**

   ___ Rent   ___ Own: ___ house   ___ apartment   ___ townhouse   ___ duplex

                            ___ condo   ___ mobile home   ___ other: _____

   Who else lives there? (relationships, ages): _____

   What kind of things do you usually make for: Frequency   Problems

   Breakfast: _____   _____   _____

   Lunch: _____   _____   _____

   Dinner: _____   _____   _____

   Physical challenges in bathing/grooming? _____   Need reminders? _____

   Daily Schedule (Include chores, shopping, meals, meds, yard work, repairs, hobbies, employment, school. In time order, in and out of the house. What the client can do independently. Note persistence, pace.)

   Time   Activity

   _____   _____

   _____   _____

   _____   _____

   _____   _____

   _____   _____

   _____   _____

   _____   _____

   _____   _____

   _____   _____

   _____   _____

   _____   _____

   _____   _____

   _____   _____

   _____   _____

   _____   _____

5 MINUTE MEMORY CHECK _____ = ___ / 3

Activities performed in the home (e.g., write letters, crafts, physical exercise, gardening, house repairs, cooking, drawing, painting, take care of pets, lifting, sewing, auto repairs, reading)

Activity	Frequency	Duration	Effects	Independent
_____	_____	_____	_____	_____
_____	_____	_____	_____	_____
_____	_____	_____	_____	_____
_____	_____	_____	_____	_____

Activities outside the home (e.g., movies, eat out, meetings, dancing, go for walks, shopping, hunting, fishing, sports, bars, biking, bowling, volunteering, clubs, organizations, religious services, AA, classes, babysitting, travel)

Activity	Frequency	Duration	Effects	Independent
_____	_____	_____	_____	_____
_____	_____	_____	_____	_____
_____	_____	_____	_____	_____
_____	_____	_____	_____	_____

Ability to focus/concentrate on these activities (in and out of house): _____
_____

When Sx's increase how are these followed? _____

___ Drive   ___ Run errands   ___ Use public transportation (___ bus,   ___ taxi)

___ Go shopping? How often? _____   Problems? _____   Independently? ___ N ___ Y

___ Walk places? How far? _____   How often? _____   Other: _____

How do you financially care for basic needs? _____

Who pays the bills? _____   Who handles the finances? _____

___ Savings account   ___ Checking account   ___ Money orders

___ Others pay/write checks   ___ Figure change

3. Living Situation

Living conditions: (___ family, ___ alone, ___ group home; ___ crowded, ___ dysfunctional; ability to follow rules/procedures)

_____

4. Ability to Relate to Others (e.g., ___ aggressive, ___ dependent, ___ defiant, ___ avoidant, ___ oppositional, ___ normal)

_____

Adults: _____   Authority figures: _____

Peers: _____   Police: _____

Family: _____   Children: _____

Neighbors: _____   Other: _____

Have best friend? _____   Group of friends? _____

Activities with friends (include frequency, duration, and problems): _____

_____

How well did client relate (examiner, office personnel) during office visit? _____

_____

5. **Substance Abuse** (if applicable)

Detailed history and current information regarding substance abuse patterns.

Last drink and/or use of drugs: _____

Age of onset: _____   Substances used historically: _____

History of usage: _____

_____

_____

_____

_____

_____

	A	B	C
Current substances used:	_____	_____	_____
Level of usage (how much?):	_____	_____	_____
Frequency (how often?):	_____	_____	_____
Duration (length of episodes):	_____	_____	_____

Effects on functioning (impact on activities, interests, ability to relate, persistence/pace): _____

_____

Reason(s) for usage: ___taste ___ escape ___ self-medicate ___ addiction ___ other: _____

___ Weekdays? What time(s) of day? _____

___ Weekends? What time(s) of day? _____

___ Alone ___ Home ___ With others ___ Bars ___ Other: _____

How often do you drink to the point of intoxication (or get high) in a given week? _____

How many binges in a given year? _____   Frequency/duration of binges? _____

Describe treatment history and medical/social consequences of the abuse (e.g., DWIs, DTs and tremors, blackouts, job loss, divorce, etc.): _____

_____

Level of functioning when not drinking or using drugs (e.g., during periods of sobriety or Tx):

_____

_____

6. **History of Arrests/Incarcerations**

_____

_____

Mental Status Exam

1. **Clinical Observations** (Entire page: Leave blank if normal. Check and comment if remarkable.)

Appearance

___ Appears age, +/-	___ Grooming	___ Hair	___ Odor
___ Posture	___ Health	___ Nails	___ Demeanor

_____

_____

Activity Level

___ Mannerisms	___ Gestures	___ Alert	___ Lethargic	___ Limp
___ Rigid	___ Relaxed	___ Combative	___ Hyperactive	___ Bored
___ Gait	___ Eye contact	___ Distracted	___ Preoccupied	___ Vigilance

_____

Speech

___ Vocabulary	___ Details	___ Volume
___ Pace	___ Reaction time	___ Pitch
___ Pressured	___ Hesitant	___ Monotonous
___ Slurred	___ Stuttering	___ Mumbled
___ Echolalia	___ Neologisms	___ Repetitions
___ Pronunciation	___ % Understood: _____	

_____

Attitude Toward Examiner

___ Attentive	___ Distracted	___ Cooperative	___ Friendly	___ Interested
___ Frank	___ Hostile	___ Defiant	___ Guarded	___ Defensive
___ Evasive	___ Hesitant	___ Manipulative	___ Humorous	___ Historian +/-

_____

2. **Stream of Consciousness**

Speech

___ Spontaneous	___ Inhibited	___ Blocked	___ Illogical	___ Vague
___ Pressured	___ Slowed	___ Disorganized	___ Rambling	___ Derailment
___ Coherent	___ Cause/effect	___ Neologisms		

Thinking

___ Relevant	___ Coherent	___ Goal directed	___ Loose & rambling

Thought Processes

___ Number of ideas	___ Flight of ideas	___ Hesitance

_____

3. **Thought Content**

Preoccupations

___ Obsessions	___ Compulsions	___ Phobias	___ Homicide	___ Antisocial

Suicidal, Current

___ Threats	___ Ideas	___ Plan

History

___ Attempts	___ Threats	___ Ideas

Hallucinations

___ Voices	___ Visions	___ Content	___ Setting	___ Sensory system

Illusions: _____

Delusions

___ Persecutory	___ Somatic	___ Grandeur

Ideas of Reference

___ Controlled	___ Broadcasting	___ Antisocial	___ Validity
___ Content	___ Mood	___ Bizarre	

4. Affect/Mood

Affective Observations

Range	___ Normal	___ Expansive	___ Restricted	___ Blunted	___ Flat
Appropriateness	___ Concordant		___ Discordant (with speech/ideas)		
Mobility	___ Normal	___ Decreased (constricted, fixed)	___ Increased (labile)		
Intensity	___ Normal	___ Mild	___ Strong		
Psychomotor	___ Normal	___ Retardation	___ Agitation		
Predominant mood	___ Neutral	___ Euthymic	___ Dysphoric	___ Euphoric	___ Manic
Level of anxiety	___ Normal	___ High (describe): _____			
Irritability	___ Normal	___ High (describe): _____			
Anger expression	___ Normal	___ High (describe): _____			

Mood (Rule in and rule out signs and symptoms)

Frequency/Intensity in Daily Life (Give specific examples or impairments/strengths, frequency, duration.)

Clearly Validate with *DSM-IV* Criteria

Affection toward others: _____

Anger: ___ anger mng't issues   ___ property destruction
       ___ explosive behaviors   ___ assaultive behaviors

How does the client act on anger?

Onset: _____   Frequency: _____

Duration: _____   Severity: _____

Examples: _____

_____

Panic Attacks: 4+, Abrupt development of:

___ palpitations	___ sweating	___ trembling
___ shortness of breath	___ feeling of choking	___ chest pain
___ nausea	___ dizziness	___ light-headed
___ derealization	___ fear of losing control	___ fear of dying
___ numbness	___ chills	___ hot flashes

___ Other: _____

_____

Onset: _____   Frequency: _____

Duration: _____   Severity: _____

Anxiety: GAD: 3+, most of time, 6 months:

___ restlessness	___ easily fatigued	___ concentration
___ irritability	___ muscle tension	___ sleep disturbance

___ Other: _____

_____

Onset: _____   Frequency: _____

Duration: _____   Severity: _____

4.9

Depression: MDE: 2+ wks, 5+:

___ usually depressed   ___ anhedonia

___ wght +/- 5%/month   ___ appetite +/-

___ sleep +/-   ___ fatigue

___ psychomotor +/-   ___ worthlessness/guilt

___ concentration   ___ other: ___ crying spells   ___ withdrawal

___ death/suicidal ideation

___ Other: _____

_____

Onset: _____   Frequency: _____

Duration: _____   Severity: _____

Dysthymia: ___ depressed most of time   ___ onset; adult 2+ child/adolescent 1+ yrs, 2+ of:

___ +/- appetite or eating   ___ in/hypersomnia   ___ low energy/fatigue

___ low self-esteem   ___ low concentration/decisions   ___ hopelessness

___ Other: _____

_____

Onset: _____   Frequency: _____

Duration: _____   Severity: _____

Mania: 3+:

___ grandiosity   ___ low sleep   ___ talkative   ___ flight of ideas

___ distractibility   ___ goals/agitation   ___ excessive pleasure

___ Other: _____

_____

Onset: _____   Frequency: _____

Duration: _____   Severity: _____

PTSD: Traumatic event with intense response: 1+:

Distressing:

___ recollections   ___ dreams   ___ reliving

___ cues   ___ physiological reactivity with cues

3+:

___ avoid thoughts   ___ avoid environmental   ___ poor recall of events

___ low interest   ___ detachment   ___ restricted range of affect

___ foreshortened future

2+:

___ sleep   ___ anger   ___ concentration

___ hypervigilance   ___ startle response

___ Other: _____

_____

Onset: _____   Frequency: _____

Duration: _____   Severity: _____

5. Sensorium/Cognition

    A) Reality Contact (How in touch with reality is the client?): _____

    Able to hold normal conversation? ____ Yes ____ No   Notes: _____

    B) Orientation X3: _____ Time ____ Place ____ Person Notes: _____

    C) Concentration:

    Attention to tasks/conversation; distractability: _____

    Count to 40 by 3s beginning at 1.

    (___ 1, ___ 4, ___ 7, ___, 10, ___, 13, ___, 16, ___, 19, ___, 22, ___, 25, ___, 28,

    ___, 31, ___, 34, ___, 37, ___, 40)

    Number of errors: _____   Time between digits: _____   Other: _____

    Count backward by 7s.

    (___ 100, ____ 93, ____, 86, ____, 79, ____, 72, ____, 65, ___, 58, ___, 51, ____, 44, ____,

    37, ____, 30, ____, 23, ____, 16, ____, 9, ____, 2)   _____

    Number of errors: _____   Time between digits: _____   Other: _____

    5 + 8 = ____   7 x 4 = _____   12 x 6 = ____   65/5 = ____   Timing: _____

    Digits forward and backward (Average adult: FWD = 5–7 BWD = 4–6)

    FWD: ___ 42 ___ 318 ___ 6385   ___ 96725   ___ 864972 ___ 5739481 ___ 31749852

    BWD: ___ 75 ___ 582 ___ 9147   ___ 74812   ___ 839427 ___ 7392641 ___ 49521863

    FWD = ____   BWD = ____   Evaluation: ___ L ____ M ___ H

    Spell WORLD ___ FWD _____ BWD   Months of year backward: _____

    Spell EARTH ___ FWD _____ BWD   Concentration evaluation: ___ L ___ M ___ H

    D) Memory:

    30 MINUTE MEMORY CHECK (5 = ___ / 3)   30 = _____ = ____ / 3

    Remote Memory

    Childhood data: ___ Schools attended ___ Teacher's names/faces ____ Street grew up on

    Historical events: Kennedy   ___ Event ___ Activities

                   M L King   ___ Event ___ Activities

                   Space Shuttle Challenger   ___ Event ___ Activities

                   World Trade Center   ___ Event ___ Activities

                   Other: _____

    Recent Memory (Y = Yes N = No V = Vague)

    ___ Activities past few months   ____ Past few days   ____ Past weekend

    ___ Yesterday (events, meals, etc.)   ____ Today (events, meals, etc.)

    ___ Activities of past holiday   ____ Other: _____

    Client's statements re: memory functioning: _____

    Specific examples of memory problems: _____

    _____

    Compared to previous functioning: _____

    _____

Evaluation of memory: _____

Long-term: ___ L ___ M ___ H   Short-term: ___ L ___ M ___ H

Immediate: ___ L ___ M ___ H

E) Information: (knowledge of current events)

Does the client: ____ read newspaper?   How often? _____

                      ____ TV/radio news?   How often? _____

Name current: ___ local ___ national news event: _____

President's name: ____   Past 3 Presidents: ___   3 large cities: ___

F) Abstractive Capacity

Interpretation of various proverbs   Interpretation Given

"Rolling stone gathers no moss": _____

"Early bird catches the worm": _____

"Strike while the iron is hot": _____

"Don't cry over spilled milk": _____

Interpretations: ____ "DK"   ____ Would not try   ____ Abstract

                 ____ Concrete   ____ Age-appropriate   ____ Unusual: _____

G) Judgment

"First one in theatre to see smoke and fire": _____

"Find stamped envelope in street": _____

Any history of problems in judgment? _____

H) Insight (awareness of issues: what level?)

____ Complete denial   ____ Slight awareness

____ Awareness, but blames others   ____ Intellectual insight, but few changes likely

____ Emotional insight, understanding, changes can occur

Client's statement regarding actions needed to get better: _____

_____

Comment on client's level of insight to problems: _____

I) Intellectual Level/Education/IQ Estimate

Education level: Formal: _____   Informal: _____

Military training: _____   Career training: _____

Intelligence: As per client: _____   Observed: _____

General knowledge: _____   School grades: _____

Career background: _____   Estimated IQ: _____

6. Somatoform & Personality Disorders

Somatoform Disorder: 4 pain Sx's:

___ head   ___ abdomen   ___ back   ___ joints   ___ extremities

___ chest   ___ rectum   ___ menstruation ___ sexual intercourse ___ urination

2 gastrointestinal Sx's:

___ nausea   ___ bloating   ___ vomiting   ___ diarrhea   ___ food intolerance

1 pseudoneurological Sx:

___ conversion Sx	___ impaired coordination	___ aphonia
___ urinary retention	___ hallucinations	___ loss of touch or pain sensation
___ double vision	___ blindness	___ deafness
___ seizures	___ dissociative Sx	___ loss of consciousness
___ Other: _____		

History of problem: _____

Primary/secondary gain: _____

Family response: _____

Selective nature of Sx: _____

Observations (pain, fatigue, gait, dizziness): _____

Personality Disorder (Fully describe any evidence of a personality disorder.)

A. Any personality disorder must result in deviation in two or more of the following enduring patterns of inner experience and behavior differing markedly from cultural expectations:

    ___ 1) cognition ___ 2) affectivity ___ 3) interpersonal functioning ___ 4) impulse control

B. The pattern is inflexible across a wide range of experiences.

C. The pattern leads to clinically significant distress or functional impairment.

D. The pattern is stable, long duration and can be traced to at least adolescence or early adulthood.

E. The pattern is not secondary to Axis I.

F. The pattern is not due to a substance or medical condition.

Cluster A

Paranoid (4+)	Schizoid (4+)	Schizotypal (5+)
____ Suspicious	____ Undesirous of friendships	____ Ideas of reference
____ Unjustified distrust	____ Solitary activities	____ Odd beliefs
____ Reluctant to confide	____ Low sexual interest	____ Unusual perceptions
____ Hidden meanings	____ Few pleasures	____ Odd thinking/speech
____ Grudges, unforgiving	____ Lacks close friends	____ Suspicious/paranoid ideation
____ Perceived character attacks	____ Indifferent to praise/criticism	____ Inappropriate/constricted affect
____ Sexual suspicions of partner	____ Emotional coldness/detachment	____ Odd appearance/behavior
		____ Lacks close friends
		____ Excessive social anxiety which does not diminish with familiarity

Cluster B

Antisocial (3+ since age 15)

____ Unlawful behaviors

____ Deceitfulness

____ Impulsivity

____ Irritability: aggressiveness, fights

____ Disregard for safety; self/others

____ Irresponsibility

____ Lack of remorse

____ Is at least 18 years old

Borderline (5+)

____ High efforts to avoid abandonment

____ Unstable intense relationships

____ Unstable identity/self-image

____ Impulsivity (2+ areas)

____ Recurrent suicidal behaviors

____ Affective instability

____ Chronic feeling of emptiness

____ Inappropriate, intense anger

____ Stress related paranoid ideations or severe dissociative symptoms

Histrionic (5+)

____ Needs center of attention

____ Interacts seductively

____ Shifting, shallow emotions

____ Appearance to draw attn.

____ Speech: impressionistic, but lacks detail

____ Self-dramatization

____ Easily suggestible

____ Considers relationships as more important than they are

Narcissistic (5+)

____ Grandiose sense of self-importance

____ Preoccupied with fantasies of success, power

____ "Special" and understood only by similar people

____ Requires excessive admiration

____ Sense of entitlement

(Narcissistic con't)

____ Interpersonally exploitive

____ Lacks empathy

____ Often envious or believes others envious of him/her

____ Arrogant, hauty

Cluster C

Avoidant (4+)

____ Avoids occupational activities due to fear of criticism

____ Unwilling to get involved unless certain of being liked

____ Restraint in personal relationships due to fear of ridicule

____ Preoccupied with being criticized or rejected in social situations

____ Inhibited in new situations

____ Views self as socially inept/ inferior

____ Reluctant to take risks due to embarrassment

Dependent (5+)

____Difficulty with decisions

____ Excessive advice seeking

____ Needs others to assume responsibility in major areas

____ Difficulty expressing disagreement

____ Difficulty initiating projects

____ Excessively seeks nuturance and support from others

____ Feels uncomfortable when alone

OCD (4+)

____ Preoccupied with details, lists, order

____ Perfectionism interferes with task completion

____ Excessive devotion to work

____ Overconscientious, inflexible about morality

____ Unable to discard items

____ Reluctant to delegate tasks

____ Miserly spending, hoarding

____ Rigidity, stubbornness

_____

_____

_____

_____

Additional information provided by client: _____

_____

Signs of malingering: _____

_____

8. **Assessment**

Summary and Diagnostic Findings (Tie together history and mental status findings and relate to diagnosis. Include onset of current Sx of the condition and how far back it goes. Include evaluation of presenting problem vs. stated limitations vs. signs and symptoms. Include prognosis. Integrate collateral information.)

This psychologist's confidence in the exam findings is ___ Poor ___ Average ___ High

. . . test findings is ___ Poor ___ Average ___ High

The claimant's ability to understand, retain, and follow instructions is

___ Poor ___ Average ___ High

Axis I   1: _____

             2: _____

             3: _____

Axis II   1: _____

             2: _____

Axis III   _____

Axis IV Current Stressors: _____

Axis V Current GAF = _____   Highest past year GAF = _____

9. **Capacity Statement**

Based on your findings:

1) ___ P ___ L ___ M ___ G ___ E   The client's ability to concentrate on and understand directions,

2) ___ P ___ L ___ M ___ G ___ E   Carry out tasks with reasonable persistence and pace,

3) ___ P ___ L ___ M ___ G ___ E   Respond appropriately to ____ co-workers, and ____ supervisors, and

4) ___ P ___ L ___ M ___ G ___ E   Tolerate the stresses in the workplace.

Prognosis: _____ Poor ___ Marginal ___ Guarded ___ Moderate ___ Good ___ Excellent

Qualifiers to prognosis:

___ Med compliance   ___ Tx compliance   ___ Home environment

___ Activity changes   ___ Behavioral changes   ___ Attitudinal changes

___ Education/training   ___ Other: _____

Comments: _____

_____

_____

_____

_____

Form 29A   Psychological Evaluation—Adult   (*Completed*)

Client's name: _George Wallington_

Phone (home): _123-8976_   ID#: _100405WD_   Date: _10/4/2005_

Address: _3579 Eddington Court_   City: _Standford_   State: _CA_ Zip: _12345_

Transportation to interview: _Car_   _X_ Alone ____ With others   _X_ Drove ____ Driven

Collateral information by: _None_   Relationship: _____

Physical Description

Identification given: _State drivers license_   Race: _Caucasian_   Gender: ___ F _X_ M

Age: _43_   Height: _5-11_   Weight: _195_   Eyes: _Brown_   Hair: _Brown_

Clothing: _Clean, casual_   Hygiene: _Normal_   Other: _Wore glasses_

History

1. **Signs and Symptoms** Client's statement of problem and impairments (e.g., social, occupational, affective, cognitive, memory, physical)

Symptoms or disability(ies)	Resulting impairment(s)
Increase anxiety in social situations, poor concentration, difficulty coping in new situations.	_Occupational: fired from job he held for 12 years due to excessive errors. Missed work 50% of time due to anxious mood._
	Social: Avoiding most people due to emerging panic symptoms. Will not go in crowds.

   As seen by professional: _Appeared confused and anxious. Some stuttering and word finding problems._

2. **History of Present Illness**

   Events or incidents leading to need for services/benefits: _Auto accident on 3/8/2004. Closed head injury left side. Since then increased symptoms. No previous history of similar impairments._

   Family Hx of Sx's: _Negative_

   Onset/Frequency/Duration/Intensity/Cycling of symptoms: _Gradual development of anxiety since auto accident. Immediate concerns in concentration. Panic symptoms since returning to work, lasting 30 minutes, moderate severity._

   Was there a clear time when Sx's worsened? _Upon retuning to work on 7/7/2004_

   Previous diagnosis (include by whom): _None_

   Course of illness: ____ Improving ____ Stable _X_ Deteriorating ____ Varies

   Current status of past diagnoses? _No previous mental health issues_

   Precipitating factors/events (e.g., emotional, environmental, social): _Any new situation or crowds of people increase anxiety and confusion._

E = Employment   V= Volunteering

Currently: ___ Yes _X_ No   Hours: _____   (Describe below. Include longest position)

	Positions	Dates	FT/PT/Temp	Problems?	Reason left
_X_ E ___ V	_Computer programmer_	_6/91–9/04_	_FT_	_None until end_	_Terminated_
_X_ E ___ V	_Computer programmer_	_5/79–6/91_	_FT_	_None_	_New position_

Usual length of employment: ___ _12 years_ ___   Usual reason(s) for leaving: ___ _Advance in career_ ___

Usual reasons for missing work or leaving early: _____   Frequency: _____

Military: _X_ N ___ Y   Dates: _____   Branch: _____

Highest rank: _____   Discharge: _____

Problems in military: _____

Medications C = Current   P = Previous   (attempt to obtain at least 5 years history)

1. ___ C ___ P   Name: ___ _None_ ___   Purpose: _____
   Dr. _____ of _____
   Dose: ___ mg X ___ /day   Dates: _____   Compliance: _____
   Last taken: _____   Effectiveness: _____
   Side effects: _____   Effect without the med: _____

2. ___ C ___ P   Name: _____   Purpose: _____
   Dr. _____ of _____
   Dose: ___ mg X ___ /day   Dates: _____   Compliance: _____
   Last taken: _____   Effectiveness: _____
   Side effects: _____   Effect without the med: _____

3. ___ C ___ P   Name: _____   Purpose: _____
   Dr. _____ of _____
   Dose: ___ mg X ___ /day   Dates: _____   Compliance: _____
   Last taken: _____   Effectiveness: _____
   Side effects: _____   Effect without the med: _____

4. ___ C ___ P   Name: _____   Purpose: _____
   Dr. _____ of _____
   Dose: ___ mg X ___ /day   Dates: _____   Compliance: _____
   Last taken: _____   Effectiveness: _____
   Side effects: _____   Effect without the med: _____

Mental Health Treatment History ___ Currently in Tx   (attempt to obtain at least 5 years history)

Dates	Purpose	In/Out pt.	Response to Tx	Professional
_____	_No history_	___ I ___ O	_____	
_____	_____	___ I ___ O	_____	

___ Check if continued on back

History of suicidality (___ ideations, ___ threats, ___ gestures, ___ plan, ___ attempts): ___ _No_ ___

Physical Health Treatment History   (attempt to obtain at least 5 years history)

Primary physician: _Betty Relberg_ of _Unity_ since _1988_ frequency _as needed_

Dates	Purpose	In/Out pt.	Response to Tx	Professional
_3/8/03–5/7/03_	_Closed head injury_	_X_ I ___ O	_Marginal_	_Jolder_
5/03 present	_Occup. therapy 2x/wk_	___ I _X_ O	_Gradual increases_	_Denlan_

___ Check if continued on back

Current special services (___ social, ___ educational, ___ legal, ___ physical): ___ _No_ ___

Note and resolve any discrepancies between stated information and records: ___ _No_ ___

BEGIN 5/30 MINUTE MEMORY CHECK

Current Level of Daily Functioning

1. **Current Hobbies, Interests and Activities**

Hobby/interest (How persistently is it followed?)	Frequency	Duration
Fishing _relaxing—as per weather_	_1x/week_	_2–3 hrs_
Yard work _enjoyable, finds something to do_	_daily_	_1 hr_
Crossword puzzles (as per MD) "boring"	_daily_	_1/2 hr_

Realistic, appropriate, compare to previous functioning: _Realistic during time of recovery_
but significantly lower than pre-morbid functioning.

2. **Activities**

___ Rent _X_ Own: _X_ house ___ apartment ___ townhouse ___ duplex

___ condo ___ mobile home ___ other: _____

Who else lives there? (relationships, ages): _Spouse, 2 daughters (4, 12), 1 son (10)_

What kind of things do you usually make for:	Frequency	Problems
Breakfast: _Cereal, toast_	_daily_	_no_
Lunch: _Sandwich_	_daily_	_no_
Dinner: _Heat up leftovers in microwave_	_1–2x/wk_	_no_

Physical challenges in bathing/grooming? _No_   Need reminders? _No_

Daily Schedule (Include chores, shopping, meals, meds, yard work, repairs, hobbies, employment, school. In time order, in and out of the house. What the client can do independently. Note persistence, pace.)

Time	Activity
_7:00_	_Get up, hygiene, bath, dressed, children off to school, spouse to work_
_8:00_	_Make breakfast independently_
_9:00_	_Go for walk, about 1/2 mile_
_10:00_	_Look at newspaper, difficulty reading/concentrating—must often reread_
_10:30_	_Crossword puzzles, very difficult to concentrate_
_11:00_	_Yard work—good job if well known task_
_12:00_	_Lunch independently_
_1:00_	_Nap (or therapy 2x/week, drives 1/2 mile)_
_3:30_	_Children home from school, watch TV_
_5:00_	_Spouse home from work, sometimes help her with dishes_
_6:00_	_TV with family_
_8:00_	_Sit on porch_
_10:00_	_Watch news "confusing"_
_11:00_	_Bed—wake up 2–3x/night. Before accident, woke up 0–1x/night._

4.18

5 MINUTE MEMORY CHECK   *"Car"*   = _1 / 3_

Activities performed in the home (e.g., write letters, crafts, physical exercise, gardening, house repairs, cooking, drawing, painting, take care of pets, lifting, sewing, auto repairs, reading)

Activity	Frequency	Duration	Effects	Independent
Physical exercise	*daily*	*1/2 hr*	*"feel less stiff"*	*yes*
Reading	*daily*	*1/2–1 hr*	*confusing*	*yes*
Lite chores	*3–4x/week*	*1 hr*	*ok, if well known*	*sometimes*
Crossword puzzles	*daily*	*1/2 hr*	*confusing*	*yes*

Activities outside the home (e.g., movies, eat out, meetings, dancing, go for walks, shopping, hunting, fishing, sports, bars, biking, bowling, volunteering, clubs, organizations, religious services, AA, classes, babysitting, travel)

Activity	Frequency	Duration	Effects	Independent
Go for walk	*daily*	*1/2–1 hr*	*relaxing if alone*	*yes*
Fishing	*1x/wk*	*2–3 hrs*	*relaxing if alone*	*yes*

Ability to focus/concentrate on these activities (in and out of house): ___*If the task is simple he does well. If new or complex, very anxiety provoking.*___

When Sx's increase how are these followed? ___*Poorly*___

_X_ Drive   ___ Run errands   ___ Use public transportation (___ bus, ___ taxi)

_X_ Go shopping? How often? _Rarely_   Problems? _Anxiety_   Independently? _X_ N ___ Y

_X_ Walk places? How far? _1/2 mile_   How often? _daily_   Other: _____

How do you financially care for basic needs? ___*Disability income*___

Who pays the bills? ___*Spouse*___   Who handles the finances? ___*Spouse*___

_X_ Savings account   _X_ Checking account   ___ Money orders

_X_ Others pay/write checks   _X_ Figure change

3. Living Situation

Living conditions: (_X_ family, ___ alone, ___ group home; ___ crowded, ___ dysfunctional; ability to follow rules/procedures)

___*Supportive family, difficult for spouse to take on increased responsibilities*___

4. Ability to Relate to Others (e.g., ___ aggressive, ___ dependent, ___ defiant, ___ avoidant, ___ oppositional, ___ normal)

_____

Adults: ___*Avoids*___	Authority figures: ___+___
Peers: ___+___	Police: ___+___
Family: ___+___	Children: ___+___
Neighbors: ___*Neutral*___	Other: _____

Have best friend? ___*Yes, lifelong*___   Group of friends? ___*Yes, little recent contact*___

Activities with friends (include frequency, duration, and problems): ___*Currently some phone calls. Previously saw friends regularly, went to sporting events.*___

How well did client relate (examiner, office personnel) during office visit? ___*Anxious, cooperative.*___

5. Substance Abuse (if applicable)

Detailed history and current information regarding substance abuse patterns.

Last drink and/or use of drugs: ___*"last night"*___

Age of onset: __*16*__   Substances used historically: __*Beer, vodka*__

History of usage: ___*Teenager, occasional usage due to peer pressure, Increased usage in*___ ___*college, especially at exam time. During a few times of unemployment has noted periods of*___ ___*drunkenness to escape guilt feelings. Recently "a slight buzz" has helped him "feel more*___ ___*sociable." Increased use of alcohol three months after accident. "I must drink if I go out in*___ ___*public." Drinks when his family is not home. Usually able to hide his drinking. No desire*___ ___*to quit.*___

	A	B	C
Current substances used:	*Vodka*	*Beer*	*(No illegal*
Level of usage (how much?):	*Up to 3 fifths/wk*	*12 pk/wk*	*substances)*
Frequency (how often?):	*Daily*	*Daily*	
Duration (length of episodes):	*2–3 hours*	*2–3 hours*	

Effects on functioning (impact on activities, interests, ability to relate, persistence/pace): *Notes* ___*effects in positive terms such as "less nervous."*___

Reason(s) for usage: ___ taste _X_ escape ___ self-medicate ___ addiction ___ other: _____

___ Weekdays? What time(s) of day? ___*When family is not home*___

___ Weekends? What time(s) of day? _____

_X_ Alone _X_ Home ___ With others ___ Bars ___ Other: _____

How often do you drink to the point of intoxication (or get high) in a given week? *1x/week*

How many binges in a given year? ___*0*___   Frequency/duration of binges? ___*0*___

Describe treatment history and medical/social consequences of the abuse (e.g., DWIs, DTs and tremors, blackouts, job loss, divorce, etc.): ___*No negative consequences to date, but has*___ ___*increasing desire/need to drink. Beginning to feel physical need for alcohol, especially on*___ ___*weekends, or when with his family in social situations.*___

Level of functioning when not drinking or using drugs (e.g., during periods of sobriety or Tx): ___*Increased anxiety*___

6. History of Arrests/Incarcerations

_____*No*_____

Mental Status Exam

1. Clinical Observations (Entire page: Leave blank if normal. Check and comment if remarkable.)

Appearance

___ Appears age, +/-	___ Grooming	___ Hair	___ Odor
___ Posture	___ Health	___ Nails	___ Demeanor

___*Normal physical appearance*___

Activity Level

___ Mannerisms	___ Gestures	___ Alert	___ Lethargic	___ Limp
_X_ Rigid	___ Relaxed	___ Combative	___ Hyperactive	___ Bored
___ Gait	___ Eye contact	___ Distracted	___ Preoccupied	___ Vigilance

Somewhat rigid and agitated _____

_____

Speech

_X_ Vocabulary	_X_ Details	___ Volume
___ Pace	_X_ Reaction time	___ Pitch
_X_ Pressured	___ Hesitant	___ Monotonous
___ Slurred	_X_ Stuttering	___ Mumbled
___Echolalia	___ Neologisms	___ Repetitions
___ Pronunciation	___ % Understood: _100_	

When anxious he began to stutter at times. Delayed reaction time some issues in word
finding. Brief sentences.

Attitude Toward Examiner

_X_ Attentive	___ Distracted	___ Cooperative	___ Friendly	___ Interested
___ Frank	___ Hostile	___ Defiant	___ Guarded	___ Defensive
___ Evasive	___ Hesitant	___ Manipulative	___ Humorous	___ Historian +/-

Attention span dwindled at times. Initially anxious, but as rapport developed he seemed
more relaxed.

2. **Stream of Consciousness**

Speech

___ Spontaneous	___ Inhibited	___ Blocked	___ Illogical	___ Vague
___ Pressured	___ Slowed	___ Disorganized	___ Rambling	___ Derailment
___ Coherent	___ Cause/effect	___ Neologisms		

Thinking

___ Relevant	___ Coherent	___ Goal directed	___ Loose & Rambling

Thought Processes

___ Number of ideas	___ Flight of ideas	___ Hesitance

All within normal limits _____

3. **Thought Content**

Preoccupations

___ Obsessions	___ Compulsions	___ Phobias	___ Homicide	___ Antisocial

Suicidal, Current

___ Threats	___ Ideas	___ Plan

History

___ Attempts	___ Threats	___ Ideas

Hallucinations

___ Voices	___ Visions	___ Content	___ Setting	___ Sensory system

Illusions: _____

Delusions

___ Persecutory	___ Somatic	___ Grandeur

Ideas of Reference

___ Controlled	___ Broadcasting	___ Antisocial	___ Validity
___ Content	___ Mood	___ Bizarre	

No evidence of thought disorder _____

4. Affect/Mood

Affective Observations

Range	___ Normal	___ Expansive	_X_ Restricted	___ Blunted	___ Flat
Appropriateness	_X_ Concordant		___ Discordant (with speech/ideas)		
Mobility	___ Normal	_X_ Decreased (constricted, fixed)	___ Increased (labile)		
Intensity	___ Normal	_X_ Mild	___ Strong		
Psychomotor	_X_ Normal	___ Retardation	___ Agitation		
Predominant mood	_X_ Neutral	___ Euthymic	___ Dysphoric	___ Euphoric	___ Manic
Level of anxiety	___ Normal	_X_ High (describe): _body/facial expression_			
Irritability	_X_ Normal	___ High (describe): _____			
Anger expression	_X_ Normal	___ High (describe): _____			

Mood (Rule in and rule out signs and symptoms)

Frequency/Intensity in Daily Life (Give specific examples or impairments/strengths, frequency, duration.)

Clearly Validate with *DSM-IV* Criteria

Affection toward others: ___ _Family only_ _____

Anger: ___ anger mng't issues   ___ property destruction
___ explosive behaviors   ___ assaultive behaviors

How does the client act on anger?

Onset: _____   Frequency: _____

Duration: _____   Severity: _____

Examples: ___ _No anger management problems._ _____

_____

Panic Attacks: 4+, Abrupt development of:

_X_ palpitations	_X_ sweating	___ trembling
_X_ shortness of breath	___ feeling of choking	___ chest pain
___ nausea	___ dizziness	___ light-headed
___ derealization	___ fear of losing control	___ fear of dying
___ numbness	___ chills	___ hot flashes

___ Other: _Increasing symptoms since returning to work after accident._ _____

_____

Onset: ___ _2–3 months ago_ ___   Frequency: ___ _2x/wk_ ___
Duration: ___ _5–30 min_ ___   Severity: ___ _Mild/moderate_ ___

Anxiety: GAD: 3+, most of time, 6 months:

___ restlessness	___ easily fatigued	___ concentration
___ irritability	___ muscle tension	___ sleep disturbance

___ Other: _Anxious only in unfamiliar situations (since head injury). No pre-morbid history_
___ _of anxiety problems._ _____

Onset: _____   Frequency: _____
Duration: _____   Severity: _____

Depression: MDE: 2+ wks, 5+:

___ usually depressed   ___ anhedonia

___ wght +/- 5%/month   ___ appetite +/-

___ sleep +/-   ___ fatigue

___ psychomotor +/-   ___ worthlessness/guilt

___ concentration   ___ other: ___ crying spells   ___ withdrawal

___ death/suicidal ideation

___ Other: _Denies clinical depression. Did not appear depressed._ _____

_____

Onset: _____   Frequency: _____

Duration: _____   Severity: _____

Dysthymia: ___ depressed most of time   ___ onset; adult 2+ child/adolescent 1+ yrs, 2+ of:

___ +/- appetite or eating   ___ in/hypersomnia   ___ low energy/fatigue

___ low self-esteem   ___ low concentration/decisions   ___ hopelessness

___ Other: _Denies_ _____

_____

Onset: _____   Frequency: _____

Duration: _____   Severity: _____

Mania: 3+:

___ grandiosity   ___ low sleep   ___ talkative   ___ flight of ideas

___ distractibility   ___ goals/agitation   ___ excessive pleasure

___ Other: _Denies_ _____

_____

Onset: _____   Frequency: _____

Duration: _____   Severity: _____

PTSD: Traumatic event with intense response: 1+:

Distressing:

___ recollections   ___ dreams   ___ reliving

___ cues   ___ physiological reactivity with cues

3+:

___ avoid thoughts   ___ avoid environmental   ___ poor recall of events

___ low interest   ___ detachment   ___ restricted range of affect

___ foreshortened future

2+:

___ sleep   ___ anger   ___ concentration

___ hypervigilance   ___ startle response

___ Other: _Denies_ _____

_____

Onset: _____   Frequency: _____

Duration: _____   Severity: _____

5. Sensorium/Cognition

A) Reality Contact (How in touch with reality is the client?): _Normal range_

Able to hold normal conversation? _X_ Yes ___ No   Notes: _____

B) Orientation X3: _X_ Time _X_ Place _X_ Person   Notes: _x 3_____

C) Concentration:

Attention to tasks/conversation; distractability: _Asked to have a few questions repeated_

Count to 40 by 3s beginning at 1.

(_X_ 1, _X_ 4, _X_ 7, _11_, 10, _14_, 13, _18_, 16, _22_, 19, _25_, 22, _29_, 25, _32_, 28,
_36_, 31, _39_, 34, _43_, 37, _46_, 40)

Number of errors: _6_   Time between digits: _6–10 sec_   Other: _____

Count backward by 7s.

(_X_ 100, _X_ 93, _84_, 86, _78_, 79, _70_, 72, _63_, 65, _59_, 58, _50_, 51, _43_, 44, _36_, 37,
___, 30, ___, 23, ___, 16, ___, 9, ___, 2)   _Gave up after 37_

Number of errors: _20_   Time between digits: _15+ sec_   Other: _Very difficult for him_

5 + 8 = _13_   7 x 4 = _28_   12 x 6 = _72_   65/5 = _(15)_   Timing: _Slow_

Digits forward and backward (Average adult: FWD = 5–7 BWD = 4–6)

FWD: _X_ 42   _X_ 318   _X_ 6385   _no_ 96725   ___ 864972   ___ 5739481   ___ 31749852

BWD: _X_ 75   _X_ 582   _no_ 9147   ___ 74812   ___ 839427   ___ 7392641   ___ 49521863

FWD = _4_   BWD = _3_   Evaluation: _X_ L ___ M ___ H

Spell WORLD _X_ FWD   _DLORW_ BWD   Months of year backward: _____No_____

Spell EARTH _X_ FWD   _HTARE_ BWD   Concentration evaluation: _X_ L ___ M ___ H

D) Memory:

30 MINUTE MEMORY CHECK (5 = _1_ / 3)   30 = _"Car"_____ = _1_ / 3

Remote Memory

Childhood data: _X_ Schools attended   _X_ Teacher's names/faces   _X_ Street grew up on

Historical events: Kennedy   _X_ Event _X_ Activities

M L King   _X_ Event _X_ Activities

Space Shuttle Challenger   _X_ Event _X_ Activities

World Trade Center   ___ Event ___ Activities

Other: _____

Recent Memory (Y = Yes   N = No   V = Vague)

___ Activities past few months   _V_ Past few days   _N_ Past weekend

___ Yesterday (events, meals, etc.)   _V_ Today (events, meals, etc.)

_N_ Activities of past holiday   ___ Other: _____

Client's statements re: memory functioning: _"Poor . . . frustrating"_

Specific examples of memory problems: _(1) Must make lists or will forget what tasks to do_
during day. (2) Hard to learn new things.

Compared to previous functioning: _Previously no memory issues, did well on challenging_
job, learned well.

Evaluation of memory: ___*Long term intact, problems with short-term and immediate*___

Long-term: ___ L __*X*__ M ___ H   Short-term: _*X*_ L ___ M ___ H

Immediate: _*X*_ L ___ M ___ H

E) Information: (knowledge of current events)

Does the client: _*X*_ read newspaper?   How often? ___*Sundays 1/2 hr*___

  _*X*_ TV/radio news?   How often? ___*Daily news on TV*___

Name current: _*X*_ local _*X*_ national news event: ___*Vague "politics, weather, crime"*___

President's name: _*X*_   Past 3 Presidents: _*No*_   3 large cities: _*Ok*_

F) Abstractive Capacity

Interpretation of various proverbs   Interpretation Given

"Rolling stone gathers no moss":   ___*"Keep busy"*___

"Early bird catches the worm":   ___*"First one up gets the best"*___

"Strike while the iron is hot":   ___*"Go for it"*___

"Don't cry over spilled milk":   _____

Interpretations: ___ "DK"   ___ Would not try   _*X*_ Abstract

          ___ Concrete   _*X*_ Age-appropriate   ___ Unusual: _____

G) Judgment

"First one in theatre to see smoke and fire":   ___*"Get out then yell fire"*___

"Find stamped envelope in street": ___*"Mail"*___

Any history of problems in judgment? _*No*_

H) Insight (awareness of issues: what level?)

___ Complete denial   ___ Slight awareness

___ Awareness, but blames others   _*X*_ Intellectual insight, but few changes likely

___ Emotional insight, understanding, changes can occur

Client's statement regarding actions needed to get better: ___*"Stay in therapy." "Get out more."*___

Comment on client's level of insight to problems: ___*Adequate*___

I) Intellectual Level/Education/IQ Estimate

Education level: Formal: ___*16 yrs B.A.*___   Informal: ___*Course work*___

Military training: ___*No*___   Career training: _____

Intelligence: As per client: _*Above average (history)*_   Observed: _____

General knowledge: _____   School grades: ___*"Above average"*___

Career background: ___*Computer programming*___   Estimated IQ: ___*110*___

6. Somatoform & Personality Disorders

Somatoform Disorder: 4 pain Sx's:

___ head   ___ abdomen   ___ back   ___ joints   ___ extremities

___ chest   ___ rectum   ___ menstruation   ___ sexual intercourse   ___ urination

2 gastrointestinal Sx's:

___ nausea   ___ bloating   ___ vomiting   ___ diarrhea   ___ food intolerance

1 pseudoneurological Sx:

___ conversion Sx	___ impaired coordination	___ aphonia
___ urinary retention	___ hallucinations	___ loss of touch or pain sensation
___ double vision	___ blindness	___ deafness
___ seizures	___ dissociative Sx	___ loss of consciousness
___ Other: _____		

History of problem: ___*Denies symptoms—History of good health*_____

_____

Primary/secondary gain: _____

_____

Family response: _____

_____

Selective nature of Sx: _____

_____

Observations (pain, fatigue, gait, dizziness): _____

_____

Personality Disorder (Fully describe any evidence of a personality disorder.)

A. Any personality disorder must result in deviation in two or more of the following enduring patterns of inner experience and behavior differing markedly from cultural expectations:

___ 1) cognition ___ 2) affectivity ___ 3) interpersonal functioning ___ 4) impulse control

B. The pattern is inflexible across a wide range of experiences.

C. The pattern leads to clinically significant distress or functional impairment.

D. The pattern is stable, long duration and can be traced to at least adolescence or early adulthood.

E. The pattern is not secondary to Axis I. _____

F. The pattern is not due to a substance or medical condition.

Cluster A

Paranoid (4+)	Schizoid (4+)	Schizotypal (5+)
___Suspicious	___Undesirous of friendships	___ Ideas of reference
___ Unjustified distrust	___ Solitary activities	___ Odd beliefs
___ Reluctant to confide	___ Low sexual interest	___ Unusual perceptions
___ Hidden meanings	___ Few pleasures	___ Odd thinking/speech
___ Grudges, unforgiving	___ Lacks close friends	___ Suspicious/paranoid ideation
___ Perceived character attacks	___ Indifferent to praise/criticism	___ Inappropriate/constricted affect
___ Sexual suspicions of partner	___ Emotional coldness/detachment	___ Odd appearance/behavior
		___ Lacks close friends
		___ Excessive social anxiety which does not diminish with familiarity

Cluster B

Antisocial (3+ since age 15)

____ Unlawful behaviors

____ Deceitfulness

____ Impulsivity

____ Irritability: aggressiveness, fights

____ Disregard for safety; self/others

____ Irresponsibility

____ Lack of remorse

____ Is at least 18 years old

Borderline (5+)

____ High efforts to avoid abandonment

____ Unstable intense relationships

____ Unstable identity/self-image

____ Impulsivity (2+ areas)

____ Recurrent suicidal behaviors

____ Affective instability

____ Chronic feeling of emptiness

____ Inappropriate, intense anger

____ Stress related paranoid ideations or severe dissociative symptoms

Histrionic (5+)

____ Needs center of attention

____ Interacts seductively

____ Shifting, shallow emotions

____ Appearance to draw attn.

____ Speech: impressionistic, but lacks detail

____ Self-dramatization

____ Easily suggestible

____ Considers relationships as more important than they are

Narcissistic (5+)

____ Grandiose sense of self-importance

____ Preoccupied with fantasies of success, power

____ "Special" and understood only by similar people

____ Requires excessive admiration

____ Sense of entitlement

(Narcissistic con't)

____ Interpersonally exploitive

____ Lacks empathy

____ Often envious or believes others envious of him/her

____ Arrogant, hauty

Cluster C

Avoidant (4+)

____ Avoids occupational activities due to fear of criticism

____ Unwilling to get involved unless certain of being liked

____ Restraint in personal relationships due to fear of ridicule

____ Preoccupied with being criticized or rejected in social situations

____ Inhibited in new situations

____ Views self as socially inept/ inferior

____ Reluctant to take risks due to embarrassment

Dependent (5+)

____ Difficulty with decisions

____ Excessive advice seeking

____ Needs others to assume responsibility in major areas

____ Difficulty expressing disagreement

____ Difficulty initiating projects

____ Excessively seeks nurturance and support from others

____ Feels uncomfortable when alone

OCD (4+)

____ Preoccupied with details, lists, order

____ Perfectionism interferes with task completion

____ Excessive devotion to work

____ Overconscientious, inflexible about morality

____ Unable to discard items

____ Reluctant to delegate tasks

____ Miserly spending, hoarding

____ Rigidity, stubbornness

No evidence of Personality Disorder _____

_____

_____

_____

Additional information provided by client: ___*None*___

___*Testing: See protocol: WAIS-IV: average*___

Signs of malingering: ___*No*___

___

8. Assessment

Summary and Diagnostic Findings (Tie together history and mental status findings and relate to diagnosis. Include onset of current Sx of the condition and how far back it goes. Include evaluation of presenting problem vs. stated limitations vs. signs and symptoms. Include prognosis. Integrate collateral information.)

This psychologist's confidence in the exam findings is ___ Poor ___ Average _*X*_ High

...test findings is ___ Poor ___ Average _*X*_ High

The claimant's ability to understand, retain, and follow instructions is

_*X*_ Poor ___ Average ___ High

Axis I   1: ___*294.0 amnestic Disorder due to closed head injury*___

2: ___*300.22 Panic attacks w/agoraphobia*___

3: ___*303.9 Alcohol dependence, early onset, Hx of above*___

Axis II   1: ___*799.9 No Dx*___

2: _____

Axis III   ___*Defer to physician*___

Axis IV Current Stressors: ___*Unemployment, social problems, changes in home functioning.*___

Axis V Current GAF = ___*50*___   Highest past year GAF = ___*80*___

9. Capacity Statement

Based on your findings:

1) ___ P _*X*_ L ___ M ___ G ___ E   The client's ability to concentrate on and understand directions,

2) ___ P _*X*_ L ___ M ___ G ___ E   Carry out tasks with reasonable persistence and pace,

3) ___ P _*X*_ L ___ M ___ G ___ E   Respond appropriately to ___ co-workers, and ___ supervisors, and

4) ___ P _*X*_ L ___ M ___ G ___ E   Tolerate the stresses in the workplace.

Prognosis: ___ Poor ___ Marginal _*X*_ Guarded ___ Moderate ___ Good ___ Excellent

Qualifiers to prognosis:

___ Med compliance   _*X*_ Tx compliance   ___ Home environment

___ Activity changes   ___ Behavioral changes   ___ Attitudinal changes

_*X*_ Education/training   ___ Other: _____

Comments: ___*Suggest: (1) med evaluation; (2) group therapy for those with closed head injuries.*___

Form 30 Psychological Evaluation—Children and Adolescents

Client's name: _____

Phone (home): _____ ID#: _____ Date: _____

Address: _____ City: _____ State: _____ Zip: _____

Collateral information by: _____ Relationship: _____

Physical Description

Identification given: _____ Race: _____ Gender: ____ F ____ M

Age: _____ Height: _____ Weight: _____ Eyes: _____ Hair: _____

Clothing: _____ Hygiene: _____ Other: _____

History

1. **Signs and Symptoms** Client's/Caregiver's statement of problems and impairments (e.g., social, academic, affective, cognitive, memory, physical)

    Symptoms or disability(ies)   Resulting impairment(s)

    _____   _____

    _____   _____

    _____   _____

    _____   _____

    _____   _____

    _____   _____

2. **History of Present Illness**

    Events or incidents leading to disabilities: _____

    _____

    _____

    Family Hx of Sx's: _____

    Onset of impairment: _____

    Was there a clear time when Sx's worsened? _____

    Previous diagnosis (by whom): _____

    Course of illness: ____ Improving ____ Stable ____ Deteriorating ____ Varies

    Current status of past diagnoses? _____

    Frequency/Duration/Intensity/Cycling of symptoms: _____

    _____

    Precipitating factors (environmental, social): _____

    _____

    Currently working/volunteering? ____ Y ____ N If Yes, describe: _____

    _____

    Previous employment/school/volunteering/other activities: _____

    _____

Medications   C = Current   P = Previous   (attempt to obtain at least 5 years history)

1. ____ C ____ P   Name: _____   Purpose: _____
   Dr. _____ of _____
   Dose: ___ mg X ____ /day   Dates: _____   Compliance: _____
   Last taken: _____   Effectiveness: _____
   Side effects: _____   Effect without the med: _____

2. ____ C ____ P   Name: _____   Purpose: _____
   Dr. _____ of _____
   Dose: ___ mg X ____ /day   Dates: _____   Compliance: _____
   Last taken: _____   Effectiveness: _____
   Side effects: _____   Effect without the med: _____

3. ____ C ____ P   Name: _____   Purpose: _____
   Dr. _____ of _____
   Dose: ___ mg X ____ /day   Dates: _____   Compliance: _____
   Last taken: _____   Effectiveness: _____
   Side effects: _____   Effect without the med: _____

4. ___ C ____ P   Name: _____   Purpose: _____
   Dr. _____ of _____
   Dose: ___ mg X ____ /day   Dates: _____   Compliance: _____
   Last taken: _____   Effectiveness: _____
   Side effects: _____   Effect without the med: _____

Mental Health Treatment History _____ Currently in Tx   (attempt to obtain at least 5 years history)

Dates	Purpose	In/Out pt.	Response to Tx	Professional
_____	_____	___ I ___ O	_____	_____
_____	_____	___ I ___ O	_____	_____
_____	_____	___ I ___ O	_____	_____

___ Check if continued on back

History of suicidality (___ ideations, ___ threats, ___ gestures, ___ plans, ___ attempts): _____
_____

Physical Health Treatment History   (attempt to obtain at least 5 years history)

Primary physician: _____ of _____ since _____ frequency _____

Dates	Purpose	In/Out pt.	Response to Tx	Professional
_____	_____	___ I ___ O	_____	_____
_____	_____	___ I ___ O	_____	_____
_____	_____	___ I ___ O	_____	_____

___ Check if continued on back

Current special services (___ social, ___ educational, ___ legal, ___ physical): _____
_____

Note and resolve any discrepancies between stated information and records: _____
_____

Current Level of Daily Functioning

1. Current Hobbies, Interests and Activities

Hobby/interest (How persistently is it followed?)   Frequency   Duration

_____   _____   _____

_____   _____   _____

_____   _____   _____

_____   _____   _____

Realistic, appropriate, compare to previous functioning: _____

_____

2. Activities

___ Rent   ___ Own: ___ house   ___ apartment   ___ townhouse   ___ duplex

                      ___ condo   ___ mobile home   ___ other: _____

Who else lives there? (relationships, ages): _____

_____

What kind of things do you usually eat for: Frequency   Problems

Breakfast: _____   _____   _____

Lunch: _____   _____   _____

Dinner: _____   _____   _____

Physical challenges in bathing/grooming? _____   Need reminders? _____

Daily Schedule (Include chores, shopping, meals, meds, yard work, repairs, hobbies, employment, school. In time order, in and out of the house. What the client can do independently. Note persistence, pace, problems.)

Time   Activity

_____   _____

_____   _____

_____   _____

_____   _____

_____   _____

_____   _____

_____   _____

_____   _____

_____   _____

_____   _____

_____   _____

_____   _____

_____   _____

_____   _____

_____   _____

_____   _____

_____   _____

5 MINUTE MEMORY CHECK _____ = ___ / 3

Activities performed in the home (e.g., write letters, crafts, physical exercise, gardening, house repairs, cooking, drawing, painting, take care of pets, lifting, sewing, auto repairs, reading)

Activity	Frequency	Duration	Effects	Independent
_____	_____	_____	_____	_____
_____	_____	_____	_____	_____
_____	_____	_____	_____	_____

Activities outside the home (e.g., movies, eat out, meetings, dancing, go for walks, shopping, hunting, fishing, sports, bars, biking, bowling, volunteering, religious services, AA, classes, babysitting, travel)

Activity	Frequency	Duration	Effects	Independent
_____	_____	_____	_____	_____
_____	_____	_____	_____	_____
_____	_____	_____	_____	_____

Ability to focus/concentrate on these activities (in and out of house): _____

When Sx's increase how are these followed? _____

___ Drive   ___ Run errands   ___ Use public transportation (___ bus, ___ taxi)

___ Go shopping? How often? _____   Problems? _____   Independently? ___ N ___ Y

___ Walk places? How far? _____   How often? _____   Other: _____

How do you financially care for basic needs? _____

Who pays the bills? _____   Who handles the finances? _____

___ Savings account   ___ Checking account   ___ Money orders

___ Others pay/write checks   ___ Figure change

3. Living Situation

Living conditions: (___ family, ___ alone, ___ group home; ___ crowded, ___ dysfunctional; ability to follow rules/procedures)

_____

4. Ability to Relate to Others (e.g., _____ aggressive, ___ dependent, ___ defiant, ___ avoidant, ___ oppositional, ___ normal)

_____

Adults: _____   Authority figures: _____

Peers: _____   Police: _____

Family: _____   Children: _____

Neighbors: _____   Other: _____

Have best friend? _____   Group of friends? _____

Activities with friends (include frequency, duration, and problems): _____

How well did client relate (examiner, office personnel) during office visit? _____

_____

5. **Substance Abuse** (if applicable)

   Detailed history and current information regarding substance abuse patterns.

   Age of onset: _____   Substances used historically: _____

   History of usage: _____

   _____

   _____

6. **Self-help Skills** (Describe child's ability and assistance needed in the following)

   Dressing: _____

   Grooming: _____

   Feeding self: _____

   Avoiding dangers: _____

   Independent activities outside the home: _____

   Making change($): _____

   Taking the bus: _____

7. **Concentration, Persistence and Pace** (age 3–18)

   (Describe ability to concentrate, attend, persist and complete tasks in a timely manner.)

   _____

   _____

   _____

Development

Pregnancy: _____   Adverse factors? _____

Delivery: _____   On time? _____

Early development: _____

Walked: _____   Talked: _____   Toilet trained: _____

(Provide specific information on how the child's symptoms impact performance of age appropriate developmental tasks and functional capacity.)

Age Group of Child (fill in appropriate age group)

A. Birth to 3 Years

Locomotion (e.g., crawling, walking, sitting up, pulling oneself into an upright position, etc.):

_____

_____

Language (e.g., vocalization, imitative sounds, talking, receptive skills, ability to follow commands, etc.): _____

_____

_____

Gross motor competence (e.g., reaching, throwing, jumping, grasping, pedaling a tricycle, etc.):

_____

_____

Fine motor competence (pincer grip, grasp, colors, uses pencils, reaches for objects, etc.):

_____

_____

Behavioral/social (e.g., excessive crying, hyperactivity, fear response to separation, aggressiveness, temper outbursts, lethargic, inability to bond, autistic features, efforts at toilet training, ability to relate to peers, siblings, parents, etc.): _____

_____

_____

B. 3 to 6 Years

Locomotion (describe any abnormalities as listed above, describe development of competency):

_____

_____

Communications (speech development, ability to form sentences, clarity of speech, expressive skills, receptive skills, ability to communicate needs, ability to respond to commands, ability to follow simple directions): _____

_____

_____

Motor (describe any abnormalities in fine or gross motor activity, can child use scissors, color within lines, copy simple designs [circle, square]. Include observations of any impairments in coordination and/or balance): _____

_____

_____

Social/emotional (toilet training, aggressiveness, hyperactivity, ability to play with others, to share with others, to separate from caregivers, competency in feeding, dressing and grooming skills, temper outbursts, night terrors, manifestations of anxiety, phobias, fear response to separation, observations of bizarre or aberrant behavior): _____

_____

_____

Ability to concentrate, attend, persist, and complete tasks in a timely manner: _____

_____

_____

C. 6 to 16 Years

Locomotion (describe any abnormalities in walking, running, mobility): _____

_____

_____

Communication (reading, writing receptive and expressive language skills, speech): _____

_____

_____

Motor skills (coordination, balance, perceptual motor skills, complex-integrated motor responses):

_____

_____

Ability to concentrate, attend, persist, and complete tasks in a timely manner: _____

_____

_____

D. 16 to 18 Years

Locomotion (describe any abnormalities in mobility): _____

_____

_____

Communications (any abnormalities noted): _____

_____

_____

Social/emotional (relationships to peer group, to school authority figures). Any evidence of oppositional, rebellious, antisocial, aggressive behavior, withdrawal. Assess stress tolerance, potential employment, potential for substance abuse, impairment in reality testing. Comment on identity issues and developing of body awareness: _____

_____

_____

Ability to concentrate, attend, persist, and complete tasks in a timely manner: _____

_____

_____

Other (Comment on any volunteer or after school work, vocational training, jobs associated with the school program in terms of work, ability to persist, complete tasks, and respond appropriately to supervision.): _____

_____

_____

Parents or Caregivers Leave Interview Room at This Time

Mental Status Exam

1. **Clinical Observations** (Entire page: Leave blank if normal. Check and comment if remarkable.)

Appearance

| ___ Appears age, +/- | ___ Grooming | ___ Hair | ___ Odor |
| ___ Posture | ___ Health | ___ Nails | ___ Demeanor |

_____

_____

Activity Level

___ Mannerisms	___ Gestures	___ Alert	___ Lethargic	___ Limp
___ Rigid	___ Relaxed	___ Combative	___ Hyperactive	___ Bored
___ Gait	___ Eye contact	___ Distracted	___ Preoccupied	___ Vigilance

_____

_____

Speech

___ Vocabulary   ___ Details   ___ Volume   ___ Pace

___ Reaction time   ___ Pitch   ___ Pressured   ___ Hesitant

___ Monotonous   ___ Slurred   ___ Stuttering   ___ Mumbled

___ Echolalia   ___ Neologisms   ___ Repetitions   ___ Pronunciation

___ % Understood: _____

_____

_____

Attitude Toward Examiner

___ Attentive   ___ Distracted   ___ Cooperative   ___ Friendly   ___ Interested

___ Frank   ___ Hostile   ___ Defiant   ___ Guarded   ___ Defensive

___ Evasive   ___ Hesitant   ___ Manipulative   ___ Humorous   ___ Historian +/-

_____

_____

2. **Stream of Consciousness**

Re: Speech:

___ Spontaneous   ___ Inhibited   ___ Blocked   ___ Illogical

___ Vague   ___ Pressured   ___ Slowed   ___ Disorganized

___ Rambling   ___ Derailment   ___ Coherent   ___ Cause/effect

___ Neologisms

Re: Thinking:

___ Relevant   ___ Coherent   ___ Goal directed   ___ Loose & rambling

Re: Thought processes:

___ Number of ideas   ___ Flight of ideas   ___ Hesitance

_____

_____

3. **Thought Content**

Preoccupations:

___ Obsessions   ___ Compulsions   ___ Phobias   ___ Homicide   ___ Antisocial

Suicidal:

Current: ___ Ideations   ___ Threats   ___ Gestures   ___ Plan   ___ Attempts

History: ___ Ideations   ___ Threats   ___ Gestures   ___ Plan   ___ Attempts

Hallucinations:

___ Voices   ___ Visions   ___ Content   ___ Setting   ___ Sensory system

Illusions: _____

Delusions:

___ Persecutory   ___ Somatic   ___ Grandeur

Ideas of reference:

___ Controlled   ___ Broadcasting   ___ Antisocial   ___ Validity

___ Content   ___ Mood   ___ Bizarre

_____

_____

4. Affect/Mood

Affective Observations

Range	___ Normal	___ Expansive	___ Restricted	___ Blunted	___ Flat
Appropriateness	___ Concordant		___ Discordant (with speech/ideas)		
Mobility	___ Normal	___ Decreased (constricted, fixed)	___ Increased (labile)		
Intensity	___ Normal	___ Mild	___ Strong		
Psychomotor	___ Normal	___ Retardation	___ Agitation		
Predominant mood	___ Neutral	___ Euthymic	___ Dysphoric	___ Euphoric	___ Manic
Level of anxiety	___ Normal	___ High (describe): _____ _____			
Irritability	___ Normal	___ High (describe): _____			
Anger expression	___ Normal	___ High (describe): _____			

Mood (Rule in and rule out signs and symptoms)

Frequency/Intensity in Daily Life (Give specific examples of impairments/strengths, frequency, duration.)

Clearly Validate with *DSM-IV* Criteria

Affection toward others: _____

Anger: ___ anger mng't issues   ___ property destruction

        ___ explosive behaviors   ___ assaultive behaviors

How does the client act on anger?

Onset: _____   Frequency: _____

Duration: _____   Severity: _____

Examples: _____

_____

Panic Attacks: 4+, Abrupt development of:

___ palpitations	___ sweating	___ trembling
___ shortness of breath	___ feeling of choking	___ chest pain
___ nausea	___ dizziness	___ light-headed
___ derealization	___ fear of losing control	___ fear of dying
___ numbness	___ chills	___ hot flashes
___ Other: _____		

_____

Onset: _____   Frequency: _____

Duration: _____   Severity: _____

Anxiety: GAD: 3+, most of time, 6 months:

___ restlessness	___ easily fatigued	___ concentration
___ irritability	___ muscle tension	___ sleep disturbance
___ Other: _____		

_____

Onset: _____   Frequency: _____

Duration: _____   Severity: _____

Depression: MDE: 2+ wks, 5+:

___ usually depressed   ___ anhedonia

___ wght +/- 5%/month   ___ appetite +/-

___ sleep +/-   ___ fatigue

___ psychomotor +/-   ___ worthlessness/guilt

___ concentration   ___ other: ___ crying spells   ___ withdrawal

___ death/suicidal ideation

___ Other: _____

_____

Onset: _____   Frequency: _____

Duration: _____   Severity: _____

Dysthymia: ___ depressed most of time   ___ onset; adult 2+ child/adolescent 1+ yrs, 2+ of:

___ +/- appetite or eating   ___ in/hypersomnia   ___ low energy/fatigue

___ low self-esteem   ___ low concentration/decisions   ___ hopelessness

___ Other: _____

_____

Onset: _____   Frequency: _____

Duration: _____   Severity: _____

Mania: 3+:

___ grandiosity   ___ low sleep   ___ talkative   ___ flight of ideas

___ distractibility   ___ goals/agitation   ___ excessive pleasure

___ Other: _____

_____

Onset: _____   Frequency: _____

Duration: _____   Severity: _____

PTSD: Traumatic event with intense response: 1+:

Distressing:

___ recollections   ___ dreams   ___ reliving

___ cues   ___ physiological reactivity with cues

3+:

___ avoid thoughts   ___ avoid environmental   ___ poor recall of events

___ low interest   ___ detachment   ___ restricted range of affect

___ foreshortened future

2+:

___ sleep   ___ anger   ___ concentration

___ hypervigilance   ___ startle response

___ Other: _____

_____

Onset: _____   Frequency: _____

Duration: _____   Severity: _____

ODD: Pattern of negativistic, hostile and defiant behaviors > 6 months: 4+ of the following:

___ loses temper	___ argues with adults
___ actively defies adults' requests	___ deliberately annoys people
___ blames others for own mistakes or misbehavior	___ touchy/easily annoyed
___ angry/resentful	___ spiteful/vindictive

1+ impairment:

___ social   ___ academic   ___ occupational

_____

_____

Conduct: Repetitive/persistent behaviors violating rights of others. 3+ (past 12 month, 1 in past 6 months)

___ Aggression to people/animals:

___ bullies, threatens, intimidates	___ initiates physical fights
___ has used harmful weapon	___ physically cruel to: ___ people ___ animals
___ stolen while confronting victim	___ forces sexual activity

Destruction of property:

___ deliberate fire setting (intended damage)   ___ deliberate property destruction

Deceitfulness or theft:

___ broken into someone's property   ___ often lies/cons   ___ has stolen without confrontation

Serious violation of rules:

___ stays out at night against parents' rules before age 13

___ has run away 2+ or one extended   ___ often truant before age 13

1+ impairment:

___ social   ___ academic   ___ occupational

_____

_____

ADHD: Inattention; 6+ Sx, 6+ months:

___ poor attn/careless mistakes	___ difficult sustaining attn.	___ forgetful
___ not listen when spoken to	___ not follow through	
___ loses things	___ easily distracted	

___ difficulty organizing, avoids tasks requiring sustained mental effort

AND/OR Hyperactivity/impulsivity, 6+, Hyperactivity:

___ fidgety	___ leaves seat often	___ runs/climbs
___ difficult being quiet	___ "on the go"	___ talks excessively

Impulsivity:

___ blurts out answers	___ difficulty awaiting turn	___ interrupts

___ Some Sx < age 7. 1+ impairment:

___ social   ___ academic   ___ occupational

_____

_____

Attention Span During Interview

___ Fidgety   ___ Remained seated   ___ Distracted

___ Blurted answers   ___ Followed directions   ___ Shifted focus

___ Talked excessively   ___ Interrupted   ___ Listened

___ Impulsivity   ___ Understood questions   ___ Attended to questions

___ Other: _____

Rule Out Clinical Syndromes

Pervasive developmental disorders, autistic disorders, specific developmental disabilities, learning disorders, incipient psychotic process, etc.: _____

_____

_____

_____

5. **Sensorium/Cognition**

   Younger Children (Provide a basic assessment of the following):

   A) **Consciousness** (ability to concentrate, confusion, attending): _____

   _____

   B) **Orientation:** ___ Time ___ Place ___ Person Notes: _____

   _____

   C) **Memory** (recent, long-term, simple facts): _____

   _____

   D) **Estimated Intellectual Functioning:** _____

   _____

   Older Children:

   A) **Reality Contact** (How in touch with reality is client?): _____

   Able to hold normal conversation? ___ Yes ___ No Notes: _____

   B) **Orientation X3:** ___ Time ___ Place ___ Person Notes:_____

   C) **Concentration** (age-appropriate measures):

   Count by 1s: _____   Count by 2s: _____   Count by 3s: _____

   Errors: ___ Time: _____   Errors: _____ Time: _____   Errors: ____ Time: _____

   Count to 40 by 3s beginning at 1.

   (___ 1, ___ 4, ___ 7, ___, 10, ___, 13, ___, 16, ___, 19, ___, 22, ___, 25, ___, 28, ___, 31, ___, 34, ___, 37, ___, 40)

   Number of errors: _____   Time between digits: _____   Other: _____

   Count backward by 7s from 100.

   (100, 93, 86, 79, 72, 65, 58, 51, 44, 37, 30, 23, 16, 9, 2.)   Errors: ___ Time: _____

   $1 + 2 =$ ___ $2 + 3 =$ ___ $3 - 2 =$ ___ $4 + 8 =$ ___

   $9 + 12 =$ ___ $2 \times 3 =$ ___ $4 \times 4 =$ ___ $7 \times 4 =$ ___

   $12 \times 6 =$ ___ $65/5 =$ ___

Digits forward and backward (for ages 6+)

FWD: ___ 42 ___ 394 ___ 6385 ___ 96725 ___ 864972 ___ 5739481 ___ 31749852

BWD: ___ 73 ___ 582 ___ 9147 ___ 74812 ___ 839427 ___ 7392641 ___ 49521863

FWD = ___ BWD = ___   Evaluation: ___ Below average ___ Average ___ Above average

Spell words: WORLD   ___ FWD ___ BWD

                STOP   ___ FWD ___ BWD

                CAT   ___ FWD ___ BWD

D) Memory

Remote Memory

Childhood data: ___ Schools attended ___ Teacher's names/faces ___ Events of past holiday
                 ___ Street grew up on ___ Mother's maiden name

Recent Memory

___ Activities past few months   ___ Past few days   ___ Activities past weekend

___ Yesterday (events, meals, etc.) ___ Today (events, meals, etc.)

___ Phone number   ___ Address

30 MINUTE MEMORY CHECK (5 = ___ / 3)   30 = _____ = ____ / 3

Client's statements re: memory functioning: _____

Long-term: ___ L ___ M ___ H   Short-term: ___ L ___ M ___ H

Immediate: ___ L ___ M ___ H

E) Information: (knowledge of current events)

Does the client: ___ read newspaper?   How often? _____

                    ___ TV/radio news?   How often? _____

Name current local/national news: _____   President's name: _____   3 large cities: ____

F) Judgment

"Find someone's purse in store": _____

"First one in theatre to see smoke and fire": _____

G) Abstractive Capacity

Interpretation of various proverbs   Interpretation Given

"Early bird catches the worm":   _____

"Strike while the iron is hot":   _____

"Don't cry over spilled milk":   _____

Interpretations: ___ "DK"   ___ Would not try   ___ Abstract
                 ___ Concrete   ___ Age-appropriate   ___ Unusual: _____

H) Insight (awareness of issues: what level?)

___ Complete denial   ___ Slight awareness

___ Awareness, but blames others   ___ Intellectual insight, but few changes likely

___ Emotional insight, understanding, changes can occur

Client's statement regarding actions needed to get better: _____

_____

Comment on client's level of insight to problems: _____

I) Intellectual Level/Education/IQ Estimate

Grade in school: ___   Ever repeat a grade? ___   Grades/Progress: _____

Special education classes: _____   Estimated IQ: _____

General knowledge: _____   Selective nature of Sx: _____

J) Adverse Factors Affecting the Child's Ability to Function

(e.g., pain, side effects of meds, dysfunctional family, abuse, physical impairments, teasing, etc.)

_____

_____

_____

_____

Additional comments by caregiver of child: _____

_____

_____

_____

_____

6. Assessment

Summary and Diagnostic Findings (Tie together history and mental status findings and relate to diagnosis. Include onset of current Sx of the condition and how far back it goes. Include evaluation of presenting problem vs. stated limitations vs. signs and symptoms. Include prognosis. Integrate collateral information.)

This psychologist's confidence in the exam findings is ___ Poor ___ Average ___ High

. . . test findings is ___ Poor ___ Average ___ High

The claimant's ability to understand, retain, and follow instructions is

___ Poor ___ Average ___ High

Axis I   1: _____

            2: _____

            3: _____

Axis II   1: _____

            2: _____

Axis III Defer to physician

Axis IV Current Stressors: _____

Axis V Current GAF = _____   Highest past year GAF = _____

Prognosis: ____ Poor ___ Marginal ___ Guarded ___ Moderate ___ Good ____ Excellent

Qualifiers to prognosis:

___ Med compliance   ___ Tx compliance   ___ Home environment

___ Activity changes   ___ Behavioral changes   ___ Attitudinal changes

___ Education/training   ___ Other: _____

Form 30A   Psychological Evaluation—Children and Adolescents   (*Completed*)

Client's name: _Christine Watters_

Phone (home): _555-0001_   ID#: _040605WC_   Date: _4/6/2005_

Address: _595959 5th Ave_   City: _Moline_   State: _MD_   Zip: _26118_

Collateral information by: _Lisa Watters_   Relationship: _Mother_

Physical Description

Identification given: _None_   Race: _Afr.-Am._   Gender: _X_ F   ___ M

Age: _6y-1m_   Height: _4-4_   Weight: _64_   Eyes: _Br_   Hair: _Bl_

Clothing: _Clean, school clothes_   Hygiene: _Normal_   Other: _____

History

1. **Signs and Symptoms** Client's/Caregiver's statement of problems and impairments (e.g., social, academic, affective, cognitive, memory, physical)

Symptoms or disability(ies)	Resulting impairment(s)
Low attention span, disruptive in school,	_Academic: 3 failing grades this term, often_
poor academic performance, needs	_disrupts entire class. School is considering_
constant reminders to stay on task.	_(EBD) special education for emotion/_
	behavioral disturbance. Social: few/no
	friends due to disruptive behaviors. Often
	teased by classmates for immaturity.

2. **History of Present Illness**

   Events or incidents leading to disabilities: _Parents noticed hyperactivity at age 3. Several comments from pre-school teachers re: "not focusing" and "always on the go." Parents thought she would "grow out of it."_

   Family Hx of Sx's: _Father was hyperactive as child. Older sister diagnosed with ADHD._

   Onset of impairment: _Noticed at age 3, but continued increases in symptoms._

   Was there a clear time when Sx's worsened? _Beginning of kindergarten: structure._

   Previous diagnosis (by whom): _None–no previous evaluations._

   Course of illness: ___ Improving   ___ Stable   _X_ Deteriorating   ___ Varies

   Current status of past diagnoses? _N/A_

   Frequency/Duration/Intensity/Cycling of symptoms: _Parents describe hyperactivity as "constant." They call her "the tornado."_

   Precipitating factors (environmental, social): _When not receiving 1-1 attention._

   Currently working/volunteering? ___ Y   _X_ N   If Yes, describe: _____

   Previous employment/school/volunteering/other activities: _None_

Medications   C = Current   P = Previous   (attempt to obtain at least 5 years history)

1. ____ C ____ P   Name: _____*None*_____   Purpose: _____
   Dr. _____ of _____
   Dose: ___ mg X ___ /day   Dates: _____   Compliance: _____
   Last taken: _____   Effectiveness: _____
   Side effects: _____   Effect without the med: _____

2. ____ C ____ P   Name: _____   Purpose: _____
   Dr. _____ of _____
   Dose: ___ mg X ___ /day   Dates: _____   Compliance: _____
   Last taken: _____   Effectiveness: _____
   Side effects: _____   Effect without the med: _____

3. ____ C ____ P   Name: _____   Purpose: _____
   Dr. _____ of _____
   Dose: ___ mg X ___ /day   Dates: _____   Compliance: _____
   Last taken: _____   Effectiveness: _____
   Side effects: _____   Effect without the med: _____

4. ___ C ____ P   Name: _____   Purpose: _____
   Dr. _____ of _____
   Dose: ___ mg X ___ /day   Dates: _____   Compliance: _____
   Last taken: _____   Effectiveness: _____
   Side effects: _____   Effect without the med: _____

Mental Health Treatment History _____ Currently in Tx   (attempt to obtain at least 5 years history)

Dates	Purpose	In/Out pt.	Response to Tx	Professional
_____	*No history*	___ I ___ O	_____	_____
_____	_____	___ I ___ O	_____	_____
_____	_____	___ I ___ O	_____	_____

____ Check if continued on back

History of suicidality (___ ideations, ___ threats, ___ gestures, ___ plans, ___ attempts): _*No*_
_____

Physical Health Treatment History   (attempt to obtain at least 5 years history)

Primary physician: _*Jill Hill, MD*_ of _*Candon*_ since _*Birth*_ frequency _*as needed*_

Dates	Purpose	In/Out pt.	Response to Tx	Professional
_____	*No significant Hx*	___ I ___ O	_____	_____
_____	*"good health"*	___ I ___ O	_____	_____
_____	_____	___ I ___ O	_____	_____

____ Check if continued on back

Current special services (___ social, ___ educational, ___ legal, ___ physical): _*None, school is*_
*considering EBD classes.*

Note and resolve any discrepancies between stated information and records: _*None*_
_____

BEGIN 5/30 MINUTE MEMORY CHECK

Current Level of Daily Functioning

1. **Current Hobbies, Interests and Activities**

Hobby/interest (How persistently is it followed?)	Frequency	Duration
Coloring	*daily*	*5–10 min intervals*
TV/video games	*daily*	*1–2 hours*
Play outdoors	*daily*	*1–2 hours*
	weekends	*varies*

Realistic, appropriate, compare to previous functioning: _*Normal range of behaviors.*_

2. **Activities**

_X_ Rent ___ Own: _X_ house ___ apartment ___ townhouse ___ duplex

___ condo ___ mobile home ___ other: _____

Who else lives there? (relationships, ages): _*Both biological parents; 1 sister (10);*_ _*1 brother (4)*_

What kind of things do you usually eat for:	Frequency	Problems
Breakfast: *Cereal*	*daily*	*no*
Lunch: *Soup-sandwiches*	*daily*	*sometimes*
Dinner: *Meat-potatoes-veg*	*daily*	*picky eater*

Physical challenges in bathing/grooming? _*No*_ Need reminders? _*Age appropriate*_

Daily Schedule (Include chores, shopping, meals, meds, yard work, repairs, hobbies, employment, school. In time order, in and out of the house. What the client can do independently. Note persistence, pace, problems.)

Time	Activity
	Typical school day as follows
6:30	*Get up, dress independently (with several prompts-prefers to play) Mother prompts her to get ready for school. Hygiene independently.*
7:45	*Catch school bus–walk 1 block with sister to bus stop*
8:15	*School, 1st grade. Mainstream classes. Breakfast and lunch at school. Increasing disruptive behaviors in school (see attached school incident reports)*
3:30	*Home changes clothes independently. Usually no homework given. Plays outside if weather is good, otherwise TV or video games. Usually with "best friend." Usually get along. Supposed to clean room before dinner. (Several prompts given) Often forgets to clean parts of room.*
5:30	*Dinner with family. Eats very quickly. Can't sit still.*
6:00	*Play outside. Sometimes goes to park with friend.*
7:30	*Home. TV. Mother says she's always "on the go" in the house. Hard to settle her down.*
9:00	*Gets ready for bed, may take 1–2 hours to fall asleep "playing with sister" in game room. Wakes up 1–2x/night. Toilet trained. No nightmares.*

4.45

5 MINUTE MEMORY CHECK   *"House-Car"*   = _2_ / 3

Activities performed in the home (e.g., write letters, crafts, physical exercise, gardening, house repairs, cooking, drawing, painting, take care of pets, lifting, sewing, auto repairs, reading)

Activity	Frequency	Duration	Effects	Independent
Coloring	daily	varies		yes
TV/videos	daily	1–2 hrs	attends if enjoyable	yes

Activities outside the home (e.g., movies, eat out, meetings, dancing, go for walks, shopping, hunting, fishing, sports, bars, biking, bowling, volunteering, religious services, AA, classes, babysitting, travel)

Activity	Frequency	Duration	Effects	Independent
Play in park	3–4x/wk	1 hr	calming	no
Sunday School	23x/m	1 hr	disruptive	N/A
	2–3x/m			

Ability to focus/concentrate on these activities (in and out of house): _If she is interested in something or receives 1-1 attention she concentrates better._

When Sx's increase how are these followed? _Tunes out everything and "climbs the walls"_

_N_ Drive   Run errands   _N_ Use public transportation (___ bus,   ___ taxi)

_N_ Go shopping? How often? _____   Problems? _____   Independently? ___ N __ Y

_N_ Walk places? How far? _____   How often? _____   Other: _____

How do you financially care for basic needs? _N/A_

Who pays the bills? _____N/A_____   Who handles the finances? _____

___ Savings account   ___ Checking account   ___ Money orders

___ Others pay/write checks   ___ Figure change

3. Living Situation

Living conditions: (_X_ family, ___ alone, ___ group home; ___ crowded, ___dysfunctional; ability to follow rules/procedures)

   Functional home environment—Eventually does most chores.

4. Ability to Relate to Others (e.g., _____ aggressive, ___ dependent, ___ defiant, _____ avoidant, ___ oppositional, ___ normal)

_____

Adults: _____Ignores_____   Authority figures: _____varies_____

Peers: __Teased often in school__   Police: _____

Family: __Normal range of rivalry__   Children: _____varies_____

Neighbors: _____Neutral_____   Other: _____

Have best friend? _____Yes_____   Group of friends? _____No_____

Activities with friends (include frequency, duration, and problems): _Play in park— video games_

How well did client relate (examiner, office personnel) during office visit? _Cooperated, but hyperactive._

5. **Substance Abuse** (if applicable)

Detailed history and current information regarding substance abuse patterns.

Age of onset: _____   Substances used historically: _____

History of usage: _____ *N/A* _____

_____

_____

6. **Self-help Skills** (Describe child's ability and assistance needed in the following)

Dressing: *OK, but needs prompts to begin task*

Grooming: *OK, but needs prompts to begin task*

Feeding self: *OK, picky eater*

Avoiding dangers: *Often runs into street w/o looking. Often gets hurt "playing too hard"*

Independent activities outside the home: *Plays in park only (next to house)*

Making change($): *N/A*

Taking the bus: *School bus only*

7. **Concentration, Persistence and Pace** (age 3–18)

(Describe ability to concentrate, attend, persist and complete tasks in a timely manner.)

Home: mother describes problems at home staying on task due to hyperactivity. Seems to pay attention but has difficulty sitting still. Maintained conversation, but hurried through tasks impulsively.

Development

Pregnancy: *Normal*   Adverse factors? *None known*

Delivery: *Caesarian*   On time? *1 week late*

Early development: *Normal milestones*

Walked: *13m*   Talked: *20m*   Toilet trained: *3 1/2 yr*

(Provide specific information on how the child's symptoms impact performance of age appropriate developmental tasks and functional capacity.)

Age Group of Child (fill in appropriate age group)

A. Birth to 3 Years

Locomotion (e.g., crawling, walking, sitting up, pulling oneself into an upright position, etc.):

N/A

_____

Language (e.g., vocalization, imitative sounds, talking, receptive skills, ability to follow commands, etc.): _____

_____

_____

Gross motor competence (e.g., reaching, throwing, jumping, grasping, pedaling a tricycle, etc.):

_____

_____

Fine motor competence (pincer grip, grasp, colors, uses pencils, reaches for objects, etc.):
_____
_____

Behavioral/social (e.g., excessive crying, hyperactivity, fear response to separation, aggressiveness, temper outbursts, lethargic, inability to bond, autistic features, efforts at toilet training, ability to relate to peers, siblings, parents, etc.): _____
_____
_____

B. 3 to 6 Years

Locomotion (describe any abnormalities as listed above, describe development of competency):
_____ *N/A* _____
_____

Communications (speech development, ability to form sentences, clarity of speech, expressive skills, receptive skills, ability to communicate needs, ability to respond to commands, ability to follow simple directions): _____
_____
_____

Motor (describe any abnormalities in fine or gross motor activity, can child use scissors, color within lines, copy simple designs [circle, square]. Include observations of any impairments in coordination and/or balance): _____
_____
_____

Social/emotional (toilet training, aggressiveness, hyperactivity, ability to play with others, to share with others, to separate from caregivers, competency in feeding, dressing and grooming skills, temper outbursts, night terrors, manifestations of anxiety, phobias, fear response to separation, observations of bizarre or aberrant behavior): _____
_____
_____

Ability to concentrate, attend, persist, and complete tasks in a timely manner: _____
_____
_____

C. 6 to 16 Years

Locomotion (describe any abnormalities in walking, running, mobility): _____*Normal range*_____
_____
_____

Communication (reading, writing receptive and expressive language skills, speech): _____
_____*Normal range*_____
_____

Motor skills (coordination, balance, perceptual motor skills, complex-integrated motor responses):
_____*Normal range*_____
_____

Ability to concentrate, attend, persist, and complete tasks in a timely manner: _____*OK when*_____ _*interested or with 1-1 adult interaction. Concentration seems to be within normal limits.*_ _*Any concentration issues seem to be secondary to hyperactivity.*_

D. 16 to 18 Years

Locomotion (describe any abnormalities in mobility): _____

_____

Communications (any abnormalities noted): _____

_____

Social/emotional (relationships to peer group, to school authority figures). Any evidence of oppositional, rebellious, antisocial, aggressive behavior, withdrawal. Assess stress tolerance, potential employment, potential for substance abuse, impairment in reality testing. Comment on identity issues and developing of body awareness: _____

_____

Ability to concentrate, attend, persist, and complete tasks in a timely manner: _____

_____

Other (Comment on any volunteer or after school work, vocational training, jobs associated with the school program in terms of work, ability to persist, complete tasks, and respond appropriately to supervision.): _____

_____

Parents or Caregivers Leave Interview Room at This Time

Mental Status Exam

1. **Clinical Observations** (Entire page: Leave blank if normal. Check and comment if remarkable.)

Appearance

| ___ Appears age, +/- | ___ Grooming | ___ Hair | ___ Odor |
| ___ Posture | ___ Health | _X_ Nails | _X_ Demeanor |

Nails bitten very short. Very active.

Activity Level

___ Mannerisms	___ Gestures	___ Alert	___ Lethargic	___ Limp
___ Rigid	___ Relaxed	___ Combative	_X_ Hyperactive	___ Bored
___ Gait	___ Eye contact	___ Distracted	___ Preoccupied	___ Vigilance

Rarely sat still. One time hid under desk. Ran out of room 3x. Agitated when didn't get her own way.

Speech

___ Vocabulary	___ Details	___ Volume	_X_ Pace
___ Reaction time	___ Pitch	___ Pressured	___ Hesitant
___ Monotonous	___ Slurred	___ Stuttering	___ Mumbled
___ Echolalia	___ Neologisms	_X_ Repetitions	___ Pronunciation

___ % Understood: _95–98_

Rapid speech. Often repeated the questions asked.

Attitude Toward Examiner

_X_ Attentive	___ Distracted	___ Cooperative	___ Friendly	___ Interested
___ Frank	___ Hostile	___ Defiant	___ Guarded	___ Defensive
___ Evasive	___ Hesitant	___ Manipulative	___ Humorous	___ Historian +/-

Held attention when interested, otherwise fidgety.

2. Stream of Consciousness

Re: Speech:

___ Spontaneous	___ Inhibited	___ Blocked	___ Illogical
___ Vague	___ Pressured	___ Slowed	___ Disorganized
___ Rambling	___ Derailment	___ Coherent	___ Cause/effect
___ Neologisms			

Re: Thinking:

___ Relevant	___ Coherent	___ Goal directed	___ Loose & rambling

Re: Thought processes:

___ Number of ideas	___ Flight of ideas	___ Hesitance

No issues

3. Thought Content

Preoccupations:

___ Obsessions	___ Compulsions	___ Phobias	___ Homicide	___ Antisocial

Suicidal:

Current: ___ Ideations ___ Threats ___ Gestures ___ Plan ___ Attempts

History: ___ Ideations ___ Threats ___ Gestures ___ Plan ___ Attempts

Hallucinations:

___ Voices	___ Visions	___ Content	___ Setting	___ Sensory system

Illusions: _____

Delusions:

___ Persecutory	___ Somatic	___ Grandeur

Ideas of reference:

___ Controlled	___ Broadcasting	___ Antisocial	___ Validity
___ Content	___ Mood	___ Bizarre	

No issues

4. Affect/Mood

Affective Observations

Range	_X_ Normal	___ Expansive	___ Restricted	___ Blunted	___ Flat
Appropriateness	_X_ Concordant		___ Discordant (with speech/ideas)		
Mobility	_X_ Normal	___ Decreased (constricted, fixed)	___ Increased (labile)		
Intensity	_X_ Normal	___ Mild	___ Strong		
Psychomotor	_X_ Normal	___ Retardation	___ Agitation		
Predominant mood	___ Neutral	_X_ Euthymic	___ Dysphoric	___ Euphoric	___ Manic
Level of anxiety	_X_ Normal	___ High (describe): _body/facial expression_			
Irritability	_X_ Normal	___ High (describe): _____			
Anger expression	_X_ Normal	___ High (describe): _____			

Mood (Rule in and rule out signs and symptoms)

Frequency/Intensity in Daily Life (Give specific examples of impairments/strengths, frequency, duration.)

Clearly Validate with *DSM-IV* Criteria

Affection toward others: ___ _Normal range_ _____

Anger: ___ anger mng't issues   _X_ property destruction

___ explosive behaviors   ___ assaultive behaviors

How does the client act on anger?

Onset: _____ _1st grade_ _____   Frequency: _____ _1x/wk_ _____

Duration: _____ _Brief_ _____   Severity: _____ _Mild_ _____

Examples: ___ _Growing concerns with temper tantrums since 1st grade_ _____

_____

Panic Attacks: 4+, Abrupt development of:

___ palpitations	___ sweating	___ trembling
___ shortness of breath	___ feeling of choking	___ chest pain
___ nausea	___ dizziness	___ light-headed
___ derealization	___ fear of losing control	___ fear of dying
___ numbness	___ chills	___ hot flashes
___ Other: _None_		

_____

Onset: _____   Frequency: _____

Duration: _____   Severity: _____

Anxiety: GAD: 3+, most of time, 6 months:

___ restlessness	___ easily fatigued	___ concentration
___ irritability	___ muscle tension	___ sleep disturbance
___ Other: _Normal range_		

_____

Onset: _____   Frequency: _____

Duration: _____   Severity: _____

Depression: MDE: 2+ wks, 5+:

___ usually depressed   ___ anhedonia

___ wght +/- 5%/month   ___ appetite +/-

___ sleep +/-   ___ fatigue

___ psychomotor +/-   ___ worthlessness/guilt

___ concentration   ___ other: ___ crying spells   ___ withdrawal

___ death/suicidal ideation

___ Other: _Normal range_ _____

_____

Onset: _____   Frequency: _____

Duration: _____   Severity: _____

Dysthymia: ___ depressed most of time   ___ onset; adult 2+ child/adolescent 1+ yrs, 2+ of:

___ +/- appetite or eating   ___ in/hypersomnia   ___ low energy/fatigue

___ low self-esteem   ___ low concentration/decisions   ___ hopelessness

___ Other: _No_ _____

_____

Onset: _____   Frequency: _____

Duration: _____   Severity: _____

Mania: 3+:

___ grandiosity   ___ low sleep   ___ talkative   ___ flight of ideas

___ distractibility   ___ goals/agitation   ___ excessive pleasure

___ Other: _No_ _____

_____

Onset: _____   Frequency: _____

Duration: _____   Severity: _____

PTSD: Traumatic event with intense response: 1+:

Distressing:

___ recollections   ___ dreams   ___ reliving

___ cues   ___ physiological reactivity with cues

3+:

___ avoid thoughts   ___ avoid environmental   ___ poor recall of events

___ low interest   ___ detachment   ___ restricted range of affect

___ foreshortened future

2+:

___ sleep   ___ anger   ___ concentration

___ hypervigilance   ___ startle response

___ Other: _No_ _____

_____

Onset: _____   Frequency: _____

Duration: _____   Severity: _____

ODD: Pattern of negativistic, hostile and defiant behaviors > 6 months: 4+ of the following:

_X_ loses temper   ___ argues with adults

___ actively defies adults' requests   ___ deliberately annoys people

___ blames others for own mistakes or misbehavior   _X_ touchy/easily annoyed

___ angry/resentful   ___ spiteful/vindictive

1+ impairment:

___ social   ___ academic   ___ occupational

Increasing symptoms but not sufficient for diagnosis.

Conduct: Repetitive/persistent behaviors violating rights of others. 3+ (past 12 month, 1 in past 6 months)

___ Aggression to people/animals:

___ bullies, threatens, intimidates   ___ initiates physical fights

___ has used harmful weapon   ___ physically cruel to: ___ people   ___ animals

___ stolen while confronting victim   ___ forces sexual activity

Destruction of property:

___ deliberate fire setting (intended damage)   ___ deliberate property destruction

Deceitfulness or theft:

___ broken into someone's property   ___ often lies/cons   ___ has stolen without confrontation

Serious violation of rules:

___ stays out at night against parents' rules before age 13

___ has run away 2+ or one extended   ___ often truant before age 13

1+ impairment:

___ social   ___ academic   ___ occupational

_No_

ADHD: Inattention; 6+ Sx, 6+ months:

___ poor attn/careless mistakes   ___ difficult sustaining attn.   ___ forgetful

___ not listen when spoken to   _X_ not follow through

___ loses things   _X_ easily distracted

___ difficulty organizing, avoids tasks requiring sustained mental effort

AND/OR Hyperactivity/impulsivity, 6+, Hyperactivity:

_X_ fidgety   _X_ leaves seat often   _X_ runs/climbs

_X_ difficult being quiet   _X_ "on the go"   _X_ talks excessively

Impulsivity:

_X_ blurts out answers   _X_ difficulty awaiting turn   _X_ interrupts

_X_ Some Sx < age 7. 1+ impairment:

_X_ social   _X_ academic   ___ occupational

Attention Span During Interview

_X_ Fidgety   _N_ Remained seated   _X_ Distracted

_X_ Blurted answers   ___ Followed directions   ___ Shifted focus

_X_ Talked excessively   _X_ Interrupted   ___ Listened

_X_ Impulsivity   _X_ Understood questions   ___ Attended to questions

___ Other: _____

Rule Out Clinical Syndromes

Pervasive developmental disorders, autistic disorders, specific developmental disabilities, learning disorders, incipient psychotic process, etc.: _____
    Oher disorders ruled out _____
_____
_____

5. **Sensorium/Cognition**

   Younger Children (Provide a basic assessment of the following):

   A) **Consciousness** (ability to concentrate, confusion, attending): ___ _N/A_ _____
   _____

   B) **Orientation:** ___ Time ___ Place ___ Person   Notes: _____
   _____

   C) **Memory** (recent, long-term, simple facts): _____
   _____

   D) **Estimated Intellectual Functioning:** _____
   _____

   Older Children:

   A) **Reality Contact** (How in touch with reality is client?): ___ _Age-appropriate_ _____

   Able to hold normal conversation? _X_ Yes ___ No   Notes: _____

   B) **Orientation X3:** _X_ Time _X_ Place _X_ Person   Notes: ___ _Age-appropriate_ _____

   C) **Concentration** (age-appropriate measures):

   Count by 1s: ___ _1–20_ ___   Count by 2s: ___ _2–10_ ___   Count by 3s: ___ _No_ ___

   Errors: _0_ Time: _Rapid_   Errors: _0_ Time: _Rapid_   Errors: ___ Time: _____

   Count to 40 by 3s beginning at 1.

   (___ 1, ___ 4, ___ 7, ___, 10, ___, 13, ___, 16, ___, 19, ___, 22, ___, 25, ___, 28, ___, 31, ___, 34, ___, 37, ___, 40)

   Number of errors: ___   Time between digits: _____   Other: _____

   Count backward by 7s from 100.

   (100, 93, 86, 79, 72, 65, 58, 51, 44, 37, 30, 23, 16, 9, 2.)   Errors: ___ Time: _____

   $1 + 2 =$ _3_ $2 + 3 =$ _5_ $3 - 2 =$ _1_ $4 + 8 =$ _12_ (fingers)

   $9 + 12 =$ _No_ $2 \times 3 =$ _No_ $4 \times 4 =$ ___ $7 \times 4 =$ ___

   $12 \times 6 =$ ___ $65/5 =$ ___

Digits forward and backward (for ages 6+)

FWD: _X_ 42 _X_ 394 _X_ 6385 ___ 96725 ___ 864972 ___ 5739481 ___ 31749852

BWD: ___ 73 ___ 582 ___ 9147 ___ 74812 ___ 839427 ___ 7392641 ___ 49521863

FWD = _4_ BWD = _0_   Evaluation: ___ Below average _X_ Average ___ Above average

Spell words: WORLD   _N_ FWD   _N_ BWD

   STOP   _X_ FWD   _N_ BWD

   CAT   _X_ FWD   _X_ BWD

D) Memory

Remote Memory

Childhood data: _X_ Schools attended   _X_ Teacher's names/faces   _X_ Events of past holiday

_X_ Street grew up on _N_ Mother's maiden name

Recent Memory

___ Activities past few months   ___ Past few days   ___ Activities past weekend

___ Yesterday (events, meals, etc.)   ___ Today (events, meals, etc.)

___ Phone number   ___ Address

30 MINUTE MEMORY CHECK (5 = _2_ / 3)   30 = _"House-Car"_   = _2_ / 3

Client's statements re: memory functioning: _____

Long-term: ___ L _X_ M ___ H   Short-term: ___ L _X_ M ___ H

Immediate: ___ L _X_ M ___ H

E) Information: (knowledge of current events)

Does the client: _N_ read newspaper? How often? _____

_N_ TV/radio news? How often? _____

Name current local/national news: _No_   President's name: _No_   3 large cities: _No_

F) Judgment

"Find someone's purse in store": _Give to mother_ _____

"First one in theatre to see smoke and fire": _____

G) Abstractive Capacity

Interpretation of various proverbs   Interpretation Given

"Early bird catches the worm":   _N/A_

"Strike while the iron is hot": _____

"Don't cry over spilled milk": _____

Interpretations: ___ "DK"   ___ Would not try   ___ Abstract

___ Concrete   ___ Age-appropriate   ___ Unusual: _____

H) Insight (awareness of issues: what level?)

___ Complete denial   _X_ Slight awareness

___ Awareness, but blames others   ___ Intellectual insight, but few changes likely

___ Emotional insight, understanding, changes can occur

Client's statement regarding actions needed to get better: _Listen to the teacher more_ ___

_____

Comment on client's level of insight to problems: _Age-appropriate_ _____

I) Intellectual Level/Education/IQ Estimate

Grade in school: _1_ Ever repeat a grade? _No_ Grades/Progress: _S's and I's_

Special education classes: _No_ Estimated IQ: _Avg_

General knowledge: _Avg_ Selective nature of Sx: _____

J) Adverse Factors Affecting the Child's Ability to Function

(e.g., pain, side effects of meds, dysfunctional family, abuse, physical impairments, teasing, etc.)

None known

_____

_____

_____

Additional comments by caregiver of child: _None—Testing WISC-III-Low normal-see profile_

_____

_____

_____

_____

6. Assessment

Summary and Diagnostic Findings (Tie together history and mental status findings and relate to diagnosis. Include onset of current Sx of the condition and how far back it goes. Include evaluation of presenting problem vs. stated limitations vs. signs and symptoms. Include prognosis. Integrate collateral information.)

This psychologist's confidence in the exam findings is

_____ Poor _____ Average _____ High

. . . test findings is

_____ Poor _____ Average _____ High

The claimant's ability to understand, retain, and follow instructions is

_____ Poor _____ Average _____ High

 ว. _____

Axis II 1: _799.9 Deferred_

 2: _____

Axis III Defer to physician

Axis IV Current Stressors: _Social & academic problems_

Axis V Current GAF = _70_ Highest past year GAF = _70_

Prognosis: ___ Poor ___ Marginal ___ Guarded _X_ Moderate ___ Good ___ Excellent

Qualifiers to prognosis:

_X_ Med compliance ___ Tx compliance ___ Home environment

___ Activity changes _X_ Behavioral changes ___ Attitudinal changes

_X_ Education/training ___ Other: _Need med eval_

Chapter 5

Treatment Planning Forms and Procedures

Individual Treatment Plans

Effective treatment plans are designed to provide a clear picture of the client's specific treatment needs. Vague intake information leads to vague treatment plans, which leads to vague treatment, which leads to vague outcomes. No one would sign a contract to have a house built which simply stated, "Build house." The blueprints and contract provide specifications regarding time frame, cost, and outcome. The treatment plan is the blueprint for therapy.

Typical problems in writing treatment plans include making statements that are too vague or generic, not indicative of the assessment, unrealistic, or not assessable, measurable, or observable. Treatment plans must directly correspond to the assessment material (e.g., purpose, impairments, diagnosis, goals). The treatment plan is driven or documented by the assessment. It must clearly reflect a plan to alleviate impairments resulting from the mental disorder. Regulating sources (such as Medicare and the Joint Commission on Accreditation of Healthcare Organizations and most third-party payers) require that treatment plans provide measurable outcomes written in behavioral, objective, or measurable terms.

The process of writing a treatment plan begins with an accurate and specific assessment of the client's concerns. Assessment sources include the clinical interview, testing, observations, historical documents, and collateral information.

The plan should reflect both the client's presenting problem and the client's stated needs and goals, and it should also reflect the clinical judgment of the therapist. Both Medicare and Joint Commission guidelines call for specific measurable treatment outcomes to be attained by the client, not the therapist.

Treatment Plan Formats

Treatment plan formats vary, but the required information is fairly consistent. A three-column format (Problems/Symptoms, Goals/Objectives, and Treatment Strategies) will be used for examples in this book.

Column One, "Problems/Symptoms."   The first column identifies specific problem areas to be addressed in treatment. The stated symptoms must correspond to, and therefore validate, the client's diagnosis and impairments. Symptoms are not vague terms or constructs such as "depression," but rather symptoms of depression that are causing functional impairment. The symptoms listed must validate and be indicative of the Axis I diagnosis.

The listed symptoms, in themselves, should clearly define the diagnosis. If not, then the diagnosis is not clearly being treated. Some mental health professionals update treatment plans regularly (e.g., every 60 days); in such cases it is obviously not possible to address every symptom of a diagnosis. But nevertheless the symptoms addressed should be indicative of the diagnosis. Prolonged treatment of other diagnoses is not justified unless other diagnoses have been given.

Ethical concerns are noted when practitioners bill insurance companies under one diagnosis but treat a different diagnosis. Potential consequences could range from services not being covered to ethical charges.

Column Two, "Goals/Objectives."   The second column lists the client's intended outcomes of treatment, written in measurable, observable, and documentable terms in which the effectiveness of the treatment can be evaluated.

Both goals and objectives are to be listed for each symptom. Goals are defined as overall, global, long-term outcomes. Goals are often the opposite of the symptoms. For example, the goal for a depressed person might be to alleviate depression. It is difficult to measure goals, but they can be broken down into objectives which are observable. Objectives are defined as incremental steps by which goals are attained. They reflect specific improvements in adaptive behaviors resulting in reduction of symptoms. Objectives are revised throughout the course of therapy depending on progress and/or setbacks.

Objectives may be measured in a variety of ways, including successive testing, charting, subjective ratings by the client and/or others, and clinical observations. It is often difficult to write all objectives in measurable, observable, or quantifiable terms, but efforts should be taken to establish a baseline and objective points of comparison. Terms such as "increase" or "decrease" should be clarified with specific quantifiers and qualifiers. For example, an objective of "increase pleasurable social activities to four per week by October 13th" is much more specific and measurable than "increase pleasurable social activities." In the latter example, *any* increase (e.g., .0001 percent) would appear as progress. Specific treatment planning keeps therapy on course. Goals and objectives must be clear in order to be followed.

Column Three, "Strategies."   The third column describes treatment interventions in and out of the sessions by which the treatment goals and objectives will be addressed. Treatment strategies may include the type of therapy (e.g., group, family, individual), school of thought (e.g., cognitive, behavioral, psychoanalytic, Rational Emotive Therapy [RET]), therapeutic techniques (e.g., dream analysis, confrontation, systematic desensitization, role playing), and homework assignments.

Each aspect of the treatment plan requires client collaboration. The client must not only agree on the symptoms, goals and treatment strategies, he or she must also be willing to submit to their integrative process in therapy. The question, "What does the client want to get out of therapy?" is too often ignored. Client/therapist cooperation and collaboration go hand in hand.

Objectives should be written in small, attainable steps. For example, if a socially withdrawn person has a treatment plan objective of initiating five social interactions per week, the likelihood of success may be quite small. But since incremental increases in objective criteria are viewed as more attainable by the client, an initial objective in this case might be to initiate one social interaction per week. The high likelihood of success is in itself rewarding. As an objective is met, new objective criteria are set, up to the point at which impairment is alleviated. Treatment plans are meant to be revised as progress and/or setbacks take place.

Success of a treatment plan also depends on how realistic and achievable the goals are. For example, a treatment plan goal to "eliminate depression" can never be reached since depression is a normal and adaptive human emotion.

Client effort and motivation to fulfill treatment plan objectives merit close attention. The relationship between performance and motivation is curvilinear. That is, low levels or drive lead to low performance because little effort and low reinforcement are perceived. Likewise, high levels of drive generally lead to high levels of anxiety about performance, and thus performance is also low. For example, if a client is suffering from agoraphobia, an objective of going to a shopping mall during the week before Christmas would probably be too anxiety-provoking for any positive performance results. But if the objective is set too low, there might be little or no motivation to change behavior. A moderate amount of drive leads to optimal performance. Discussing specific goals and objectives with the client can certainly help determine the success of a treatment plan and subsequent treatment.

FORM 31
Individual Treatment Plan

FORM 31A—Example of a Poor Treatment Plan

In the example of vague treatment plan statements on page 5.8, entries are neither descriptive, observable, measurable, nor client-specific with respect to functional impairments. No target dates are set. Goals are not broken down into objectives. It is not signed by the client or therapist.

Adult

Judy Doe's treatment plan (Form 31B) is the culmination of the presenting problem, testing, intake questions, clinical observations, and biographical information. During the second session, she and the therapist collaboratively set a course of treatment that met both the professional abilities of the therapist and the therapeutic wants and needs of the client.

The concerns noted in column 1 of the treatment plan serve a variety of functions. First, they validate the diagnosis. Her diagnosis of major depression is validated in her treatment plan for each of the following concerns:

1. Decreased energy level.

2. Low ego strength.

3. Difficulty concentrating.

4. Hopelessness feelings.

5. Diminished pleasure.

6. Social withdrawal.

The goals and objectives are based on, first, alleviation of the symptoms noted in Column 1, and second, on agreed-upon outcomes for Judy Doe to work on in a given time frame. Since not all mental health professionals are competent to treat all clients' concerns, the treatment strategies include referrals to other professionals when necessary. Judy Doe is to receive talk therapy from the psychologist but is referred to her physician for medication and to monitor a physical exercise program.

In this case, the psychologist's training does not permit her to prescribe medications or monitor physical procedures; therefore, a referral is given in these areas. Serious ethical violations may occur when mental health professionals practice outside of their competencies. For example, if a mental health professional were to suggest, or even monitor, a diet or exercise program and the client developed physical problems related to the program, the practitioner could be subject to litigation and possible license revocation.

Child

A treatment plan for children (Form 31C) differs from an adult treatment plan in that the initial sessions are not direct therapy; rather, the initial objectives are to establish a therapeutic relationship, acclimate the child to therapy, and establish rapport and trust. Without these initial sessions the prognosis would be poor.

FORM 32
Short-Term Therapy Treatment Plan

Form 32 depicts a sample treatment plan for short-term therapy in which session content is preplanned according to treatment goals and objectives. It differs from the traditional treatment plans in this book in that it outlines in advance the objectives for each session. Therapy is defined by a set number of sessions in which the focus of each is planned in the initial sessions.

FORM 33
Treatment Review

A Treatment Review (Form 33) is generally used in settings in which care is monitored by a supervisor or review committee. Organizations such as JCAHO require case reviews periodically or when changes are made in areas such as diagnosis, treatment plan, therapist, or an additional evaluation is requested. This document is designed for quality control within the clinic.

As treatment plan goals are met, they should be documented. New goals should be added as needed to best suit the client's needs. Clearly describe the purpose for any changes in treatment, rather than only listing changes. Changes such as progress and setbacks are documented to help assess the effectiveness of treatment.

When the estimated number of sessions to completion of treatment has been reached, but more sessions are needed, it should be clearly documented why more sessions are necessary. In such cases, the treatment plan is being changed. Any information that affects the course of treatment, such as additional life stressors, is documented to justify the changes. Diagnosis changes must be clearly validated according to the *DSM-IV-TR*.

FORM 34
Treatment Update

The Treatment Update (Form 34) does not provide clinical details as in the Treatment Review. Rather, it summarizes the client's current standing in treatment and allows for a response from its recipient. It is communication between the therapist and a third-party. The form is usually used in cases such as when a third party (county social worker, guardian, parent, court, attorney, physician, etc.) has requested periodic summaries of the client's progress, or by others involved as collaterals or supports in therapy. Some clients may benefit from receiving this brief report of progress. A legal release of information is required to share this material in most cases.

Form 31   Individual Treatment Plan

Client's name: _____ DOB: _____ Date _____

Presenting problem: _____ Therapist: _____

Axis I: _____ Axis II: _____

Services Needed

Anticipated Number of Sessions

Treatment	0	1	2	3–5	6–10	11–20	21–40	40+
___ Assessment	___	___	___	___	___	___	___	___
___ Individual	___	___	___	___	___	___	___	___
___ Group	___	___	___	___	___	___	___	___
___ Family	___	___	___	___	___	___	___	___
___ Other	___	___	___	___	___	___	___	___

Problems/Symptoms	GOALS/Objectives	Treatment Strategies

I have discussed the information listed above, various treatment strategies, and their possible outcomes. I have received and/or read my copy of my rights as a client and procedures for reporting grievances. I concur with the above diagnosis and treatment plan.

Client's signature: _____ Date: ____/____/_____

Guardian's signature: _____ Date: ____/____/_____

Therapist's signature: _____ Date: ____/____/_____

Clinical supervisor: _____ Date: ____/____/_____

Client's name: _JD_____   Date: _____

Problems/Symptoms	GOALS/Objectives	Treatment Strategies
Depression	*Eliminate depression*	*Individual therapy and Prozac*
Irritability	*Stop mood swings*	*Therapy*
Sadness	*Increase outlook*	*Counseling*
Conduct	*Stop negative behaviors*	*Discuss feelings*
Anger	*Anger management*	*Listen to tapes*
Budgeting	*Balance budget*	*Marriage counseling*
Marital discord	*Communication skills*	*Talk therapy*

Therapist's signature: _____

Form 31B Individual Treatment Plan—Adult (*Completed*)

Client's name: _Doe, Judy_   DOB: _7/6/1954_   Date _3/15/2005_
Presenting problem: _Depressed mood, irritability_   Therapist: _DLB_
Axis I: _296.32 Major depression, recurrent, moderate_   Axis II: _Deferred_

Services Needed

Anticipated Number of Sessions

Treatment	0	1	2	3–5	6–10	11–20	21–40	40+
_X_ Assessment	___	___	_X_	___	___	___	___	___
_X_ Individual	___	___	___	___	___	_X_	___	___
___ Group	___	___	___	___	___	___	___	___
___ Family	___	___	___	___	___	___	___	___
___ Other	___	___	___	___	___	___	___	___

Problems/Symptoms	GOALS/Objectives	Treatment Strategies
DEPRESSED MOOD Address following symptoms:	Develop plan to alleviate emotional, occupational, and social impairment due to depressed mood. Return to previous functioning levels.	Individual therapy (cognitive behavioral). Med referral. Possible marital therapy. Successive BDIs. Charting.
1. Decreased energy level	INCREASE ENERGY LEVEL Participate in appropriate physical exercise daily	Medical evaluation referral. Physical program approved by physician.
2. Low ego strength	INCREASE EGO STRENGTH Accomplish at least one weekly homework assignment which leads to positive outcomes. Log at least one positive self-statement daily. Verbalize awareness of negative self-beliefs.	Focus on positive qualities. Chart and reinforce progress. Role playing. Logging. Experiencing and sharing feelings in session.
3. Difficulty concentrating	IMPROVE ABILITY TO FOCUS ON THOUGHTS/ACTIVITIES Complete an appropriate lesson plan in 45–60 minutes (as per previous functioning).	Learn strategies to break problems down into components.
4. Hopelessness feelings	RESTRUCTURE DYSFUNCTIONAL THOUGHTS/PROCESSES Chart one future plan daily. Develop insight as to relationship between stressors, anger, and depression.	Analyze dysfunctional thoughts. Keep dysfunctional thought record. Positive outcomes homework.
5. Diminished pleasure	INCREASE PLEASURE IN DAILY ACTIVITIES Increase/maintain selected pleasurable activities to 3x/week.	Incorporate effective time management of pleasurable vs. nonpleasurable activities. Chart and reinforce progress.
6. Social withdrawal	INCREASE SOCIAL INTERACTIONS Increase and maintain at least 2 new social interactions/week.	Role playing. Psychoeducational training. Chart and reinforce progress.

I have discussed the information listed above, various treatment strategies, and their possible outcomes. I have received and/or read my copy of my rights as a client and procedures for reporting grievances. I concur with the above diagnosis and treatment plan.

Client's signature: _Judy Doe_   Date: _3 / 15 / 2005_
Guardian's signature: _____   Date: __ / __ /
Therapist's signature: _Darlene L. Benton, PhD_   Date: _3 / 15 / 2005_
Clinical supervisor: _Sharon Bell, PhD_   Date: _3 / 16 / 2005_

Form 31C Individual Treatment Plan—Children and Adolescents (*Completed*)

Client's name: _Rentschler, Johnny_ DOB: _3/6/1998_ Date _1/29/2005_
Presenting problem: _Anger management, coping, withdrawal_ Therapist: _DLB_
Axis I: _Adjustment reaction/depressed mood and conduct_ Axis II: _None_

Services Needed

Anticipated Number of Sessions

Treatment	0	1	2	3–5	6–10	11–20	21–40	40+
_X_ Assessment	___	___	X	___	___	___	___	___
_X_ Individual	___	___	___	___	___	X	___	___
___ Group	___	___	___	___	___	___	___	___
_X_ Family	___	___	___	___	X	___	___	___
___ Other	___	___	___	___	___	___	___	___

Problems/Symptoms	GOALS/Objectives	Treatment Strategies
Behavioral and affective dysfunctioning since recent divorce of parents.	*Develop plan to alleviate emotional, behavioral, and social impairment, and increase coping skills.*	*Individual play therapy. Collateral sessions with mother. Charting.*
INITIAL CONCERNS *1. Lack of trust*	*INCREASE LEVEL OF TRUST* *Develop nonthreatening therapeutic relationship.* *ENGAGE IN PLAY THERAPY* *Enactment of psychological conflicts in therapy session.*	*Initial sessions incorporating drawings (e.g., draw pictures of family as an expression of affect and to help become comfortable in therapeutic setting). Increasing use of play therapy and rapport- and trust-building strategies.*
SYMPTOMS *2. Anger/behavioral management* • *Recurrent outbursts toward mother* • *Property damage in the home* • *Bullying/hitting younger sister*	*INCREASE ABILITY TO EXPRESS, CLARIFY, AND LABEL ANGER FEELINGS POSITIVELY* *Current: 4–5 daily outbursts toward family.* *3-month objective: 0–2 daily outbursts.* *Current: 0 interactions discussing feelings.* *3-month objective: discuss, label feelings 1/day.*	*Play therapy utilizing safe expression of hostility. Role playing means of appropriately verbalizing related feelings.* *Charting at home with selective reinforcers such as verbal praise.*
3. Difficulties coping with changes in environment resulting in increased stress levels	*Learn socially acceptable means of coping with loss and resultant anger management issues.*	*Play therapy. Psychoeducation. Role playing.*
4. Social withdrawal	*INCREASE TIME SPENT WITH SIGNIFICANT OTHERS, ACTIVITIES, AND RECREATION* *Current hours in above activities: 4/week.* *3-month objective: 20/week.*	*Family assignments encouraging positive social activities. Charting.*

I have discussed the information listed above, various treatment strategies, and their possible outcomes. I have received and/or read my copy of my rights as a client and procedures for reporting grievances. I concur with the above diagnosis and treatment plan.

Client's signature: _____ Date: ___/___/_____
Guardian's signature: _Linda Rentschler_ Date: _1_/_29_/_2005_
Therapist's signature: _Darlene L. Benton, PhD_ Date: _1_/_29_/_2005_
Clinical supervisor: _Sharon Bell, PhD_ Date: _2_/_3_/_2005_

Form 32   Short-Term Therapy Treatment Plan

Client's name: _____ DOB: _____ Date _____

Presenting problem: _____ Therapist: _____

Axis I: _____ Axis II: _____

Services Needed

Anticipated Number of Sessions

Treatment	0	1	2	3–5	6–10	11–20	21–40	40+
___ Assessment	___	___	___	___	___	___	___	___
___ Individual	___	___	___	___	___	___	___	___
___ Group	___	___	___	___	___	___	___	___
___ Family	___	___	___	___	___	___	___	___
___ Other	___	___	___	___	___	___	___	___

Problems/Symptoms   **GOALS/Objectives**   **Treatment Strategies**

Schedule of Topics

Session(s)	Topic(s)	Session(s)	Topic(s)

I have discussed the information listed above, various treatment strategies, and their possible outcomes. I have received and/or read my copy of my rights as a client and procedures for reporting grievances. I concur with the above diagnosis and treatment plan.

Client's signature: _____ Date: _____/_____/_____

Guardian's signature: _____ Date: _____/_____/_____

Therapist's signature: _____ Date: _____/_____/_____

Clinical supervisor: _____ Date: _____/_____/_____

Form 32A   Short-Term Therapy Treatment Plan   (*Completed*)

Client's name: _Roe, Sheila_____   DOB: _6/4/1964_   Date _5/7/2005_____

Presenting problem: _Depressed mood, irritability_____   Therapist: _PS____

Axis I: _300.4 Dysthymic Disorder_____   Axis II: _Deferred_____

Services Needed

Anticipated Number of Sessions

Treatment	0	1	2	3–5	6–10	11–20	21–40	40+
_X_ Assessment	___	___	X	___		___	___	___
_X_ Individual	___	___	___	___	X	___	___	___
___ Group	___	___	___	___		___	___	___
___ Family	___	___	___	___		___	___	___
___ Other	___	___	___	___		___	___	___

Problems/Symptoms	GOALS/Objectives	Treatment Strategies
DEPRESSED MOOD Address following symptoms:	Develop plan to alleviate emotional, occupational, and social impairment due to depressed mood.	Individual therapy (cognitive behavioral). Possible marital therapy. Successive BDIs.
1. Decreased energy level	INCREASE ENERGY LEVEL Participate in increased physical activities.	Medical evaluation referral. Discuss exercise program (M.D. approval).
2. Hopelessness feelings	RESTRUCTURE THOUGHTS TO VIEW FUTURE MORE POSITIVELY Chart one future plan daily.	Analyze dysfunctional thoughts. Keep dysfunctional thought record. Positive outcomes homework.
3. Diminished pleasure	INCREASE PLEASURE IN DAILY ACTIVITIES Increase/maintain selected pleasurable activities to 3x/week.	Incorporate effective time management of pleasurable vs. nonpleasurable activities. Chart progress.
4. Social withdrawal	INCREASE SOCIAL INTERACTIONS Increase/maintain at least 2 new social interactions per week.	Role playing. Psychoeducational training. Chart progress.

Schedule of Topics

Session(s)	Topic(s)	Session(s)	Topic(s)
1	Assessment	5–6	Social withdrawal
2	Treatment planning		Diminished pleasure
3	Diminished pleasure	7	Review progress
4	Hopelessness feelings	8–9	Hopelessness feelings
	Diminished pleasure		Social withdrawal
		10	Closure

I have discussed the information listed above, various treatment strategies, and their possible outcomes. I have received and/or read my copy of my rights as a client and procedures for reporting grievances. I concur with the above diagnosis and treatment plan.

Client's signature: _____Sheila Roe_____   Date: _5_ / _7_ / _2005_

Guardian's signature: _____   Date: ___ / ___ /_____

Therapist's signature: _____Phillip Schultz, MSW_____   Date: _5_ / _7_ / _2005_

Clinical supervisor: _____Sharon Bell, PhD_____   Date: _5_ / _7_ / _2005_

Form 33   Treatment Review

Client's name: _____ DOB: _____ Date: _____

ID no: _____ No. of sessions since last review: _____ Intake date: _____

Initial Diagnosis   **Current Diagnosis**

Axis I   _____   Axis I   _____

          _____   _____

Axis II   _____   Axis II   _____

Axis III _____   Axis III _____

Axis IV   _____   Axis IV   _____

Axis V   _____   Axis V   _____

Purpose of Treatment Review

____ Change in diagnosis   ____ Significant change in treatment plan

____ Estimated length of treatment reached   ____ Change in treatment or therapist

____ Required periodic review   ____ Significant change in functioning level

____ Increased or attempted suicidal concerns   ____ Other: _____

Describe any changes in the client's condition noted above: _____

_____

_____

_____

Progresses: _____

_____

_____

_____

Setbacks/Impairments: _____

_____

_____

What actions are needed at this time?   Describe needed services:

____ Referral   _____

____ Transfer   _____

____ Psychiatric eval _____

____ Psychological eval _____

____ Physical eval   _____

____ Other   _____

5.13

Treatment Plan Review Refer to previous Treatment Plan or Treatment Review

Current Goal 1

Met yet? Target date if not met yet

_____ __ Y __ N _____

Describe current progress toward objectives: _____

_____

_____

Current Goal 2

Met yet? Target date if not met yet

_____ __ Y __ N _____

Describe current progress toward objectives: _____

_____

_____

Current Goal 3

Met yet? Target date if not met yet

_____ __ Y __ N _____

Describe current progress toward objectives: _____

_____

_____

Current Goal 4

Met yet? Target date if not met yet

_____ __ Y __ N _____

Describe current progress toward objectives: _____

_____

_____

New Goal 1

_____ Target date: _____

Problem area: _____

Objectives: _____

_____

Treatment: _____

Services (and frequency) needed: _____

_____

New Goal 2

_____ Target date: _____

Problem area: _____

Objectives: _____

_____

Treatment: _____

Services (and frequency) needed: _____

_____

Therapist: _____ Date: ____/____/_____

Reviewed by: _____ Date: ____/____/_____

Form 33A   Treatment Review   (*Completed*)

Client's name: _William Olden_   DOB: _3/7/1979_   Date: _7/9/2005_

ID no: _OW040498_   No. of sessions since last review: _12_   Intake date: _4/4/2005_

Initial Diagnosis

Axis I   _Oppositional Defiant Disorder_
         Adj Disorder, conduct, Chronic

Axis II   _No diagnosis_

Axis III   _Defer to physician_

Axis IV   _Social, family, academic problems_

Axis V   _58_

Current Diagnosis

Axis I   _Oppositional Definant Disorder_

Axis II   _No diagnosis_

Axis III   _Defer to physician_

Axis IV

Axis V

Purpose of Treatment Review

____ Change in diagnosis

____ Estimated length of treatment reached

_X_ Required periodic review

____ Increased or attempted suicidal concerns

____ Significant change in treatment plan

____ Change in treatment or therapist

____ Significant change in functioning level

____ Other: _____

Describe any changes in the client's condition noted above: _School year ended, is in required_ _summer school. Decreased conduct and defiance._

Progresses: _Catching up in school in summer program. Seldom over 1 or 2 disruptive behaviors_ _in school weekly for past month. Is initiating cooperative behaviors to family and peers._

Setbacks/Impairments: _Continued blaming mother for "ruining my family." Was found sneaking_ _alcohol one time at home. Continued foul language._

What actions are needed at this time?

_X_ Referral

____ Transfer

____ Psychiatric eval

____ Psychological eval

____ Physical eval

____ Other

Describe needed services:

Join summer anger management

group for adolescents

_____

_____

_____

_____

_____

5.15

Treatment Plan Review Refer to previous Treatment Plan or Treatment Review

Current Goal 1   Met yet?   Target date if not met yet
Decrease oppositional behaviors   ___ Y _X_ N   _9/30/2005_

Describe current progress toward objectives: _Has decreased oppositional behaviors at home_
and school by 50%.

Current Goal 2   Met yet?   Target date if not met yet
Initiate and maintain one peer friendship   _X_ Y ___ N

Describe current progress toward objectives: _Has maintained positive and cooperative friendship_
with neighbor (same age).

Current Goal 3   Met yet?   Target date if not met yet
Decrease temper tantrums   ___ Y _X_ N   _6/20/2005_

Describe current progress toward objectives: _Mother reports that temper tantrums have decreased_
from 6/week to 2/week.

Current Goal 4   Met yet?   Target date if not met yet
Cease initiating fights with peers   _X_ Y ___ N

Describe current progress toward objectives: _Has not initiated a fight with peers for three weeks._

New Goal 1
Develop positive relationship with step-father   Target date: _10/5/2005_

Problem area: _Ignores step-father 80% of time, often sarcastic_

Objectives: _—Initiate at least one conversation with step-father daily_
—Attend one outing 2x/month with step-father

Treatment: _Incorporate into individual and family counseling_

Services (and frequency) needed: _Behavioral assignments, cognitive therapy_

New Goal 2
Target date: _____

Problem area: _____

Objectives: _____

Treatment: _____

Services (and frequency) needed: _____

Therapist: _Samuel Jones, MSW_   Date: _7_ / _9_ / _2005_

Reviewed by: _Charles Wollat, LICSW_   Date: _7_ / _14_ / _2005_

Form 34   Treatment Update

Client's name: _____   Report prepared for: _____

Therapist: _____   No. of sessions since last update: _____

Current treatment Plan Goals Being Addressed in Therapy

_____

_____

_____

_____

Recent Progresses

_____

_____

_____

_____

Recent Setbacks or Lack of Progress

_____

_____

_____

_____

Suggestions for Improved Progress

_____

_____

_____

_____

Summary Checklist of Therapeutic Progress

Topic	Progress				
	Low		Moderate		High
Attendance	(__)	(__)	(__)	(__)	(__)
Discusses ongoing issues	(__)	(__)	(__)	(__)	(__)
Acknowledges problem areas	(__)	(__)	(__)	(__)	(__)
Developing insight into behaviors/emotions	(__)	(__)	(__)	(__)	(__)
Motivation to change	(__)	(__)	(__)	(__)	(__)
Objectives being met in timely manner	(__)	(__)	(__)	(__)	(__)
Therapy seems beneficial	(__)	(__)	(__)	(__)	(__)

Therapist: _____   Date: ____/____/_____

Form 34 Treatment Update (*Completed*)

Client's name: _William Olden_   Report prepared for: _Lanna Olden, mother_

Therapist: _Samuel Jones, MSW_   No. of sessions since last update: _4_

Current treatment Plan Goals Being Addressed in Therapy

(1) Decreased temper tantrums

(2) Develop positive relationship with step-father

Recent Progresses

(1) Role played and discussed four alternative behaviors which have better consequences

(2) Revised roles in an attempt to empathize with step-father

Recent Setbacks or Lack of Progress

States that he still has little desire to get close to step-father. Seems to believe that he will betray

biological father.

Suggestions for Improved Progress

Do not allow his behavior to visibly affect marriage and family relationships. Reinforce his

efforts to control temper tantrums.

Summary Checklist of Therapeutic Progress

Topic	Progress				
	Low		Moderate		High
Attendance	(__)	(__)	(__)	(_X_)	(__)
Discusses ongoing issues	(__)	(__)	(_X_)	(__)	(__)
Acknowledges problem areas	(__)	(_X_)	(__)	(__)	(__)
Developing insight into behaviors/emotions	(__)	(__)	(_X_)	(__)	(__)
Motivation to change	(__)	(_X_)	(__)	(__)	(__)
Objectives being met in timely manner	(__)	(__)	(__)	(_X_)	(__)
Therapy seems beneficial	(__)	(__)	(_X_)	(__)	(__)

Therapist: _Samuel Jones, MSW_   Date: _8_ / _1_ / _2005_

Chapter 6

Progress Notes

In-Session Progress Notes

Progress notes are designed to document the course of therapy. They should clearly reflect the implementation of the treatment plan and assessment. The treatment plan symptoms, objectives, and treatment strategies must be documented regularly in the progress notes.

Various formats for writing progress notes such as DAP and SOAP are commonly used. Organized progress notes provide structure to progress note writing, rather than simply summarizing a session. The acronym DAP stands for data, assessment, and plan. SOAP stands for subjective, objective, assessment, and plan. Other formats, such as the acronym IIII or 4-I (information, interpretation, intervention, and instruction), provide similar information, but in a different format. The DAP format will be used for examples in this book.

As a higher level of security for psychotherapy notes, HIPAA allows progress notes to be kept in a separate file. It is the therapist's discretion whether to allow the client to review these records. If these progress notes are not kept in a separate file, this stipulation does not apply.

Data

The Data section of the progress notes is oriented to address a number of clinical concerns or questions. Although the progress notes may not specifically cover each of the following areas of documentation, overall they should reflect:

What specifically took place in the session.

Therapeutic interventions.

Clinical observations.

Test results.

Homework assignments.

Current documentation of the diagnosis.

Current stressors, impairments, and affective and cognitive concerns.

Current behavioral concerns.

As in the scientific method, data provides information by which to assess a client's current condition, assess the progress of therapy, and plan upcoming interventions based on current data and assessment. Specifically, documentation in the Data section includes the following.

Clinical Diagnosis.   An outside reader should be able to determine the diagnosis, current issues, treatment, and interventions by the content of the progress notes. For example, if the diagnosis is an adjustment disorder, the progress notes should document an adjustment disorder by addressing the current stressor(s) and the resulting affective/behavioral issues noted in the diagnosis. Likewise, if the diagnosis is a conduct disorder, progress notes should clearly address treatment of conduct, not depression, unless there is a secondary diagnosis of depression. Of course, secondary issues may be documented and noted, but progress notes must be consistent with the primary diagnosis and treatment objectives of the session.

Functional Impairments. Medical necessity of treatment is defined as "significant impairment or dysfunction as a result of a mental disorder." Symptoms and impairments differ in that symptoms help define the *DSM-IV-TR* diagnosis, but do not adequately specify which areas of the client's life are adversely affected. The specific ways in which symptoms adversely affect the client's life are referred to as impairments. The course of treatment is aimed at alleviating the functional impairments resulting from the *DSM* symptoms of the diagnosis. As treatment progresses, functional impairments decrease. Regular charting of ongoing functional impairments is crucial to documentation of the course of treatment. When functional impairments no longer validate or justify a diagnosis, most third-party payers no longer cover services. But if progress notes do not validate functional impairments, there is no "documented behavioral evidence"; thus an audit or case review could result in funds paid for services being returned. As the treatment is revised, it addresses current functional impairments.

Types of functional impairments include social, family, occupational, affective, physical, cognitive, sexual, educational, biopsychological, and other areas in life that could lead to dysfunction. Documentation of functional impairments includes providing specific examples that are measurable. For example, a client with major depression might be impaired occupationally by significant decreases in work production; thus his or her job future might be in jeopardy. Documentation could include comparisons of previous functioning (e.g., producing 10 widgets per week) to current functioning (e.g., producing 3 widgets per week due to fatigue, low motivation, missing work, etc.). Progress notes could document specific interventions to alleviate fatigue, low motivation, and missing work, and subsequently document the resulting production at work. Charting such as Figure 6.1 could aid the documentation. The goal of such documentation is not to produce a graph, but rather to provide evidence of progress or setbacks in order to monitor and document therapeutic effectiveness of therapy and client participation.

Treatment Plan Symptoms, Goals, and Objectives. The documentation of clinical symptoms is similar to that of functional impairments. In the previous example, a functional impairment was less production at work, while symptoms include fatigue, low motivation, and missing work. Documentation of symptoms includes noting ongoing frequency, duration, and intensity of symptoms. Charting techniques may be employed, and may include simple notation in the chart for later comparisons. Each therapeutic session has specific objectives taken directly from the treatment plan.

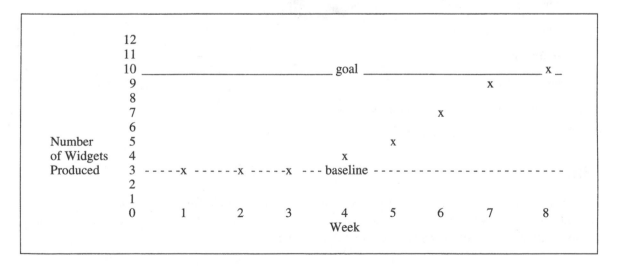

Figure 6.1 Graph Charting Patient Progress Based on Effectiveness of Therapy.

Therapeutic Interventions.   Documentation of clinical interventions is required in progress notes. Charting statements both reflect and document accepted therapeutic interventions. Most third-party payers require that the techniques employed in therapy are not experimental in nature. Notes should reflect specific techniques, interventions, and their outcomes. Such information will provide an empirical rationale to continue, discontinue, or modify the specific course of therapy. Intervention statements also include evaluation of client homework assignments prescribed in therapy.

Current Issues/Stressors.   Progress notes should provide ongoing evidence of current stressors and problems, as well as positive aspects in the client's life. Documented therapeutic interventions are directed at alleviating impairments resulting from these stressors. Therapeutic techniques are noted that document interventions designed to cope with current issues and stressors. Ongoing documentation assesses therapeutic results.

Observations.   Clinical observations written in the progress notes provide ongoing statements in areas such as affect, mental status, contact with reality, nonverbal behaviors, unusual behaviors or statements, contradictory statements, and so forth that provide additional documentation of the need for services. Examples of affective observations include psychomotor retardation/agitation and level of affect (e.g., normal, restricted, blunted, or flat). Other examples may be found on pages 3.89–3.92 in the Mental Status Exam section of the Diagnostic Assessment Report and in the Diagnostic Interview Form. Several publications are available describing such terminology (see Bibliography).

Assessment

The Assessment section of the progress notes is used for evaluation of the course of therapy based on the most recent data (results of the current session). Assessment may include the current session and a cumulative assessment of the therapy in general. The following areas may be evaluated:

> The session.
>
> The course of therapy.
>
> Client cooperation/insight/motivation.
>
> Client progress/setbacks.
>
> Areas needing more work.
>
> Impairments.
>
> Treatment strategies.
>
> How treatment plan objectives are being met.
>
> Changes needed to say on target.

Plan

The Plan section of the progress notes is based on the Assessment. The question asked is, "Based on the current assessment, what will be done to most effectively meet the treatment plan objectives?" A confirmation and/or revision of the treatment plan, this section may include plans for:

Homework assignments.

Upcoming interventions.

The next session or series of sessions.

Treatment plan revisions in objectives or strategies.

Common Errors in Progress Notes

Form 35A illustrates several common errors.

Errors of Omission

1. No date (M/D/Y).

2. No stated objectives for the session. The content of the session should follow specific treatment plan objectives and be documented in the progress notes.

3. No signature of therapist. Initials are not sufficient.

4. No start and ending time. Notations such as "1 hr" are often not sufficient for documentation unless exact times are documented in a ledger or date book.

Errors of Commission. Each progress note statement is quite vague and does not validate any diagnosis or impairments.

5. "Did his homework."

   Although this statement may suggest client compliance, it does not provide information on the therapeutic effectiveness of the activity or suggest how it meets treatment plan objectives. Homework assignments should be documented concerning their therapeutic effectiveness and should be consistent with accepted procedures in the mental health field.

6. "Took test."

   Ongoing testing is certainly an effective means of documentation, but the specific test given and the results are needed to provide data for reference. It is possible to chart results of ongoing testing. A brief interpretation is also suggested.

7. "Talked about. . . . Went over. . . . Discussed. . . ."

   Statements such as these indicate to some degree the content of the session, but provide no indication of how the treatment plan is being followed or documented.

8. There should be no open spaces left where additional information could later be added to the progress notes. Lines should fill up this space to prevent fabricating information after the fact. When a

therapist recalls information at a later date, it should be written as an addendum, rather than simply penciled in.

9. "Waive co-payment. . . ."

Such procedures are illegal and constitute insurance fraud.

Saving Time in Progress Note Writing

Approximately 75 percent of the therapists surveyed by this author have indicated that they write progress notes after the session (see pages 6.11 and 6.12). They believe that if they took progress notes during the session they would not be able to attend to the client as well and that writing progress notes after the session helps to provide an overall picture of the session.

However, other therapists have stated that their progress notes details and accuracy have increased when they started writing the notes during the session. They add that the transition often takes a few months. The form on page 6.13 entitled Progress Notes—Outline can be used during the transition from taking progress notes after the session to taking them during the session.

In some cases, writing progress notes during the session can increase rapport and empathy. When the therapist nonverbally portrays the message, "What you say is important, so I must write it down," progress note writing during the session can be both time-saving and therapeutic.

FORM 35
Progress Notes

Two sample progress notes are included. The first, on page 6.11 is for an adult client named John Doe and is designed to document evidence of the course of therapy and follow the DAP guidelines discussed previously. The second, on page 6.12, is for a child. It follows the treatment plan from page 5.10.

FORM 36
Progress Notes—Outline

Form 36 provides structure and reminders to the therapist as to what areas of documentation are helpful in progress notes. Although the information contained in the progress notes is the same as previous examples, this form breaks down the DAP format into specific content areas. The form is not designed to model a particular type of treatment, but rather to provide evidence of on-target treatment for any therapeutic stance.

Some therapists using this form prefer to jot brief notes during the session to be used as reminders when they write the final copy of their progress notes. Others use this form as a final product. This form can also serve as a transition for therapists in the process of changing their procedure from writing progress notes after the session to writing them during the session.

A Progress Note—Outline form for Judy Doe's third session in therapy is provided as Form 36A. The DAP format is used, but the specific documentation needed for each section is addressed.

FORM 37
Group Therapy Progress Notes

Few group therapists have time to write separate and concise progress notes for an entire group. Some therapists have reported that they spend more time after the session writing progress notes than the time spent in the session. Others report that they use the same progress note for the entire session, noting contributions for each client. The latter practice poses ethics problems due to confidentiality being broken if any of the group members' files are released to an outside source.

The Group Therapy Progress Notes form on page 6.15 is designed to enable the therapist to take separate notes on each group member during the session. Information that is common to all group members (treatment plan objectives for the session) is listed under Group Topics Discussed. Twelve group behaviors are rated in the Group Behavior Ratings section. Over the course of group therapy these ratings can be assessed for various areas of progress. The remaining space on the form allows for Individual Contributions, which may be documented as the client speaks.

The group progress note form also includes a periodic summary that is helpful when progress notes are regularly forwarded to others such as parents, guardians, social workers, or group homes.

FORM 38
Psychiatric Medication Management
Progress Notes

The Psychiatric Medication Management Progress Notes form is designed for a psychiatrist to evaluate the client's current problem areas, mental status, current risk factors, and medications. If additional concerns or therapeutic services are needed, a progress notes form is also suggested.

Form 35   Progress Notes

Client's name: _____   Session: _____   Date: _____

Diagnosis: _____

Tx goals: _____   Therapist: _____

Time started: _____   Time finished: _____   Duration: _____

Next appointment: Date: _____   Time: _____

Therapist's signature: _____

6.8

Form 35A   Progress Notes   (*Poor Example*)

Client's name: _____*John*_____   Date: _____*Monday*_____

John was on time for his appointment. Did his homework. Took test. Talked about his homework. Went over marital relationship. Discussed events of week and how they relate to counseling. Was happy about talking to his uncle on the phone.

Went over homework and made plans. Worked on communication skills. Positive communication is important. Will come again.

(Note: waive co-payment if insurance pays their portion)

Therapist's signature: _____   Date: ____/____/____

Form 35B   Progress Notes—Adult   (*Completed*)

Client's name: _____*John Doe*_____   Session: __*5*__   Date: __*2/13/2005*__

Diagnosis: __*300.4 Dysthymia*_____

Tx goals: __*Ego strength/Positive thoughts*_____   Therapist: ___*PS*___

(**D**) *Completed homework assignment of identifying dysfunctional thoughts. Reviewed five positive qualities and five perceived negative characteristics from previous session. Several self-deprecating statements. Current BDI score = 29 (previous week = 32). Difficulties believing that he is capable of being happy. Describes self as being easily irritated and less capable than most other people. Fairly upset about continued spousal discord. Two divorce threats this week. Now sleeping in guest room; angry, frustrated, sad. States much guilt and remorse over his irritability, which he believes causes others to reject him. Charted progress of social contacts. Continues to meet current homework goals of one new social interaction per week. Describes affective level past week as sad about 50% of the time. (Charting indicates previous four weeks = 60–75% of time feeling sad.) Missed one day at work this week due to feelings of boredom/fatigue.* **Sessions Topics: Ego strength.** *Role-played speaking with assertiveness to spouse, employer, and in job interview.* **Positive thoughts.** *States no positive plan or goals for future. History of others making his decisions (parents, relatives, spouse). Identified three attainable short-term goals that he is interested in pursuing: 1) enrolling in community education course or seminar, 2) weekend trip, 3) volunteering at nursing home once per week.*

(**A**) *Increased focus on personal responsibility for behavioral/affective change and in self-direction. Viewing self more positively in past few weeks. Continued concerns with level of irritability and spousal discord. Progress in individual concerns, but low motivation in spousal issues and missing work. Compliant in homework assignments, but level of insight moderately low. Behavioral techniques seem most helpful.*

(**P**) *Homework: Implement one of three above listed short-term goals. Continue dysfunctional thought record. Client is considering spousal involvement in therapy in 3–4 weeks.*

Time started: __*4:00 p.m.*__   Time finished: __*4:51 p.m.*__   Duration: __*51 minutes*__

Next appointment: Date: __*2/20/2005*__   Time: __*2:00 p.m.*__

Therapist's signature: __*Phillip Schultz, MSW*_____

Form 35C   Progress Notes—Children and Adolescents   (*Completed*)

Client's name: _____*Johnny Rentschler*_____ Session: __*3*__ Date: __*2/12/2005*__

Diagnosis: ___*Adjustment reaction with depressed mood/conduct*___

Tx goals: ___*Establish trust/Engage in play therapy*___ Therapist: ___*SB*___

(D) *1st session since assessment.* **Mother present.** *Began session with mother bringing in chart of 38 physical aggressions in past week directed toward people, and 12 incidents of property damage in the home. Major aggression toward sister after two attempts by Johnny to phone father who did not return phone calls. Mother further noted receiving two notes from teacher describing initiating fights in school. Possible suspension impending. Mother further notes that Johnny refused to go on family outing to visit friends in old neighborhood. Spend most of weekend in his room watching TV and playing video games. Refused to play with same-aged cousin, whom mother invited to home. Loaned mother copy of "Parental Consistency Manual."* **Mother not present.** *Asked Johnny to draw portrait of his family. Quickly drew colorful picture with all family members in a boxing ring. Everyone in the family except Johnny had hands tied. Mother was kicking at him. He was the only one able to fight with his hands. (See drawing dated 2/12/2005.) Note father's placement on other side of ropes in opposite corner. When invited to discuss the drawing, Johnny stated that dad is far away and can't be reached because his mother is in the way and his sister is on his mother's side. He further noted that his mother and sister cannot hurt him, like his father did before, or they will also get in trouble.*

(A) *Much blaming of mother for father's absence. Resentment and anger toward family, whom he views as responsible for father now being unapproachable. Deep sense of loss. Seems to view family as choosing sides against him, but they are unable to control his behaviors without getting into legal trouble. Views situation as having few available options to cope with perceived rejection. Insight into source of anger slowing developing. Views control as rewarding.*

(P) *"Functional Analysis of Behavior" from to be completed by mother. Continue with drawings in which he draws/discusses changes he desires and related affect. Continue nonthreatening enactments of family dynamics. Continue rapport/trust building.*

Time started: __*2:00 p.m.*__   Time finished: __*2.49 p.m.*__   Duration: ___*49 minutes*___

Next appointment: Date: __*2/19/2005*__   Time: __*2:00 p.m.*__

Therapist's signature: ___*Sharon Bell, PhD*___

Form 36 Progress Notes—Outline

Name: _____ Therapist: _____ Date: _____

Axis I: _____ Axis II: _____

Session goals/objectives: _____

Data

Homework from past session(s): _____

_____

_____

Functional impairment (e.g., emotional, social, occupational, legal, behavioral; include degree,

frequency, duration): _____

_____

_____

_____

Current issues/topics/stressors: _____

_____

_____

_____

Interventions: _____

_____

_____

_____

Observations: _____

_____

_____

_____

Other: _____

_____

Assessment (Progress/Impairment/Effectiveness of interventions): _____

_____

_____

_____

Plan (Homework, objectives next session, changes, testing): _____

_____

_____

_____

Time started: _____ Time finished: _____ Duration: _____

Next appointment: Date: _____ Time: _____

Therapist's signature: _____

Form 36A Progress Notes—Outline (*Completed*)

Name: _____*Judy Doe*_____ Therapist: __*DLB*__ Date: ___*3/22/2005*___

Axis I: __*296.32 Major depression, recurrent, moderate*__ Axis II: ___*Deferred*___

Session goals/objectives: ___*Hopelessness: Restructure dysfunctional thoughts*___

Data

Homework from past session(s): ___*Completed homework assigned; identified uncomfortable*___ ___*situations leading to depression and hopelessness.*___

Functional impairment (e.g., emotional, social, occupational, legal, behavioral; include degree, frequency, duration): ___*Poor appetite. One meal/day, increasing fatigue. Little social support at*___ ___*home. Very little time spent with spouse or children this week, no sexual desire in 2–3 months.*___ ___*Continues usually feeling depressed, guilty, and angry. Low motivation to teach students. Missed*___ ___*one day of work; no energy, motivation.*___

Current issues/topics/stressors: ___*Angry because both students and her family will not become*___ ___*motivated to her expectations. States it is her fault. Increasing anger toward spouse due to not*___ ___*supporting her parenting decisions. Much self-blame for others not performing. Notes guilt*___ ___*feelings if she does not chauffeur her children like "other parents."*___

Interventions: ___*Discussed and identified 3 dysfunctional thoughts and their respective situations*___ ___*and associated feelings. Vented feelings of anger toward her family and students via empty chair.*___ ___*Confronted defensiveness about accepting others' negative treatment toward her as acceptable.*___

Observations: ___*Poor eye contact, slumped posture, closed body position, monotonous speech,*___ ___*restricted affect, less psychomotor agitation during periods of insight.*___

Other: ___*SUDs level of depression = 88. Baseline = 95. See Subjective Units of Distress (SUDs)*___ ___*charts.*___

Assessment (Progress/Impairment/Effectiveness of interventions): ___*Increased insight into*___ ___*relationship between "shoulds" from parents and current affective/behavioral concerns.*___ ___*Differentiating thoughts and feelings is quite helpful. Difficulties accepting that she is angry at*___ ___*others.*___

Plan (Homework, objectives next session, changes, testing): ___*Dysfunctional thought record as*___ ___*homework. Read "Escape from Co-dependency." Next session: Pleasurable activities.*___

Time started: __*1:00 p.m.*__ Time finished: __*1:52 p.m.*__ Duration: _____*52 minutes*_____

Next appointment: Date: ___*3/29/2005*___ Time: __*1:00 p.m.*__

Therapist's signature: ___*Darlene L. Benton, PhD*___

6.13

Form 37   Group Therapy Progress Notes

Client: _____   Group: _____   Date: _____

Agenda: Group Topics Discussed

_____

_____

Group Behavior Ratings

	Low		Medium		High
Seemed interested in the group	(__)	(__)	(__)	(__)	(__)
Initiated positive interactions	(__)	(__)	(__)	(__)	(__)
Shared emotions	(__)	(__)	(__)	(__)	(__)
Helpful to others	(__)	(__)	(__)	(__)	(__)
Focused on group tasks	(__)	(__)	(__)	(__)	(__)
Disclosed information about self	(__)	(__)	(__)	(__)	(__)
Understood group topics	(__)	(__)	(__)	(__)	(__)
Participated in group exercises	(__)	(__)	(__)	(__)	(__)
Showed listening skills/empathy	(__)	(__)	(__)	(__)	(__)
Offered opinions/suggestions/feedback	(__)	(__)	(__)	(__)	(__)
Seemed to benefit from the session	(__)	(__)	(__)	(__)	(__)
Treatment considerations addressed	(__)	(__)	(__)	(__)	(__)

Monthly Evaluation (fill out last group of each month)

Topic		Progress	
	Low	Medium	High
Participation	(__)	(__)	(__)
Discusses issues	(__)	(__)	(__)
Insight	(__)	(__)	(__)
Motivation	(__)	(__)	(__)
Emotional expression	(__)	(__)	(__)
Stays on task	(__)	(__)	(__)
Objectives being met	(__)	(__)	(__)

Suggestions

____ Individual counseling   ____ Evaluation for meds   ___Other: _____

Individual Contributions This Session

_____

_____

_____

_____

_____

_____

_____

Time started: _____   Time finished: _____   Duration: _____

Therapist: _____

Cotherapist: _____

Form 37A   Group Therapy Progress Notes   (*Completed*)

Client: ___*Pat Anderson*___   Group: ___*Grief*___   Date: ___*3/10/2005*___

Agenda: Group Topics Discussed

___*Session 6 Agenda: 1) Expressing grief; 2) Coping with changes*___

___*Next week: 1) Saying "good-bye"; 2) Future plans*___

Group Behavior Ratings

	Low		Medium		High
Seemed interested in the group	(__)	(__)	(_X_)	(__)	(__)
Initiated positive interactions	(__)	(_X_)	(__)	(__)	(__)
Shared emotions	(__)	(__)	(_X_)	(__)	(__)
Helpful to others	(__)	(_X_)	(__)	(__)	(__)
Focused on group tasks	(__)	(__)	(_X_)	(__)	(__)
Disclosed information about self	(__)	(__)	(_X_)	(__)	(__)
Understood group topics	(__)	(__)	(_X_)	(__)	(__)
Participated in group exercises	(__)	(__)	(_X_)	(__)	(__)
Showed listening skills/empathy	(__)	(__)	(__)	(_X_)	(__)
Offered opinions/suggestions/feedback	(__)	(__)	(_X_)	(__)	(__)
Seemed to benefit from the session	(__)	(__)	(_X_)	(__)	(__)
Treatment considerations addressed	(__)	(__)	(__)	(_X_)	(__)

Monthly Evaluation (fill out last group of each month)

Topic	Progress		
	Low	Medium	High
Participation	(__)	(_X_)	(__)
Discusses issues	(__)	(_X_)	(__)
Insight	(__)	(_X_)	(__)
Motivation	(__)	(__)	(_X_)
Emotional expression	(__)	(__)	(_X_)
Stays on task	(__)	(_X_)	(__)
Objectives being met	(__)	(_X_)	(__)

Suggestions

____ Individual counseling   ___ Evaluation for meds   ___Other: _____

Individual Contributions This Session

___*Pat was 20 minutes late for the session. Did not seem interested in discussing how he is currently*___
___*handling death of his parents in auto accident. During a group exercise he disclosed that he cries*___
___*every night before going to sleep and wakes up 3–4 times per night thinking that his parents are*___
___*in the room. Has not been doing most of his homework in college, but reports slight increases in*___
___*homework compliance in past 2 weeks. Generally quiet (but seemed to listen/empathize) when*___
___*other people discussed their coping strategies dealing with loss of loved ones.*___

Time started: ___*7:00 p.m.*___   Time finished: ___*8:30 p.m.*___   Duration: ___*90 minutes*___

Therapist: ___*Katie Anderson, MA*___

Cotherapist: ___*Grant Bauste, MA*___

Form 38   Psychiatric Medication Management Progess Notes

Patent's name: _____   Date: _____

__Inpatient __Outpatient   ID/Chart No. _____

PATIENT'S
STATEMENTS   PROBLEM   SEVERITY   COMMENTS
Appetite   __No __Yes   __Mild __Mod __Severe   _____
Energy   __No __Yes   __Mild __Mod __Severe   _____
Concentration   __No __Yes   __Mild __Mod __Severe   _____
Guilt/Hopelessness __No __Yes __Mild __Mod __Severe   _____
Libido   __No __Yes   __Mild __Mod __Severe   _____
Sleep   __No __Yes   __Mild __Mod __Severe   _____
Social   __No __Yes   __Mild __Mod __Severe   _____
Injurious/Suicidal __No __Yes __Mild __Mod __Severe   _____
Weight   __No __Yes   __Mild __Mod __Severe   _____
Anxiety/Panic   __No __Yes   __Mild __Mod __Severe   _____
Cognition   __No __Yes   __Mild __Mod __Severe   _____
Thoughts   __No __Yes   __Mild __Mod __Severe   _____
Drugs/Alcohol   __No __Yes   __Mild __Mod __Severe   _____
Other statements _____
_____
_____

Overall Mood: Negative 1 2 3 4 5 6 7 8 9 10   Positive

MENTAL STATUS EXAM   COMMENTS   AbN = Abnormal
Appearance   __Normal __AbN   _____
Activity Level   __Normal __AbN   _____
Mood   __Normal __AbN   _____
Motor/Gait   __Normal __AbN   _____
Cognition   __Normal __AbN   _____
Insight/Judgment   __Normal __AbN   _____
Speech   __Normal __AbN   _____
Attention/Concentration __Normal __AbN   _____
Memory (recent/remote)   __Normal __AbN   _____
Orientation   __Normal __AbN   _____
Associations   __Normal __AbN   _____
Thought Content   __Normal __AbN   _____
Other _____

Suicidal   __No __Yes, Describe   __Ideations __Gestures __Threats __Plan
                         Actions taken _____

Homicidal   __No __Yes, Actions taken _____

Chemical Abuse __No __Yes, Actions taken _____

Current meds _____
Compliance problems __No __Yes, Describe _____
Side effects __None __Yes, Describe _____
Changes in meds _____ # Refills _____

DSM Diagnosis
Axis I _____   _____
        _____   _____
Axis II _____   _____
Axis III _____
Axis IV _____   Axis IV GAF= _____ Highest in past year _____

PLAN _____ LABS _____

Next Appt. _____ Signature _____

Chapter 7

Other Forms Used During the Course of Treatment

Forms in this chapter can elicit helpful information that could come up in treatment depending on the client's current concerns. Areas such as suicidality, informed consent for medication, and dealing with target behaviors are covered.

Although this text provides a few examples of client handouts, it is not the book's purpose. The reader is referred to the *Wiley Homework Planner Series* for several examples of homework assignments and handouts.

FORM 39
Informed Consent for Medication

The purpose of this form is two-fold. First, the client signs a statement of informed consent stating that he or she understands the potential benefits, risks, and side effects of the prescribed medications. In addition, the client agrees to inform the clinic when discontinuing the medication and agrees to remain in therapy while taking medication prescibed by the clinic.

FORM 40
Suicide Contract

A suicide contract serves several purposes. Although it is not a legal contract, it represents the client's commitment to take responsible actions when feeling suicidal. It is a signed agreement between the client and the therapist that suicide will not take place. It further provides evidence that the therapist has provided help for the client.

Most therapists ask clients to keep the contract with them at all times. It contains important contact telephone numbers that may not otherwise be immediately available or thought of during a crisis period. It also represents the therapist's commitment to the client, by providing means to contact the therapist in times of emergency or crisis.

FORM 41
Cooperating in Child Rearing

Form 41 begins on page 7.5 with a narrative regarding various reasons why parents' diverse backgrounds and personalities may make it difficult for them to agree on child-rearing practices, followed by a discussion regarding various ways in which the parents may have been raised and how the disparity could cause conflict with the partner's view of parenting. In a homework assignment, each partner is asked to provide information regarding his or her upbringing compared to the partner's. Understanding and compromises are subsequently suggested.

FORM 42
Couple's Analysis of
Target Behaviors

The Couple's Analysis of Target Behaviors form (Form 42) is designed to increase communication by breaking down negative behaviors in the relationship into causal and affective components. In this homework assignment, clients are asked to indicate how they believe their partner felt after each disagreement and also to list positive alternative actions that could have been taken in place of the negative behavior.

FORMS 43 and 43A
Third-Party Prior Authorization
Request for Continued Services

Many third-party payers initially approve fewer than three initial sessions for assessment and then request a prior authorization (PA) for continued services at regular intervals. Every third-party payer has its own form for requesting continued services. Therapists often complain of their requests usually being turned down, causing services to be quickly terminated due to lack of insurance coverage. As a result, cognitive dissonance persists. Often, the true issue is the therapist's lack of training in writing the PA request, rather than the third-party payer's refusal to continue services. Requesting a PA for services requires concise writing skills in which documenting medical necessity is essential.

The forms on pages 7.17 and 7.18 represent PAs from the file of Judy Doe. These samples represent a typical PA format. The first is completed vaguely and does not provide sufficient documentation of diagnosis, symptoms, impairments, therapeutic progress/setbacks, and so on. It is written in a manner suggesting that the client has improved significantly and does not need further services. If this were the case, further services should not be requested. But, if additional mental health services are medically necessary, the documentation provided in this form would be a disservice to the client.

Some therapists have noted that writing a PA request is a "Catch-22" situation. That is, if significant improvements are noted as in this form, the PA will be denied because goals apparently have been met sufficiently. On the other hand, if continued severe impairments are noted, it may appear that treatment is ineffective, so the PA will likewise be denied.

The form on page 7.18 provides specific examples of Judy Doe's progress in therapy and documents a continued need to work on other treatment plan goals. This one-page document attempts to summarize the entire course of treatment. The quantified examples are taken directly from the well-documented progress notes, rather than offering a nondocumented opinion at the time of writing the PA request.

Form 39   Informed Consent for Medication

Name: (last) _____ (first) _____ (I) _____ Chart Number _____

_____ (name of MD) _____ has explained that the best treatment for my problem would include the use of the following medications:

Medication   **Dosage Range**

_____   _____

_____   _____

_____   _____

_____   _____

_____   _____

I have been given a copy of the:
( ) USP Patient Information Sheet   ( ) Other written information

I have had the opportunity to discuss the risks, benefits and potential side effects of the listed medications with my doctor, and have received a reasonable explanation.

I understand that the medications of this type have been successful in treatment of similar symptoms in others. Further, I understand that there is no guarantee that these agents will be as effective with my particular symptoms. I agree to notify my physician in the event that I experience any side effects or problems with the above medications.

I have informed my doctor that: ( ) I am pregnant   ( ) I am not pregnant   ( ) NA
                                        ( ) I have other known physical disorders:

                                        _____

                                        _____

I understand that if I discontinue receiving individual counseling services, or have not seen an individual counselor at _____ (name of clinic) _____ within the past 30 days, I can no longer receive medication services from my physician at _____ (name of clinic) _____. In such cases, I must first complete an individual counseling session at _____ (name of clinic) _____ or make an appointment with my family doctor to continue medication services.

I voluntarily consent to take this medication. I also understand that I have the right to withdraw my consent and stop taking medication at any time. If I decide to discontinue the medication, I will tell my doctor immediately, he/she may explain how to safely stop the medication.

_____   _____
Patient/Parent/Guardian Signature   **Date**

As a physician, I certify that these instructions have been disclosed to the patient (parent or guardian, if appropriate), and they express understanding and agree to take the medications.

_____   _____
Physician Signature   **Date**

Form 40   Suicide Contract

Date: _____

I, _____ , (client), hereby contract with _____
(therapist), that I will take the following actions if I feel suicidal.

1. I will not attempt suicide.

2. I will phone _____ at _____ .

3. If I do not reach _____ , I will phone any of the following services:

Name/Agency	Phone
_____	_____
_____	_____
_____	_____
_____	_____
_____	_____

4. I will further seek social supports from any of the following people:

Name	Phone
_____	_____
_____	_____
_____	_____
_____	_____
_____	_____

5. If none of these actions are helpful or not available, I will check-in the ER at one of the following:

Hospital	Address	Phone
_____	_____	_____
_____	_____	_____
_____	_____	_____
_____	_____	_____
_____	_____	_____

6. If I am not able to receive help I will phone 911, or 0.

Client's signature: _____   Date: ____/____/_____

Therapist's signature: _____   Date: ____/____/_____

Form 41   Cooperating in Child Rearing

No two people totally agree on all child-rearing principles. The same individual will often seem strict in some matters but quite lax in others. What you view as strict may be thought of as lenient by your partner. What you consider to be fun might be seen as dangerous by your partner.

Most parents tend to raise their children in a similar manner to how they grew up. Of course there are exceptions, but many of the child-rearing techniques we use were learned because our parents (by their example) taught them to us. Unless your parents were just like your partner's parents, your schooling was identical to your partner's schooling, your ideas are the same as your partner's ideas, and so forth, it is inevitable that some of your child-rearing techniques will conflict with those of your partner.

Two important issues involved in child-rearing practices include:
1. the degree of **warmth vs. hostility** in the household, and
2. the degree of **independence vs. control** rendered to the child.

1. WARMTH VS. HOSTILITY. The amount of warmth shown in a family can range from extremely warm (too much smothering and affection) to extremely hostile (little or no love shown).

Extremely warm families often smother their children with so much affection that the children may grow up demanding that others take care of their needs. If you were raised in an extremely warm family it is possible that you might have some difficulties separating your identity from that of your children and family.

Being raised in a warm, loving family can be quite rewarding provided that it doesn't lead to constant smothering. Warm families tend to be affectionate, accepting, and low in physical punishment; parents don't openly criticize one another and are family-centered, rather than self-centered.

Extremely hostile families are often prone to extreme disciplinary measures toward their children. The words "I love you" are rarely spoken. Parents are often rejecting, cold, disapproving, and quite critical of family members. If you were raised in a hostile family it is possible that you might have some difficulties listening to your children's points of view, showing affection, and controlling your temper.

Some families seem to go back and forth between warmth and hostility. When things are going quite well (e.g., children are obeying, finances are in order, parents are getting along, etc.) these families tend to be warm. But when pressures confront the family, there may be times when the parents vent their hostilities on each other and/or the children. This type of situation becomes confusing to the children because of the mixed messages they are receiving. These parents must learn how to be consistent.

2. INDEPENDENCE VS. CONTROL. The amount of independence granted to children can range from extreme independence (children having few or no rules) to extreme control (children allowed to make few or no decisions).

Extreme independence in a family allows the children to do almost whatever they want to do. Parents reason that the children will learn from their mistakes and grow from the experiences. Few restrictions are imposed, and little enforcement is provided for these restrictions. If you were raised in an extremely independent child-rearing family, it is quite possible that you are somewhat uncomfortable when it comes to setting limits or enforcing family rules.

Extreme control in a family allows few decisions to be made without the approval of the "head of the house." Children are expected to do exactly what they are told, even when no logical reason is given. There are many restrictions and high enforcement of the rules. If you were raised in an extremely controlling family, perhaps you experience great discomfort or anger whenever someone doesn't agree with you or behaves contrary to your ideas, advice, or rules.

Most people were raised in families in which the family atmosphere is somewhere between extremely warm and extremely hostile. Perhaps there was some hostility, but most of the time warmth was shown. Likewise, few people were raised on either extreme of independence or control. Most children are gradually granted more independence as they get older.

CONSIDERATIONS: You and your partner might find it difficult agreeing or cooperating on how to raise your children. You learned from different teachers! Now is the time for both of you to objectively appraise the benefits and drawbacks of your own upbringing, and purposely create the type of family atmosphere that is best for your family.

Your children need stability and consistency in their family life. When they are presented with dissimilar messages from you and your partner it may be quite difficult for them to develop a consistent value system. Although you both may not at present agree on certain techniques of child rearing, you must come to some agreement for the children's sake. Although compromise and cooperation may be difficult at first, you will find that the harmony they eventually produce will enhance your relationship and your family stability.

First, make compromises. Families function more smoothly when each partner practices the give-and-take process of cooperation. The will of one spouse should not impose on the rights of the other partner. Selfish desires of one partner may often lead to long-lasting hurts and resentments on the part of the other. Many compromises may not immediately feel good to the individual, but cooperation and agreement lead to a more stable relationship.

Second, be consistent. When you agree upon how you will handle certain issues, tell the children about the process you went through to come to your decisions. That is, let them know that the rules of the house have been formulated by both you and your partner. When issues come up you may be tempted to go back to your old ways of dealing with them, but stay consistent for the family's sake. In the long run your children will respect the newfound strength of family unity.

Third, be patient. Change takes time. Your children will do their best to test the parent they see as the more lenient. At first expect a certain amount of protest when family rules are changed or added. But over time the children will realize that you and your spouse are together when it comes to discipline. Remember, a parent is a child's most influential teacher.

Your name: _____ Date _____

Partner's name: _____

Please respond to the following items. Do not share this information with your partner until the next counseling session.

1) Which of the following best describes the family in which you grew up?

WARM AND ACCEPTING				AVERAGE			HOSTILE AND FIGHTING	
1	2	3	4	5	6	7	8	9

Comments: _____

_____

_____

2) Which of these describes the way in which your parents raised you?

ALLOWED ME TO BE VERY INDEPENDENT				AVERAGE			ATTEMPTED TO CONTOL ME	
1	2	3	4	5	6	7	8	9

Comments: _____

_____

_____

3) Which of the following best describes the family in which your partner grew up?

WARM AND ACCEPTING				AVERAGE			HOSTILE AND FIGHTING	
1	2	3	4	5	6	7	8	9

Comments: _____

_____

_____

4) Which of these best describes the way in which your partner's parents raised your partner?

ALLOWED MY PARTNER TO BE VERY INDEPENDENT				AVERAGE			ATTEMPTED TO CONTROL MY PARTNER	
1	2	3	4	5	6	7	8	9

Comments: _____

_____

_____

5) Which of the following best describes your family style?

I AM WARM AND ACCEPTING				AVERAGE			I AM HOSTILE AND FIGHTING	
1	2	3	4	5	6	7	8	9

Comments: _____

_____

_____

6) Which of these describes the way in which you are raising your children?

I ALLOW THEM
TO BE VERY
INDEPENDENT   AVERAGE   I ATTEMPT TO
CONTROL THEM

 1 2 3 4 5 6 7 8 9

Comments: _____

_____

_____

7) Which of the following best describes your partner's family style?

PARTNER IS
WARM AND
ACCEPTING   AVERAGE   PARTNER IS
HOSTILE AND
FIGHTING

 1 2 3 4 5 6 7 8 9

Comments: _____

_____

_____

8) Which of these describes the way in which your partner is raising your children?

PARTNER ALLOWS
THEM TO BE VERY
INDEPENDENT   AVERAGE   PARTNER
ATTEMPTS TO
CONTROL THEM

 1 2 3 4 5 6 7 8 9

Comments: _____

_____

_____

9) Which of the following best describes the family style you would like you and your partner to have?

WARM AND
ACCEPTING   AVERAGE   HOSTILE AND
FIGHTING

 1 2 3 4 5 6 7 8 9

Comments: _____

_____

_____

10) Which of these describes the way in which you would like you and your partner to raise you children?

BOTH ALLOW
TO BE VERY
INDEPENDENT   AVERAGE   BOTH
ATTEMPT TO
CONTROL THEM

 1 2 3 4 5 6 7 8 9

Comments: _____

_____

_____

11) List the child-rearing issues about which you and your partner have very different opinions or practices:

A) Issue: _____

How do you differ? _____

_____

Problems arising: _____

_____

Your willingness to compromise: _____

_____

Comments: _____

_____

B) Issue: _____

How do you differ? _____

_____

Problems arising: _____

_____

Your willingness to compromise: _____

_____

Comments: _____

_____

C) Issue: _____

How do you differ? _____

_____

Problems arising: _____

_____

Your willingness to compromise: _____

_____

Comments: _____

_____

D) Issue: _____

How do you differ? _____

_____

Problems arising: _____

_____

Your willingness to compromise: _____

_____

Comments: _____

_____

Form 42   Couple's Analysis of Target Behaviors

Your name: _____   Date: _____

Spouse's name: _____

Every couple encounters misunderstandings, disagreements, hurt, and anger, as well as happy times, fulfillment, encouragement, and cooperation. Unfortunately, when relationships are on the down side, too many people dwell on the negatives. Not all people intentionally try to hurt their partners, but, when arguments heat up, they often fall back into selfish attitudes and behaviors that only serve as ammunition for their own cause. Such defenses never facilitate a happy relationship.

A few examples of detrimental behaviors include the following:

- Belittling/putting down
- Blaming or accusing
- Bringing up the past
- Constantly refusing sex
- Controlling
- Dwelling on negatives
- Flirting with others
- Guilt trips
- Lack of affection
- Lying
- Not sharing responsibilities

- Physical abuse
- Pouting
- Refusing to talk/shunning
- Sarcasm
- Shifting attention to family/friends
- Spending or hoarding money
- Substance abuse
- Threatening suicide
- Threatening to leave
- Verbal abuse
- Yelling

Enjoying a successful relationship involves much more than simply eliminating negative behaviors. Some couples would leave therapy with little to talk about if the counseling only involved discarding the negative. Mutually rewarding, positive actions must replace the negative.

Directions: During the next week list all interactions between you and your partner in which negative interactions (such as those above) take place. Mark down the day and approximate time when each take place. Do not share this list with your partner or compare notes. We will go over the lists in the next counseling session. Use as many of the attached sheets as necessary.

This list must contain behaviors acted out by you, your partner, and both. The purpose of this exercise is to learn about and enrich your relationship, not to blame or find fault. We are not interested in determining "who is right," but rather "what is right" for your relationship.

Also include alternative positive actions that could have been taken instead of the negative behavior, and what seemed to cause the behavior (if you know).

Date: _____   Time: _____

Negative behavior(s): _____
_____
_____
_____

Acted out by whom: _____   ___ Both

What caused it to happen? _____
_____
_____
_____

How did you feel afterward? _____
_____

How do you think your partner felt afterward? _____
_____

What positive actions could have been taken instead of the negative: _____
_____
_____
_____
_____

Date: _____   Time: _____

Negative behavior(s): _____
_____
_____
_____

Acted out by whom: _____   ___ Both

What caused it to happen? _____
_____
_____
_____

How did you feel afterward? _____
_____

How do you think your partner felt afterward? _____
_____

What positive actions could have been taken instead of the negative? _____
_____
_____
_____
_____

Your name: _____ *Linda Schommer* _____   Date: _____ *3/9/2005* _____

Spouse's name: _____ *Paul Schommer* _____

Every couple encounters misunderstandings, disagreements, hurt, and anger, as well as happy times, fulfillment, encouragement, and cooperation. Unfortunately, when relationships are on the down side, too many people dwell on the negatives. Not all people intentionally try to hurt their partners, but, when arguments heat up, they often fall back into selfish attitudes and behaviors that only serve as ammunition for their own cause. Such defenses never facilitate a happy relationship.

A few examples of detrimental behaviors include the following:

- Belittling/putting down
- Blaming or accusing
- Bringing up the past
- Constantly refusing sex
- Controlling
- Dwelling on negatives
- Flirting with others
- Guilt trips
- Lack of affection
- Lying
- Not sharing responsibilities

- Physical abuse
- Pouting
- Refusing to talk/shunning
- Sarcasm
- Shifting attention to family/friends
- Spending or hoarding money
- Substance abuse
- Threatening suicide
- Threatening to leave
- Verbal abuse
- Yelling

Enjoying a successful relationship involves much more than simply eliminating negative behaviors. Some couples would leave therapy with little to talk about if the counseling only involved discarding the negative. Mutually rewarding, positive actions must replace the negative.

Directions: During the next week list all interactions between you and your partner in which negative interactions (such as those above) take place. Mark down the day and approximate time when each take place. Do not share this list with your partner or compare notes. We will go over the lists in the next counseling session. Use as many of the attached sheets as necessary.

This list must contain behaviors acted out by you, your partner, and both. The purpose of this exercise is to learn about and enrich your relationship, not to blame or find fault. We are not interested in determining "who is right," but rather "what is right" for your relationship.

Also include alternative positive actions that could have been taken instead of the negative behavior, and what seemed to cause the behavior (if you know).

Date: _3/12/2005_   **Time:** _6:45 a.m._

Negative behavior(s): _Paul kept telling me that the only reason I spend so much time getting_ _ready in the morning is to impress the men at work. Even though there are no other men, I told_ _him, "At least some people care about me."_

Acted out by whom: _____   _X_ Both

What caused it to happen? _When pressure between us build up we become quite sarcastic and_ _belittling of each other. When he accuses me I don't try to reason, but rather I try to hurt his_ _feelings and make him feel inadequate._

How did you feel afterward? _Guilty for implying I might have admirers and good because I was_ _one up on him._

How do you think your partner felt afterward? _Angry and put down._

What positive actions could have been taken instead of the negative: _We could let the other_ _know on a regular basis how important we are to each other. When I feel like I'm being put down,_ _I could discuss my feelings with him rather than spout off. He could avoid making judgmental_ _statements about me by telling me when he is down._

Date: _3/15/2005_   **Time:** _8:30 p.m._

Negative behavior(s): _He yelled at me for spending $200 on a new outfit. I shouted back that he_ _is not my father and I can spend what I want. Then I drove off and did not come back until_ _3:00 a.m. and said, "I went where people appreciate me."_

Acted out by whom: _____   _X_ Both

What caused it to happen? _We have several unpaid bills, but I spent $200 on a whim. He was_ _very upset and I reacted._

How did you feel afterward? _Angry because he has no right to tell me how much I can spend._ _Guilty, because we are in debt. Childish, because he lectured me._

How do you think your partner felt afterward? _Frustrated, because I often overspend when we_ _have other bills to pay._

What positive actions could have been taken instead of the negative? _This could have been_ _prevented if we had an agreed-on budget. He didn't have to yell at me. I didn't have to drive off_ _for several hours. We should agree on expenditures over a certain amount._

Form 43   Third-Party Prior Authorization Request for Continued Services

(Provider information): _____

(Patient information):

	ICD	or	DSM
Primary diagnosis: _____	_____		_____
Secondary diagnosis: _____	_____		_____

Initial service date: _____   Dates requested: From: _____ through _____

Hours used: _____   Type(s) of service(s) and hours requested: _____

Describe mental health history and current mental status with documentation of diagnosis.

_____

_____

_____

Current stressors and functional impairment. Include psychological impairment as a result of this disorder.

_____

_____

_____

Rating of patient's progress in therapy.   Poor   1   2   3   4   5   6   High
Documentation of progress.

_____

_____

Rating of patient's cooperation.   Poor   1   2   3   4   5   6   High
Describe willingness to follow treatment plan.

_____

_____

_____

Current medications. Therapist's contact with primary care physician.

_____

_____

_____

Discharge plans. Include objective criteria.

_____

_____

_____

Signature: _____   Date: ____/____/____

Form 43A Third-Party Prior Authorization Request for Continued Services (*Poor Example*)

(Provider information): _Judy Doe_   (Patient information):

                                                     ICD   or   DSM

Primary diagnosis: _____ _Depression_ _____   _____   _____

Secondary diagnosis: _____   _____   _____

Initial service date: _____   Dates requested: From: _____ _9/7/2005_ ___ through _9/7/2006_

Hours used: _10_   Type(s) of service(s) and hours requested: _Counseling_ _____

Describe mental health history and current mental status with documentation of diagnosis.

Has been in counseling several times in life. History of marital issues. Mental status indicates ___

need for counseling. Continues to meet diagnostic criteria for depression. _____

Current stressors and functional impairment. Include psychological impairment as a result of this disorder.

Marital conflict. Does not like her job. Psychological impairment due to issues relating to people ___

who upset her. _____

Rating of patient's progress in therapy.   Poor   1   2   3   4   5   (6)   High
Documentation of progress.

Client is doing very well in therapy. Able to discuss issues which are difficult to discuss with ___

spouse. _____

Rating of patient's cooperation.   Poor   1   2   3   4   5   (6)   High
Describe willingness to follow treatment plan.

Always willing to participate in discussions in treatment sessions. _____

Current medications. Therapist's contact with primary care physician.

None needed. No referrals necessary. _____

Discharge plans. Include objective criteria.

Client agrees to remain in treatment until marriage issues are resolved. _____

Signature: _____   Date: ____/____/____

Form 43B   Third-Party Prior Authorization Request for Continued Services   (*Completed*)

(Provider information): *Judy Doe*

(Patient information):

ICP   or   DSM

Primary diagnosis: *Major depression, moderate, recurrent* _____ *296.32*

Secondary diagnosis: _____ _____ _____

Initial service date: *1/27/2005*   Dates requested: From: *3/29/2005* through *12/7/2005*

Hours used: *6*   Type(s) of service(s) and hours requested: *Individual psychotherapy—15 hrs*

Describe mental health history and current mental status with documentation of diagnosis. *Hx of mental health; Dx of Major depression since 1976. Three in-patient hospitalizations due to suicidal threats/attempts. Other Tx since 1976 includes 6 months of group therapy. 3 attempts of individual therapy (each <10 sessions), and ongoing med management. Appears depressed/psychomotor retardation/fatigued/low motivation/weight loss of 20# in past 3 months/sleeping 12 hrs/day. Oriented x3. No evidence of thought disorder. Family Hx of depression (Dx, Tx, hospital).*

Current stressors and functional impairment. Include psychological impairment as a result of this disorder. *Unemployment due to being fired from job (excessive absences). Few/no friends. Divorced six weeks ago. No immediate family in geographic area. Excessive social withdrawal (spends most of day in home, has refused invitations of former friends to attend social functions). Sad most of time, low motivation. Notes difficulty concentrating when filling out job applications.*

Rating of patient's progress in therapy.   Poor   1   2   3   (4)   5   6   High

Documentation of progress. *Documentation of Progress. Client notes that she wants to change her outlook on life. Has successfully accomplished two of four homework assignments involving initiating social interactions, time management, and involving herself in pleasurable activities. Increase insight regarding dysfunctional thought processes. Gains in ability to make positive self-statements. Continued concerns in social withdrawal and low motivation. Presently focusing on assertiveness skills.*

Rating of patient's cooperation.   Poor   1   2   3   4   5   (6)   High

Describe willingness to follow treatment plan. *High degree of cooperation, but perhaps due to overdependence. Generally agrees with interpretative statements, but in a seemingly dependent manner. Recent attempts at role playing assertiveness have been facilitative.*

Current medications. Therapist's contact with primary care physician. *Current meds include Prozac from MD. Noted compliance. Collaborative treatment with MD. Shared Tx plans. Summary of sessions exchanged monthly.*

Discharge plans. Include objective criteria. *See attached Tx plan for specific goals to be accomplished during course of therapy including: Consistent BDI score of < 15. 8 hrs of sleep per night/5 job applications per week until job is acquired/acceptable subjective rating of level of impairment due to depression. Tapering off of sessions. Current weekly visits will become every other week as of session 10.*

Signature/Professional title: *Darlene L. Benton, PhD, Clinical Psychologist* Date: *3 / 15 / 2005*

Chapter 8

Chart Review
and Outcomes
Documentation

The following forms are not used directly in client care, but the type of information monitored is necessary in areas of accreditation, outcome research, and quality improvement. Most of the forms presented in this section would be used in larger, accredited clinics in which there is a utilization review committee. However, individual practitioners benefit from the content of the forms when monitoring outcomes of their therapy.

FORM 44
Chart Review

This form is used within a clinic for periodic chart review. It covers documentation of treatment throughout therapy. The format is designed for criteria of third-party reviews in audits by accreditation agencies and insurance companies. It provides an overall score in documentation areas such as integrating the client's information in background information, diagnosis, treatment planning, progress notes, and termination procedures.

FORM 45
Utilization Review Committee
Guide to Review Charts for Audit

Accreditation agencies require utilization review of records for quality improvement. Generally, a utilization review committee reviews charts, providing feedback to the therapists on a regular basis. The Utilization Review Committee Guide to Review Charts for Audit covers several areas of administrative and clinical procedures for evaluation by the committee. It includes specific corrective actions to be taken by the therapist.

FORM 46
Utilization Review Committee—
Chart Review Summary

This form is designed to meet accreditation agency requirements of chart review. It summarizes the charts reviewed in a committee action.

FORM 47
Medical Records Audit Chart

This form is used by the medical records reviewer, not to monitor the quality of documentation, but rather to inform the therapist and clinical supervisors as to what is missing or incomplete in various clients' medical records. It is designed to follow the policies, procedures, time-frames, and forms used in a given clinic.

FORM 48
Statement of Confidentiality
for Those Auditing or
Reviewing Client Charts

A statement of confidentiality signed by outside sources reviewing records is required by certain accrediting agencies, requiring a specific agreement between the clinic and those reviewing the charts.

FORM 49
Client Satisfaction Survey

Accreditation agencies require ratings of client satisfaction for various aspects of the clinic such as convenience, treatment, office staff, and other related functions of the clinic. Statistical analyses can be conducted comparing various aspects of clinical services or to review client satisfaction of individual therapists. Client cooperation is much higher with a brief, one-page form.

FORM 50
Clinical Outcomes Questionnaire

The Clinical Outcomes Questionnaire (Form 50) provides a brief checklist for the client to fill out after treatment has been terminated. Some clinics mail it to the client with a self-addressed, stamped envelope at the time the termination letter is sent. It is designed to measure consumer satisfaction within a number of realms of services provided. It provides feedback to both the clinician and the therapist as to areas of strengths and weakness in a quantified manner. Agencies such as JCAHO may request that evidence is shown how the clinic attains and responds to the client feedback.

Form 44   Chart Review

Client's name: _____ ID#: _____ Date of review: _____

Therapist: _____ Reviewed by: _____

Check the appropriate column.   Key: 0 = No   1 = Somewhat   2 = Yes

Background Information

0   1   2

___ ___ ___   Do the signs and symptoms coincide with and clarify the presenting problem?

___ ___ ___   Are the signs and symptoms clearly documented?

___ ___ ___   Does the history indicate stressors and/or circumstances demonstrating a need for services?

___ ___ ___   Is a relevant medical history included?

___ ___ ___   Does the biopsychosocial information include relevant areas of strength/weakness?

___ ___ ___   Does the biopsychosocial information depict cultural/spiritual concerns?

_____/12 total

Remarks: _____

_____

Diagnostic Information

0   1   2

___ ___ ___   Is the diagnosis concordant with observations?

___ ___ ___   Is the diagnosis clearly validated by *DSM-IV-TR* symptoms criteria?

___ ___ ___   Are specific impairments due to the diagnosis listed?

_____/6 total

Remarks: _____

_____

Treatment Plan

0   1   2

___ ___ ___   Are the treatment plan problem areas concordant with the diagnosis?

___ ___ ___   Does the treatment plan outline the type and number of sessions needed?

___ ___ ___   Are the goals and objectives realistic or attainable within the estimated time frames?

___ ___ ___   Are the specific objectives measurable or observable?

___ ___ ___   Are the treatment strategies appropriate?

_____/10 total

Remarks: _____

_____

Progress Notes

0   1   2

___ ___ ___   Do the progress notes reflect the diagnosis and treatment plan?

___ ___ ___   Do the progress notes include specific data supporting continued need for services?

___ ___ ___   Are treatment strategies (including meds) clearly identified and assessed?

___ ___ ___   Are progress and setbacks of each session assessed?

___ ___ ___   Is a specific plan for each subsequent session noted?

___ ___ ___   If there are health/safety issues, are they addressed?

_____/12 total

Remarks: _____

_____

Termination Procedures

0   1   2

___ ___ ___   Is the reason for termination noted?

___ ___ ___   Is the progress toward each goal documented?

___ ___ ___   Is the timing of termination appropriate?

___ ___ ___   Was a termination letter sent?

___ ___ ___   Is a 5 Axis discharge diagnosis included?

_____/10 total

Remarks: _____

_____

Total score: _____ 50

Areas of concern: _____

Areas of strength: _____

Reviewers Comments/Suggestions: _____

_____

_____

_____

_____

_____

_____

_____

_____

_____

Reviewer's signature: _____ Date: ____/____/_____

Therapist's signature: _____ Date: ____/____/_____

Form 45   Utilization Review Committee Guide to Review Charts for Audit

Therapist _____   Case # _____ _____
Client   _____   MM/YY _____ / _____
Reviewed for Appropriateness of: __Admissions   __Continued Stay   __Discharge   __Other: _____
Initial Session _____   # of visits _____   Reviewer _____

> Important Note: In the following items, if "No" is checked, but no additional written notations are made in the Comments section, the "Corrective Action" is considered self-explanatory, based on the specific statement marked "No."

1. ORIENTATION CHECKLIST   Complete (to date)
  __Yes   __No
Comments/Corrective Actions _____

2. PERSONAL HISTORY FORM
  a) Why did the patient seek services and what are the client's expectations of therapy? Is it related to a mental illness?
  __Yes   __No
  b) Is it consistent with the diagnosis? If not, has it been explained to the client?
  __Yes   __No
Comments/Corrective Actions _____

3. COMPREHENSIVE ASSESSMENT
  a) Do the documented signs, symptoms, and severity of impairment in different areas of the patient's life support the existence of a mental illness?
  __Yes   __No
  b) Is specific *DSM-IV-TR* criteria present that support the diagnosis?
  __Yes   __No
  c) Does the GAF score seem appropriate?
  __Yes   __No
  d) Are the concerns from the Personal History Form addressed in, and concordant with, the Biopsychosocial information?
  __Yes   __No
  e) Are the client's Strengths, Needs, Abilities, and Preferences (S.N.A.P.'s) sufficiently documented?
  __Yes   __No
  f) Do the Mental Status Exam observations coincide with the diagnosis?
  __Yes   __No
  g) Are areas of suicidality, threat to others, medical problems, and substance abuse appropriately followed through?
  __Yes   __No
  h) Does the Interpretive Summary adequately portray the documentation and need for treatment?
  __Yes   __No
Comments/Corrective Actions _____

4. INDIVIDUAL TREATMENT PLAN
  a) Is the treatment plan consistent with the diagnosis, symptoms, and impairments?
  __Yes   __No
  b) Does the treatment plan address S.N.A.P.'s (strengths, needs, abilities, preferences) that are found in the Comprehensive Assessment?
  __Yes   __No
  c) Are the goals and objectives measurable and/or observable?
  __Yes   __No
  d) Are the treatment strategies specific and appropriate?
  __Yes   __No
  e) Are the target dates (EDC's) appropriate?
  __Yes   __No
  f) Was the treatment plan completed by the second session?
  __Yes   __No
  g) Did the client or guardian sign and provide input in the plan?
  __Yes   __No
  h) Is the Discharge Plan present?
  __Yes   __No
Comments/Corrective Actions _____

5. TREATMENT PLAN STATUS REVIEW

    a) Do status reviews support continued treatment?
    __Yes   __No
    b) If target dates (EDC's) have been extended, has it been documented?
    __Yes   __No
    c) Is the patient's perception of progress noted on the status review?
    __Yes   __No
    d) Is there a steady improvement in the GAF score, or, if not, is it documented adequately?
    __Yes   __No
Comments/Corrective Actions _____

6. PROGRESS NOTES

    a) Are the Progress Notes in correct format? (current clinical status, signs/symptoms, session content, interventions, progress)
    __Yes   __No
    b) Do Progress Notes focus on treatment of the identified mental illness?
    __Yes   __No
    c) If treatment is not Partner Relational, do the Progress Notes avoid relationship issues?
    __Yes   __No
    d) Is there specific reference to the Treatment Plan Goals/objectives?
    __Yes   __No
    e) Do the Progress Notes reflect current setbacks and improvements?
    __Yes   __No
    f) Does Progress Note contain a procedure code?
    __Yes   __No
Comments/Corrective Actions _____

7. DISCHARGE SUMMARY

    a) Did the course of treatment seem appropriate?
    __Yes   __No
    b) Is there a clear post-termination plan (e.g., psychiatric care, follow-up, etc.)?
    __Yes   __No
    c) GAF at Admission   _____   GAF at Discharge_____
Comments/Corrective Actions _____

8. OVERALL

    a) Is all documentation timely and completed in its entirety?
    __Yes   __No
    b) Are all needed signatures present?
    __Yes   __No
    c) Did the therapist follow through on any doctor's orders?
    __Yes   __No
Comments/Corrective Actions _____

Additional Comments by Committee _____
_____
_____
_____
_____
_____
_____
_____
_____

(Written by committee)

Item(s) Requiring Corrective Action: _____

(Items I and II written by therapist)

I) Check one of the options (A,B,C) below:

__ **A)** **I will comply with all of the "Corrective Actions" determined by the committee.** Please indicate which actions were taken by listing items checked "No" on pages 1–2 and listed above. Use the chart below to list the actions taken.

Items in which corrective action will be taken

Item Number (e.g., 3c)	Date Action(s) Taken	Specific Corrective Action(s) Taken by Therapist

__ **B)** **I will comply with some of the "Corrective Actions" determined by the committee.** Please indicate: 1) in the chart above, which actions were taken; and 2) in the chart below, those in which you are in disagreement. For those actions in which you disagree, appeal the committee's decision, per the attached Appeal Process Policy.

Items in which you are appealing (e.g., 2b, 3c)

Items in which you disagree with the committee's decision; to be appealed: _____

__ **C)** **I disagree with all of the "Corrective Actions" determined by the committee** and will appeal the committee's decision, per the attached Appeal Process Policy.

<u>**Signatures and Credentials**</u>

II) Therapist

_____   _____
Therapist   Date

III) Committee

_____ _____   _____ _____
UR Chairperson   Date   Psychiatrist (as needed)   Date

Form 46 Utilization Review Committee—Chart Review Summary

REVIEW FINDINGS OF DATE: _____

Therapist	Client's Name	Case #	Admission Appropriate Mental Health Dx DSM Criteria 2a–f	Assessment Justifies Care 2g	Treatment Plan Shows Continuity with Assessment 3a,b	Goals, Objectives, & Treatment Relate to Problem 3b	Objectives are measurable and Client Focused 3c–e	Justification for extended Treatment 4	Progress Notes Support Treatment 5	Discharge was Appropriate 6	GAF Increase 6d	Services Billed Correctly 7	Overall Procedures 8
1			Y N N/A	Y N N/A	Y N N/A	Y N N/A	Y N N/A	Y N N/A	Y N N/A	Y N N/A	Y N N/A	Y N N/A	Y N N/A
2			Y N N/A	Y N N/A	Y N N/A	Y N N/A	Y N N/A	Y N N/A	Y N N/A	Y N N/A	Y N N/A	Y N N/A	Y N N/A
3			Y N N/A	Y N N/A	Y N N/A	Y N N/A	Y N N/A	Y N N/A	Y N N/A	Y N N/A	Y N N/A	Y N N/A	Y N N/A
4			Y N N/A	Y N N/A	Y N N/A	Y N N/A	Y N N/A	Y N N/A	Y N N/A	Y N N/A	Y N N/A	Y N N/A	Y N N/A
5			Y N N/A	Y N N/A	Y N N/A	Y N N/A	Y N N/A	Y N N/A	Y N N/A	Y N N/A	Y N N/A	Y N N/A	Y N N/A
6			Y N N/A	Y N N/A	Y N N/A	Y N N/A	Y N N/A	Y N N/A	Y N N/A	Y N N/A	Y N N/A	Y N N/A	Y N N/A
7			Y N N/A	Y N N/A	Y N N/A	Y N N/A	Y N N/A	Y N N/A	Y N N/A	Y N N/A	Y N N/A	Y N N/A	Y N N/A
8			Y N N/A	Y N N/A	Y N N/A	Y N N/A	Y N N/A	Y N N/A	Y N N/A	Y N N/A	Y N N/A	Y N N/A	Y N N/A
9			Y N N/A	Y N N/A	Y N N/A	Y N N/A	Y N N/A	Y N N/A	Y N N/A	Y N N/A	Y N N/A	Y N N/A	Y N N/A
10			Y N N/A	Y N N/A	Y N N/A	Y N N/A	Y N N/A	Y N N/A	Y N N/A	Y N N/A	Y N N/A	Y N N/A	Y N N/A
11			Y N N/A	Y N N/A	Y N N/A	Y N N/A	Y N N/A	Y N N/A	Y N N/A	Y N N/A	Y N N/A	Y N N/A	Y N N/A
12			Y N N/A	Y N N/A	Y N N/A	Y N N/A	Y N N/A	Y N N/A	Y N N/A	Y N N/A	Y N N/A	Y N N/A	Y N N/A
13			Y N N/A	Y N N/A	Y N N/A	Y N N/A	Y N N/A	Y N N/A	Y N N/A	Y N N/A	Y N N/A	Y N N/A	Y N N/A
14			Y N N/A	Y N N/A	Y N N/A	Y N N/A	Y N N/A	Y N N/A	Y N N/A	Y N N/A	Y N N/A	Y N N/A	Y N N/A
15			Y N N/A	Y N N/A	Y N N/A	Y N N/A	Y N N/A	Y N N/A	Y N N/A	Y N N/A	Y N N/A	Y N N/A	Y N N/A
16			Y N N/A	Y N N/A	Y N N/A	Y N N/A	Y N N/A	Y N N/A	Y N N/A	Y N N/A	Y N N/A	Y N N/A	Y N N/A
17			Y N N/A	Y N N/A	Y N N/A	Y N N/A	Y N N/A	Y N N/A	Y N N/A	Y N N/A	Y N N/A	Y N N/A	Y N N/A
18			Y N N/A	Y N N/A	Y N N/A	Y N N/A	Y N N/A	Y N N/A	Y N N/A	Y N N/A	Y N N/A	Y N N/A	Y N N/A
19			Y N N/A	Y N N/A	Y N N/A	Y N N/A	Y N N/A	Y N N/A	Y N N/A	Y N N/A	Y N N/A	Y N N/A	Y N N/A
20			Y N N/A	Y N N/A	Y N N/A	Y N N/A	Y N N/A	Y N N/A	Y N N/A	Y N N/A	Y N N/A	Y N N/A	Y N N/A
21			Y N N/A	Y N N/A	Y N N/A	Y N N/A	Y N N/A	Y N N/A	Y N N/A	Y N N/A	Y N N/A	Y N N/A	Y N N/A
22			Y N N/A	Y N N/A	Y N N/A	Y N N/A	Y N N/A	Y N N/A	Y N N/A	Y N N/A	Y N N/A	Y N N/A	Y N N/A
23			Y N N/A	Y N N/A	Y N N/A	Y N N/A	Y N N/A	Y N N/A	Y N N/A	Y N N/A	Y N N/A	Y N N/A	Y N N/A
24			Y N N/A	Y N N/A	Y N N/A	Y N N/A	Y N N/A	Y N N/A	Y N N/A	Y N N/A	Y N N/A	Y N N/A	Y N N/A
25			Y N N/A	Y N N/A	Y N N/A	Y N N/A	Y N N/A	Y N N/A	Y N N/A	Y N N/A	Y N N/A	Y N N/A	Y N N/A

Form 47   Medical Records Audit Chart

Client:_____   Case Number: _____

Therapist:_____   Date of Termination: _____

Reviewed by:_____   Date Submitted for Review:_____
                                             Date Reviewed:_____

Please return to medical Records by ___(date)___ with all corrections complete.

HIPAA Compliance

_____   Privacy of Information form signed by client   _____

Consent for Treatment: (must have each time client is re-admitted for treatment and/or at client's 18th birthday)

Auditor   Dated:_____   Needs correction
_____   Client name completed   _____
_____   Chart number completed   _____
_____   Guarantor name completed (guardian if possible)   _____
_____   Signed & dated by client/legal guardian   _____
_____   Signed & dated by witness   _____

Comments:_____
_____

Personal History Form:

Auditor   Dated: _____   Needs correction
_____   Completed in its entirety   _____
_____   Child immunizations records present   _____
_____   Signed by client/guardian   _____
_____   Signed by therapist (with credentials)   _____
_____   Signed by psychiatrist (physician) (with credentials)   _____

Comments:_____
_____

Comprehensive Assessment

Auditor   Dated: _____   Needs correction
_____   Completed within 48 hours   _____
_____   Completed in its entirety   _____
_____   Axis I–V completed   _____
_____   Signed by therapist (with credentials)   _____
_____   Signed by psychiatrist (with credentials)   _____
_____   Signed by therapist if notation by doctor   _____

Comments:_____
_____

8.11

Progress Notes

Auditor   Dated: _____   Needs correction

_____   All progress notes present

_____   Errors corrected appropriately   _____

Missing Information

Missing Note	Missing In/Out Time	Missing Procedure Code	Missing Therapist Signature	Incorrect Billing Code	Should be …	For this DOS

Comments: _____

_____

Biopsychosocial Update

Auditor   Dated:_____   Needs correction

_____   Completed 1 year from Comprehensive Assessment   _____

                  Should have been completed by _____

_____   Completed in its entirety

_____   Signed by therapist (with credentials)   _____

Comments: _____

_____

Individual Treatment Plan

Auditor   Dated:_____   Needs correction

_____   (Adjunctive serviced checked by auditor)

_____   Completed by end of 2nd session   _____

_____   Completed in its entirety   _____

_____   Signed by client/legal guardian   _____

_____   Signed by therapist (with credentials)   _____

_____   Signed by psychiatrist (with credentials)   _____

Comments: _____

_____

8.12

Status Review

Auditor   Dated:_____   Needs correction

_____ All status reviews present   _____

Missing Information

Review date	Not done in time frame	Note entirely complete	Missing client's perceived progress	Missing therapist signature	Missing psychiatrist signature

Comments: _____

_____

Discharge Summary

Auditor	Dated: _____	Needs correction
_____	(Post termination plan checked auditor)	_____
_____	Completed in its entirety	_____
_____	Post termination plan completed	_____
_____	Psychiatric intervention stated if applicable	_____
_____	No abbreviation present (unless key given)	_____
_____	Signed by therapist (with credentials & date)	_____
_____	Last date of service within 15 days of termination	_____
_____	Signed by psychiatrist (with credentials and date)	_____
_____	Psychiatrist signed within 10 days of therapist's sign.	_____

Comments: _____

_____

Psychological Testing

Auditor	Dated:_____	Needs correction
_____	Completed in its entirety	_____
_____	Psychological testing request form present	_____
_____	Psychiatrist authorized before testing was done	_____
_____	Report	_____
_____	Test battery	_____
_____	Signature of psychologist/supervisor	_____

Comments: _____

_____

8.13

Psychiatric Evaluation

Auditor	Dated:_____	Needs correction
_____	Request for psychiatric evaluation present & complete	_____
_____	Signed by therapist	_____
_____	Approved by psychiatrist prior to evaluation	_____
_____	Evaluation report completed in its entirety	_____
_____	Signed by psychiatrist	_____

Comments: _____
_____

Medication Review

Auditor	Dated:_____	Needs correction
_____	Notes completed in their entirety	_____
_____	Signed by psychiatrist	_____
_____	Medication information/consent form completed	_____
_____	Signed by client	_____
_____	Signed by psychiatrist	_____

Comments: _____
_____

Medication Record

Auditor	Dated:_____	Needs correction
_____	Each column completed in its entirety	_____
_____	All scripts present	_____

Comments: _____
_____

Request for client information

Auditor	Dated:_____	Needs correction
_____	Completed in its entirety	_____
_____	Signed by the client	_____
_____	Signed by the witness	_____
_____	Appropriate copy sent to agency	_____
_____	Reviewed (when applicable)	_____

Comments: _____
_____

Readmit Forms (2) (within 1 year of discharge only)

Auditor	Dated:_____	Needs correction
_____	Completed in its entirety	_____
_____	Signed by therapist	_____
_____	Appropriate copy sent to agency	_____
_____	Reviewed (when applicable)	_____

Comments: _____
_____

Substance Abuse Clients

Auditor   Dated:_____   Needs correction

_____   Forms completely in entirety   _____

_____   Physical exam (by 30 days from admission)   _____

_____   Substance intake form   _____

_____   Signed by therapist   _____

Comments: _____

_____

Auditor   Dated:_____   Needs correction

_____   Only blank ink used by therapist   _____

_____   Errors corrected appropriately   _____

_____   Fee agreement form filed in chart   _____

Additional comments: _____

_____

_____

_____

Corrective Action Status

_____   No corrections needed. Great job? Please sign, date, and return this form to medical records.

_____   Corrections needed. Please make the needed corrections and complete the following.

Therapist Response Section

_____   All corrections have been made.

_____   All corrections have been made, except as indicated below.

Comments/Questions: _____

_____

_____

_____

_____

_____

_____

_____   _____

Therapist Signature and Credentials   Date

Form 48   Statement of Confidentiality for Those Auditing or Reviewing Client Charts

The purpose of this form is to protect client confidentiality for those authorized to review client charts from _____(name of clinic)_____.

I, _____, am reviewing client charts at

_____(name of clinic)_____ for the purpose of

   __ audit

   __ accreditation review

   __ consultation

   __ other (describe) _____

I agree that no client identifying information will be removed from the premises, copied, or related to others in verbal, written or any other form within the legal bounds of confidentiality in accordance with 42 C.F.R. 2.53(b)(2).

_____   _____

Signature of person reviewing records   Date

_____

Name of agency

_____   _____

Witness   Date

Form 49   Client Satisfaction Survey

*In order to help us provide quality services to our clients, we regularly conduct the **Client Satisfaction Survey**. The information is used to increase our strengths and learn what needs improvement. Your cooperation is extremely helpful and appreciated. You do not have to identify yourself.*

Primary type of services received. *(check only one)*
__Marriage/Family   __Adult mental health   __Child/Adolescent   __Substance abuse
__Other *(describe)* _____

Circle the most fitting responses on a 1–5 scale.   ***1= Strongly Agree with statement***
5= Strongly Disagree with statement
NA=Not applicable

Implications of Response: *"1" is very positive, "2" is positive, "3" is neutral, "4" is negative, "5" is very negative*

<u>**Circle the most fitting response**</u>

1) **"I (or client, if child) feel satisfied with the services I received."**   NA (Agree) 1 2 3 4 5 (Disagree)

2) **"If later, there is a need, I (or client, if child) would reenter treatment."**   NA (Agree) 1 2 3 4 5 (Disagree)

3) **"I have experienced a reduction in the problems that I was experiencing before entering treatment."**   NA (Agree) 1 2 3 4 5 (Disagree)

4) **"Transportation and/or scheduling problems influenced my decision to terminate."**   NA (Agree) 1 2 3 4 5 (Disagree)

5) **"The office staff was helpful."**   NA (Agree) 1 2 3 4 5 (Disagree)

6) **"The therapist addressed issues related to my problems"**   NA (Agree) 1 2 3 4 5 (Disagree)

7) Comments _____
_____

Staff use: Date information received _____
Comments _____
_____
_____
_____

Form 50   Clinical Outcomes Questionnaire

Name (optional): _____   Therapist: _____   Date: _____

No. of sessions attended: _____   Purpose of counseling (e.g., depression, anxiety): _____

Type(s) of counseling: ____ Individual ___ Group ____ Family ___ Marriage ___ Other: _____

Please circle the response under each statement which most closely indicates your level of agreement or disagreement.

Highly Disagree 1	Moderately Disagree 2	Slightly Disagree 3	Neutral 4	Slightly Agree 5	Moderately Agree 6	Highly Agree 7

"I was given choices about my treatment."

| 1 | 2 | 3 | 4 | 5 | 6 | 7 |

"The therapist explained the benefits and risks of therapy to me."

| 1 | 2 | 3 | 4 | 5 | 6 | 7 |

"I was treated with respect and dignity by the therapist."

| 1 | 2 | 3 | 4 | 5 | 6 | 7 |

"The therapist listened to my concerns."

| 1 | 2 | 3 | 4 | 5 | 6 | 7 |

"The treatment plan was clearly explained to me."

| 1 | 2 | 3 | 4 | 5 | 6 | 7 |

"Services were performed in a time-efficient manner."

| 1 | 2 | 3 | 4 | 5 | 6 | 7 |

"The clinic's policies were clearly explained to me."

| 1 | 2 | 3 | 4 | 5 | 6 | 7 |

"The counseling was directed toward helping my problem areas."

| 1 | 2 | 3 | 4 | 5 | 6 | 7 |

"I was satisfied with the counseling I received."

| 1 | 2 | 3 | 4 | 5 | 6 | 7 |

"The services I received were helpful."

| 1 | 2 | 3 | 4 | 5 | 6 | 7 |

"I would return to the therapist for services in the future if needed."

| 1 | 2 | 3 | 4 | 5 | 6 | 7 |

Comments: _____

_____

_____

_____

Chapter 9

Termination and Aftercare

Clients are not officially terminated from treatment simply because they stop attending therapy sessions. Accreditation agencies and potential liability concerns require official discharge planning. A client is not officially discharged until a termination letter is sent.

FORM 51
Discharge Summary

The Discharge Summary form (Form 51) is intended to summarize the effects of therapy. It lists the initial and final diagnoses, dates of service, progress, and reasons for termination. It provides a brief overview of changes in symptomology and the client's level of functioning as the result of therapy. Both the client's and therapist's evaluation are included.

Material from the Discharge Summary is helpful in assessing outcome measures. For example, changes in diagnosis, GAF, and current stressors can provide quantifiable information deemed necessary by several managed care organizations and third-party reviewers. An evaluation of the reasons for termination may help the clinic assess the quality, type, and number of services provided by both individual therapists and the clinic. Such information is helpful in clinic planning.

FORM 52
Termination Letter

The Termination Letter (Form 52) is sent to the client when services from the therapist or clinic are no longer being utilized. It serves at least two purposes. First, it is designed to free the clinic from any responsibility for any of the client's actions (which had nothing to do with the therapy received) after therapy has taken place. A clinic may bear some responsibility for a nonterminated client. Second, it provides a transition point to the client.

Certain ethical principles must be considered at a termination. Terminating a client is not abandoning a client. A proper termination implies that sufficient progress was made or attempted at the clinic, and the client is ready for a change to treatment elsewhere, or has made sufficient progress so that treatment is no longer necessary.

The clinic should provide the client with resources at termination to handle emergencies or crises. These may include crisis hot-line numbers, hospitals, walk-in clinics, or availability of the therapist or clinic in the future. Clearly document in progress notes that this information was provided to the client.

At the time of termination, the therapist should document the reason for termination and the estimated risk of relapse. Relapse is beyond the clinic's control. Therefore, the therapist should assure the client that help is available if needed in the future.

Some therapists suggest that the client receives periodic "booster sessions" such as at 6 months, then 12 months. It is important to clearly explain to a client the purpose of termination and that a termination letter will be sent, even though there may be booster sessions in the future.

Form 51   Discharge Summary

Client's name: _____ DOB: _____ Case # _____

Initial Diagnosis   Axis I _____   Code # _____

Axis II _____   Code # _____

Axis III _____   Code # _____

Axis IV _____

Axis V GAF _____

Discharge Diagnosis   Axis I _____   Code # _____

Axis II _____   Code # _____

Axis III _____   Code # _____

Axis IV _____

Axis V GAF _____

Services and Termination Status

Opening date: _____   Termination date: _____   Total number of sessions: _____

Which of the following services were used during client's stay?

_____ Individual   __ Group _____ Family _____ Marital _____ Psychiatric

_____ Psych. Testing _____ Other (specify) _____

Overall Status at Termination

___ Marked improvement ___ Moderate improvement ____ No change ___ Regressed ___ Unknown

Reason(s) for Termination

___ Discharged as planned   ____ Terminated against therapist's advice

___ Referred for other services   ____ Therapist is leaving the clinic or area

___ No longer making appointments   ____ Insufficient progress in therapy

___ Have missed excessive appointments   ____ Client is leaving the area

___ Other _____

Presenting Problem and Assessment

(Subjective Evaluation: Summarize specific symptomatology, onset, duration, and frequency of Sx's. Include client's assessment of presenting problem and reason(s) for seeking services. Also include factors such as family or environmental factors affecting functioning.)

_____

_____

_____

_____

_____

_____

9.3

Clinical Course

(Impact of services upon each problem identified in Treatment Plan. What the client and therapist did to become healthy and was there any improvement in client's condition in regards to specific problem areas.)

_____

_____

_____

_____

_____

Medical/Psychiatric Status

(Was the client seen by the psychiatrist for either a psychiatric evaluation or for medications. Discharge meds, dosages, instructions.)

_____

_____

_____

_____

_____

Post-Termination Plan

(Include referrals, appointments, disposition, client's reaction.)

_____

_____

_____

_____

_____

Client's Statement Regarding Satisfaction of Treatment Rendered

_____

_____

_____

_____

_____

Endorsements

Therapist signature/certification: _____ Date: _____/_____/_____

I concur with the Final Diagnosis and Termination Plan, as delineated.

Comments: _____

_____

Supervisor signature/certification: _____ Date: _____/_____/_____

Form 51A Discharge Summary (*Completed*)

Client's name: _Judy Doe_   DOB: _7/6/1954_   Case # _DJ 030805_

Initial Diagnosis   Axis I   _Major Dep. Mod. Recurrent_   Code # _296.32_

                                   Axis II   _Deferred_   Code # _799.9_

                                   Axis III   _Defer to physician_   Code # _____

                                   Axis IV   _Marital, social, occupational problems_

                                   Axis V   GAF _55_

Discharge Diagnosis   Axis I   _Major Dep. Recurrent (full remission)_   Code # _296.32_

                                   Axis II   _No diagnosis_   Code # _V71.09_

                                   Axis III   _Defer to physician_   Code # _____

                                   Axis IV   _Mild occupational problems_

                                   Axis V   GAF _74_

Services and Termination Status

Opening date: _3/8/2005_   Termination date: _1/8/2006_   Total number of sessions: _30_

Which of the following services were used during client's stay?

       _X_ Individual   __ Group   Family   _X_ Marital   ____ Psychiatric

       ____ Psych. Testing   ____ Other (specify) _____

Overall Status at Termination

___ Marked improvement _X_ Moderate improvement ____ No change ___ Regressed ___ Unknown

Reason(s) for Termination

_X_ Discharged as planned   ____ Terminated against therapist's advice

___ Referred for other services   ____ Therapist is leaving the clinic or area

___ No longer making appointments   ____ Insufficient progress in therapy

___ Have missed excessive appointments   ____ Client is leaving the area

___ Other _____

Presenting Problem and Assessment

(Subjective Evaluation: Summarize specific symptomatology, onset, duration, and frequency of Sx's. Include client's assessment of presenting problem and reason(s) for seeking services. Also include factors such as family or environmental factors affecting functioning.)

Depressed mood most of time with extreme social withdrawal resulting in missing work and loss

of friends in past year. Exacerbated by marital discord. Wants to return to previous functioning.

Clinical Course

(Impact of services upon each problem identified in Treatment Plan. What the client and therapist did to become healthy and was there any improvement in client's condition in regards to specific problem areas.)

(1) Regular exercise and nutrition led to increased energy level. (2) Self-esteem gradually increased as step-by-step behavioral assignments and assertiveness training yielded positive results. (3) Analyzing dysfunctional thoughts led to viewing situations more positively.

Medical/Psychiatric Status

(Was the client seen by the psychiatrist for either a psychiatric evaluation or for medications. Discharge meds, dosages, instructions.)

4/1/2005—Placed on Prozac 30 mg by Dr. Holtz. No side effects. Gradual improvement in mood stabilization over next 3–4 weeks. Remains on Prozac. Med. check-ups as per physician.

Post-Termination Plan

(Include referrals, appointments, disposition, client's reaction.)

Therapist is available for future needs. Names of 3 crisis centers given to client. She feels satisfied with the course of therapy status.

Client's Statement Regarding Satisfaction of Treatment Rendered

She states that she is satisfied with the treatment and outcomes and agrees with discharge status.

Endorsements

Therapist signature/certification: *Darlene Benton, PhD* Date: *1 / 7 / 2006*

I concur with the Final Diagnosis and Termination Plan, as delineated.
Comments: *Discharge seems appropriate.*

Supervisor signature/certification: *Sharon Bell, PhD* Date: *1 / 9 / 2006*

Form 52   Termination Letter

Name: _____   Date: _____

Address: _____

City, State, Zip: _____

Dear (name of client) _____:

We thank you for using our services. Our records indicate that you are no longer receiving counseling at our clinic due to:

_____ Discharged as planned   _____ Terminated against therapist's advice

_____ Referred for other services   _____ Therapist is leaving the clinic or area

_____ No longer making appointments   _____ Insufficient progress in therapy

_____ Have missed excessive appointments   _____ Client is leaving the area

_____ Other _____

If you are in need of further services at this time, or in the future, please feel free to phone us to discuss continuing services or a referral.

Sincerely,

Therapist: _____   Date: _____/_____/_____

Bibliography and Suggested Readings

American Psychiatric Association. (2000). *Diagnostic and Statistic Manual of Mental Disorders* (Text Revision). Washington, DC: American Psychiatric Association.

American Psychological Association. (1992). *Ethical Principles for Psychologists and Code of Conduct.* Washington, DC: American Psychological Association.

_____. (1987). General Guidelines for Providers of Psychological Services. *American Psychologist, 42,* 7.

Arzuaga, P. (2004). HIPAA privacy rules: Protecting patient information requested through discovery, subpoenas and court orders. *Employee Benefits Journal, 29*(2), 28–35.

Barlow, D. H. (2001). *Clinical Handbook of Psychological Disorders: A Step-by-Step Treatment Manual* (3d ed.). New York, NY: Guilford Press.

Brown, S. L. (1991). *The Quality Management Professional's Study Guide.* Pasadena, CA: Managed Care Consultants.

Browning, C. H., & Browning, B. J. (1996). *How to Partner with Managed Care.* New York, NY: John Wiley & Sons, Inc.

Code of Federal Regulations. (2002). 45 CFR Parts 160 and 164. *Standards for privacy of individually identifiable health information.* Retrieved June 6, 2004, from http://www.hhs.gov/ocr/_hipaa/privacy.html.

English, A., & Ford, C. A. (2004). The HIPAA privacy rule and adolescents: Legal questions and clinical challenges. *Perspectives on Sexual and Reproductive Health, 36*(2), 80–86.

Galasso, D. (1987). Guidelines for Developing Multi-Disciplinary Treatment Plans. *Hospital and Community Psychiatry, 38,* 394–397.

Goldstein, G., & Hersen, M. (2000). *Handbook of Psychological Assessment* (3d ed.). New York, NY: Pergamon Press.

Goodman, M., Brown, J., & Deitz, P. (1992). *Managing Managed Care: A Mental Health Practitioner's Guide.* Washington, DC: American Psychiatric Press.

Grant, R. L. (1981). "The Capacity of the Psychiatric Record to Meet Changing Needs." In C. Siegel & S. K. Fischer (Eds.), *Psychiatric Records in Mental Health Care.* New York, NY: Brunner/Mazel.

Groth-Marnat, G. (2003). *Handbook of Psychological Assessment* (4th ed.). New York, NY: John Wiley & Sons, Inc.

Health Insurance Portability and Accountability Act of 1996, Public Law 104-91, section 1176.

Health Privacy Project, Institute for Health Care Research and Policy, Georgetown University. (2002). *Summary of HIPAA Privacy Rule.* Retrieved June 6, 2004, from http://www.healthprivacy.org/usr_do0c?RegSummary 2002.pdf.

Joint Commission on Accreditation of Healthcare Organizations. (2003). *Accreditation Manual for Mental Health, Chemical Dependency, and Mental Retardation Developmental Disabilities Services.* OakBrook Terrace, IL: Joint Commission on Accreditation of Healthcare Organizations.

Jongsma, A. E., & Peterson, L. M. (2002). *The Complete Adult Psychotherapy Treatment Planner* (3d ed.). New York, NY: John Wiley & Sons, Inc.

Bibliography

Jongsma, A. E., Peterson, L. M., & McInnis, W. P. (2002). *The Child Psychotherapy Treatment Planner* (3d ed.). New York, NY: John Wiley & Sons, Inc.

Jongsma, A. E., Peterson, L. M., & McInnis, W. P. (2002). *The Adolescent Psychotherapy Treatment Planner* (3d ed.). New York, NY: John Wiley & Sons, Inc.

Kennedy, J. A. (2003). *Fundamentals of Psychiatric Treatment Planning* (2d ed.). Washington, DC: American Psychiatric Press.

Maxmen, J. S., & Ward, N. G. (1994). *Essential Psychopathology and Its Treatment.* New York, NY: W. W. Norton, Inc.

*Medicare Program: Prospective Payment for Medicare Final Rule: Federal Register 49 (January 3):*234–240. (1984).

Morrison, J. R. (1994). *The First Interview.* New York, NY: Guilford Press.

Othmer, E., & Othmer, S. C. (2001). *The Clinical Interview Using DSM IV,* Vol. 1: *Fundamentals;* Vol. 2: *The Difficult Patient.* Washington, DC: American Psychiatric Press.

Social Security Regulations. (1981). *Rules for Determining Disability and Blindness.* Washington, DC: U.S. Department of Health and Human Services, Social Security Administration, Office of Operational Policy and Procedures, SSA No. 64-014, ICN 436850.

Soreff, S. M., & McDuffee, M. A. (1997). *Documentation Survival Handbook: A Clinician's Guide to Charting for Better Care, Certification, Reimbursement, and Risk Management* (2d ed.). Seattle, WA: Hogrefe & Huber.

Stanton, T. J., Scheidt, K. S., & Bassler, S. A. (2002). *What every employer needs to know about the HIPAA privacy rules.* Retrieved June 6, 2004, from http://www.ged.com.

Trull, E., & Phares, E. J. (2001). *Clinical Psychology: Concepts, Methods, and Profession* (6th ed.). Pacific Grove, CA: Brooks/Cole Publishing Co.

Trzepacz, P. T., & Baker, R. W. (1993). *The Psychiatric Mental Status Examination.* New York, NY: Oxford University Press.

U.S. Department of Health and Human Services. (1983). Medicare Program: Prospective Payments for Medicare Inpatient Hospital Services. *Federal Register 48(171):*39752-890.

U.S. Department of Health and Human Services—Office for Civil Rights. (2003). *Summary of the HIPPAA privacy rule.* Retrieved June 6, 2004, from http://www.hhs.gov/ocr/privacysummary.pdf.

Wiger, D. E. (1999). *The Clinical Documentation Sourcebook: A Comprehensive Collection of Mental Health Practice Forms, Handouts, and Records* (2d ed.). New York, NY: John Wiley & Sons, Inc.

Wiger, D. E. (in press). *The Clinical Documentation Primer* (2d ed.). New York, NY: John Wiley & Sons, Inc.

Zuckerman, E. L. (2000a). *Clinician's Thesaurus: A Guidebook for Writing Psychological Reports* (5th ed.). New York, NY: Guilford Press.

Zuckerman, E. L. (2000b). *The Paper Office: Forms, Guidelines, and Resources* (3d ed.). New York, NY: Guilford Press.

CD-ROM Information

CD-ROM Table of Contents

PAGE	FILE NAME	TITLE
5.11	form32.doc	Short-Term Therapy Treatment Plan
5.13	form33.doc	Treatment Review
5.17	form34.doc	Treatment Update
6.8	form35.doc	Progress Notes
6.12	form36.doc	Progress Notes—Outline
6.14	form37.doc	Group Therapy Progress Notes
6.16	form38.doc	Psychiatric Medication Management Progress Notes
7.4	form39.doc	Informed Consent for Medication
7.5	form40.doc	Suicide Contract
7.6	form41.doc	Cooperating in Child Rearing
7.11	form42.doc	Couple's Analysis of Target Behaviors
7.15	form43.doc	Third-Party Prior Authorization Request for Continued Services
8.5	form44.doc	Chart Review
8.7	form45.doc	Utilization Review Committee Guide to Review Charts for Audit
8.10	form46.doc	Utilization Review Committee—Chart Review Summary
8.11	form47.doc	Medical Records Audit Chart
8.16	form48.doc	Statement of Confidentiality for Those Auditing or Reviewing Client Charts
8.17	form49.doc	Client Satisfaction Survey
8.18	form50.doc	Clinical Outcomes Questionnaire
9.3	form51.doc	Discharge Summary
9.7	form52.doc	Termination Letter

Introduction

This appendix provides you with information on the contents of the CD that accompanies this book. For the latest and greatest information, please refer to the ReadMe file located at the root of the CD.

System Requirements

- A computer with a processor running at 120 Mhz or faster

- At least 32 MB of total RAM installed on your computer; for best performance, we recommend at least 64 MB

- A CD-ROM drive

NOTE: Many popular word processing programs are capable of reading Microsoft Word files. However, users should be aware that a slight amount of formatting might be lost when using a program other than Microsoft Word.

Using the CD with Windows

To install the items from the CD to your hard drive, follow these steps:

1. Insert the CD into your computer's CD-ROM drive.

2. The CD-ROM interface will appear. The interface provides a simple point-and-click way to explore the contents of the CD.

If the opening screen of the CD-ROM does not appear automatically, follow these steps to access the CD:

1. Click the Start button on the left end of the taskbar and then choose Run from the menu that pops up.

2. In the dialog box that appears, type *d:\setup.exe*. (If your CD-ROM drive is not drive d, fill in the appropriate letter in place of *d*.) This brings up the CD Interface described in the preceding set of steps.

WHAT'S ON THE CD

The following sections provide a summary of the software and other materials you'll find on the CD.

Content

The CD-ROM includes files for each of the 52 blank forms from the book in Word format. Forms can be customized and printed out. All documentation is included in the folder named "Content."

Applications

The following applications are on the CD:

Microsoft Word Viewer

Microsoft Word Viewer is a freeware viewer that allows you to view, but not edit, most Microsoft Word files. Certain features of Microsoft Word documents may not display as expected from within Word Viewer.

OpenOffice.org

OpenOffice.org is a free multi-platform office productivity suite. It is similar to Microsoft Office or Lotus SmartSuite, but OpenOffice.org is absolutely free. It includes Word Processing, Spreadsheet, Presentation, and Drawing applications that enable you to create professional documents, newsletters, reports, and presentations. It supports most file formats of other Office software. You should be able to edit and view any files created with other Office solutions.

Shareware programs are fully functional, trial versions of copyrighted programs. If you like particular programs, register with their authors for a nominal fee and receive licenses, enhanced versions, and technical support.

Freeware programs are copyrighted games, applications, and utilities that are free for personal use. Unlike shareware, these programs do not require a fee or provide technical support.

GNU software is governed by its own license, which is included inside the folder of the GNU product. See the GNU license for more details.

Trial, demo, or evaluation versions are usually limited either by time or functionality (such as being unable to save projects). Some trial versions are very sensitive to system date changes. If you alter your computer's date, the programs will "time out" and no longer be functional.

User Assistance

If you have trouble with the CD-ROM, please call the Wiley Product Technical Support phone number at (800) 762-2974. Outside the United States, call 1(317) 572-3994. You can also contact Wiley Product Technical Support at **http://www.wiley.com/techsupport**. John Wiley & Sons will provide technical support only for installation and other general quality control items. For technical support on the applications themselves, consult the program's vendor or author.

To place additional orders or to request information about other Wiley products, please call (800) 225-5945.